Between Speaking and Silence

Between Speaking and Silence

A Study of Quiet Students

Mary M. Reda

Published by State University of New York Press, Albany

Printed in the United States of America

For information, contact State University of New York Press, Albany, NY
www.sunypress.edu

Production by Ryan Morris
Marketing by Fran Keneston

Library of Congress Cataloging-in-Publication Data

Reda, Mary M.
    Between speaking and silence : a study of quiet students / Mary M. Reda.
        p. cm.
    Includes bibliographical references and index.
    ISBN 978-0-7914-9361-8 (hardcover : alk. paper)
    ISBN 978-0-7914-9362-5 (pbk. : alk. paper) 1. Communication in education.
2. Teacher-student relationships.   3. College teaching.   I. Title.
    LB1033.5.R43 2009
    378.1'25—dc22
                                                                    2008028050

10 9 8 7 6 5 4 3 2 1

For my father,
a musician at heart.
He taught me the
value of silence—the rests—in a
piece of music.
He was also one hell
of a storyteller.

Contents

Acknowledgments

First I want to thank all of those students who participated in my research for this project, particularly the five who agreed to be interviewed. Their generosity of time, eloquent stories, and spirit touches me, and I am honored they shared these gifts.

Much appreciation to Peter Elbow and Anne Herrington for their thoughtful consideration, feedback, and willingness to listen and challenge me through this process. I continue to be amazed by them. My appreciation to Elizabeth Petroff for agreeing to work on this project with me. And I am grateful to Lad Tobin as well, who got me into Composition in the first place.

I am grateful to my friends and colleagues. Kate Dionne and Susan Kirtley are two of the finest teachers and best friends a person could ever hope to know. Although it sounds like a cliché, it is no exaggeration to say that I would not have gotten through this without them; their wit, compassion, and boundless intelligence were a life raft. Kim De Vries, Sone Filipo, Mike Mattison, Pam Hollander, Linda Fernsten, Justine Murison, Greg Tulonen, and Chris De Vries also deserve enormous thanks for their support and friendship. Likewise, I thank all of my colleagues from Boston College, the University of Massachusetts at Amherst, and The College of Staten Island, The City University of New York who have shared with me their stories of "quiet students"; they convinced me that this project was one worth pursuing. Finally, thanks to my family. I am particularly grateful to my sister Ann. Words cannot describe her support or my appreciation.

This work was supported (in part) by two grants from The City University of New York PSC-CUNY Research Award Program.

Chapter 1

Listening to the
Silences in Our Classrooms

A Study of Quiet Students

No one dared
Disturb the sound of silence.

—Simon and Garfunkel, *Sounds of Silence*

It is any Tuesday, 2:29 p.m. I walk into the room that houses my College Writing class. Students are pulling desks into a haphazard circle we'll need to dismantle later. As class begins, Frank writes frantically, and I choose to believe he's so enthralled by the discussion of organization or academic language or audience that he's feverishly taking notes. A placid half-smile flickers across Maggie's face as she turns to study each speaker, nodding mechanically. Alice blinks at me, pensively munching the end of her ponytail. And there's a distinct possibility that Steve, my fraternity-brother-student, is asleep under the brim of the baseball cap that shades his eyes.

By the end of class, not much seems to have changed with these students. Frank writes, Maggie smiles, Alice chews, Steve's baseball cap bobs. They've written; they've been physically present; sometimes, they've even tried to laugh at my jokes. But not one of them has spoken. Their silence, their sheer determination *not* to say anything, their presence reproaches me.

Within a discipline that elevates dialogue and constructed knowledge, and within a home writing program that supports this theoretical standpoint by mandating practices such as student publications and peer feedback, I work to develop a pedagogy of dialogue. For me

1

this means a writing class that centers on student voices. Through the exercises I choose and the daily routine we follow, I try to transmit this vision of learning to my students.

Still, every semester I find a Frank, a Maggie, an Alice, a Steve—students whose silences overpower the voices that fill class discussions. And on rough days, I'm startled to realize that I've begun to resent these students and whatever it is that drives them into their silences.

I know what I see: hostility, passiveness, resistance, lack of preparation. I begin to construct explanations that account for the silences—explanations that coincidentally define my students' behaviors in terms of their flaws. But these explanations offer me little that is useful: my students remain quiet. And I remain tense, unable to coax or tease or shock them out of silence.

This is the introduction to a paper I presented at the Conference on College Composition and Communication; I continued, tracing how my students saw their own silences. But my audience focused on this scene, these all-too-familiar students, my frustration. For many in the audience, the tension I alluded to was compounded by their sense that a required course such as College Writing (the single compulsory course at the university where I was teaching) often evokes resistance that students express passively through their silences. During the discussion, audience members enumerated for each other the crimes of student silence: students who do not volunteer to speak in class; students who seem uncomfortable, even resentful, when called on; students who appear unwilling to speak to partners and small groups; students who seem to strive for single-word answers whenever possible. We talked about the particular topics that seemed to provoke student silence, challenging texts, the wisdom of our professional discourse, and the imperative to get students talking.

The audience shied away from what I saw as the real heart of the paper: that how I saw these students was often radically different from how they saw themselves, that students see their silences through a different lens than we do, that they use a different vocabulary to talk about classroom dynamics. It was as if we were unable to move beyond *our* visions of failure to seriously consider the challenges students' perspectives might fruitfully offer us. In retrospect, perhaps I should not have been surprised at the direction this conversation took, given how deeply ingrained in many of us compositionists is the desire for student dialogue. Since then, I have heard countless colleagues say (in tones ranging from desperation to undisguised contempt), "*They just won't talk. How do I get them to/convince them to/encourage them to talk in class? I want to hear* their *voices.*"

So the questions of this conference presentation have lingered for me. How *do* the Franks, the Maggies, the Alices, and the Steves see the silences in our classrooms? How do they construct their own experiences in relation to this issue that is so highly charged for teachers? What narratives, discourses, and values do they draw on in these constructions? How do such constructions affect students' perceptions of and experiences in composition classes, in particular? In this book, I attempt to address these questions through a qualitative study of one College Writing class at the University of Massachusetts at Amherst.

Returning to my conference presentation and the responses of the audience will clarify my goals for this current, larger project: to question the teacher-constructions of student silence as always negative, and to try to understand the ways students may see silence differently than we do. While I believe our perspectives and theoretical orientations are important, these constructions are, by their very nature, limited. And yet these limited constructions have virtually achieved (for teachers, at least) the status of *a priori* knowledge about quiet students. Linda Brodkey argues:

> We can only hope to transform a hegemonic practice with a narrative that insists on interrupting a story told in a classroom or in the academy that has acquired the status of lived experience, reality, logic, science, or any of the other seemingly unassailable stories that have acquired the status of authoritative discourse. The only way to fight a hegemonic discourse is to teach ourselves and others alternative ways of seeing the world.[1]

I believe these quiet students' stories call into question *our* authoritative discourse, our seemingly unassailable stories about classroom silence. While the stories we teachers may tell about classroom silence and quiet students may seem irrefutable, the perspectives of students offer us an important way of re-seeing the classroom. A consideration of the experiences, constructions, and reactions of these students invites us to redefine and expand how we think about these students, our classrooms, and the value of silence.

Background

In *Teaching with Your Mouth Shut,* Donald L. Finkel persuasively critiques our culture's image of the "great teacher" as one rooted in the archetypal act of *Telling.* He claims that we mistakenly equate the "great teacher" with a brilliant lecturer who inspires students with her displays of profound knowledge and mastery of the subject. She has a contagious enthusiasm about the subject, and she appears to be able to speak endlessly (to the enjoyment of her rapt students). In telling, she gives knowledge.[2] And the docile student—the one who can be taught—must be silent in order to receive that knowledge.

However, I see in our culture a second, perhaps even more powerful image of the "great teacher": the discussion leader who is able to inspire each student's passion, intellect, self-reflection, personal growth, and political awareness. Such teachers, through their skillful combination of probing questions, inspiring comments, and willingness to listen to students' voices, not only teach their subject more effectively but also teach their students to become better people. Both inside and outside the academy, this type of teacher (mythologized in mainstream culture through such films as *Dead Poets Society* or *Dangerous Minds* and even the more complex *Half Nelson*) is often represented as subversive in overthrowing the traditional Telling-model of education that Finkel critiques.

In the movement away from a model of education that is centered on the lecturing voice of a teacher and the monologic delivery of knowledge from teacher to receptive student, the model of the "good student" has likewise changed. Rather than celebrating the silent student (one therefore receptive to the knowledge doled out by the teacher in lecture-sized portions), this new paradigm imagines a vocal, "active" student whose classroom activity is an integral part of the construction of knowledge. In particular, much contemporary composition pedagogy is premised on this notion of dialogic education rooted in the work of theorists such as John Dewey, Paulo Freire, and Kenneth Bruffee.

Dewey's notion of "active participation . . . expression and cultivation of individuality . . . learning through experience"[3] anticipates contemporary pedagogy's postmodern interest in collaborative learning. Like Dewey, Freire claims that "authentic thinking" can only take place through dialogue; a teacher's fundamental mission is to engage in a dialogue with her students about her views *and* theirs. Freire argues for the centrality of dialogue and its liberatory potential:

> To speak is to transform the world. . . . Dialogue is the encounter between men, mediated by the world, in order to name the world. . . .
> If it is in speaking their word that people, by naming the world, transform it, dialogue imposes itself as the way by which they achieve significance as human beings. Dialogue is thus an existential necessity . . . trust is established by dialogue. . . . Without dialogue there is no communication, and without communication there can be no true education.[4]

In the work of composition scholars such as Bruffee and Harvey Weiner, "dialogue" and student talk have become a central component of the classroom. As Bruffee claims:

> Our task must involve engaging students in conversation among themselves at as many points in both the writing and the reading

process as possible, and that we should contrive to ensure that students' conversation about what they read and write is similar in as many ways as possible to the way we would like them eventually to read and write. The way they talk with each other determines the way they will think and the way they will write.[5]

This emphasis on student talk and dialogue (sometimes represented as "voice") is one of the few issues uniting compositionists from divergent political orientations within the field—from Mary Rose O'Reilley to David Bartholomae. While *voice* has become a contested term and while some might dispute Bruffee's expansive claims for student dialogue (most notably, John Trimbur in "Consensus and Difference in Collaborative Learning"), few compositionists would argue against "dialogue" as representing all that is productive, empowering, and valuable in our often fragmented efforts as a field.

Hepzibah Roskelly summarizes composition's disciplinary concern with dialogue in this way:

All of us compositionists believe in group work. In this post-Vygotskian, post-Freirian age it's impossible not to. The terms that dominate our collective conversations in conferences and in our journals—collaboration, peer response, discourse community, constructed knowledge—have become symbols for a pedagogical agenda that values talk and activity as learning tools. . . . A person learns in groups as he listens and speaks, and he learns about himself as well as the culture he inhabits. He may act to change that culture; he most certainly will be changed by it.[6]

However, the ideal student-learners of composition's "group work" are not always those we see in our classrooms when this paradigm of education is implemented. Rather than embracing dialogue, our students often appear to resist teacherly efforts at collaborative learning and constructed knowledge. While the silences initiated by teachers are seen as productive and natural (and generally unremarked upon), those silences initiated by students are troubling, problematic, and disruptive. These quiet students constitute a central classroom tension for many teachers—those who have a theoretical grounding in dialogic and collaborative learning; those who value it on a practical or an experiential level; and those who construct themselves as simply wanting to hear the voices of their students.

I do not wish to argue against this model of dialogic education; in fact, it underlies much of my own teaching.[7] But I do wish to consider what limitations this model imposes. In this paradigm, the good student, the student who learns, is the "active" student; *active* has become synonymous with highly vocal. When our model of education posits highly vocal students, those quiet or silent students in our classrooms, then, may appear to mark some sort of failure or breakdown of this pedagogy. And while many teachers internalize a student's silence as marking the failure of the *teacher* to sufficiently engage her students or to implement a theoretical vision, others focus on the failure of the *student* to meet the teacher's or institution's expectations. As I will explore in chapter 2, in either of these visions, inevitably someone must be held accountable for the perceived failure that is marked by silence.

Much of the scholarship about so-called "silent students" connects silence with a literal or metaphorical lack or absence. Janet Collins's remarks in *The Quiet Child*, a study of elementary schoolchildren, typify such a position: "Allowing children to be passive observers deprives them of important learning experiences."[8] Such accounts are based on the implicit theorizing that students are silent because they are passive, unprepared, or uncritical, and that without outwardly visible and measurable manifestations (such as speaking), students are not engaged. These students are constructed through a deficit model: they fail to meet the minimum standards a teacher sets. Again, Collins's work characterizes a prevalent view: "Quiet pupils have to be encouraged to be more assertive and find their voice in the classroom."[9] Such an assertion assumes that if a teacher cannot hear a student's voice then she does not have one, and that an optimal combination of pedagogical strategies will enable a student to move beyond whatever keeps her unproductively silent.

Other explorations of silence cluster around a concern for the political and social implications of silence and what Michelle Fine and Lois Weis call "the dynamics of power and privilege that nurture, sustain, and legitimate silencing."[10] Feminist theory, critical pedagogy, and multicultural studies help us define silence as a response to the oppressive mechanisms and the politics of a particular culture perpetuating or enforcing particular codes of silence, what Tillie Olsen has called "unnatural silences." For example, in *Organizing Silence*, Robin Patric Clair theorizes how such silencing is effected through coercion, the exertion of force, and hegemony—the systems of control "'normalized' through institutions such as the family, education, religion, systems of law and systems of enforcement, medicine, and general administration."[11] The assumption of such examinations is clear: as the title of Fine and Weis's volume suggests, our efforts should be directed toward moving "beyond silence."

Here it is important to acknowledge the growing body of literature that argues that silence can be a legitimate choice. Cheryl Glenn, George Kalamaras, Adrienne Rich, and others challenge the more prevalent culturally inscribed definitions and interpretations of "the problem of silence." In the final chapter, I will explore this thinking in light of my students' observations about the value they perceive in choosing to be silent. At this point in my argument, however, I suggest that these perspectives and rereadings of silence still carry far less weight in our conversations about the silences and quiet students in our classrooms. Students who choose not to speak are described through a rhetoric of failure: these students are seen by what they do not do rather than by what they *choose* to do.

Strikingly absent from most of these explorations of silence are the perspectives of students. It is a noticeable lack. Typically our literature shows the attempts of teachers and theorists to understand, even to rationalize, the silence of their students, with varying degrees of criticism or political justification. Yet we have failed to consider the insights our students' constructions could offer us about this dynamic.[12]

With Linda Brodkey, I believe that "we see the world from a particular vantage point . . . what can be seen by either the human eye or a human theory is necessarily partial, that is, both an *incomplete* and an *interested* account of whatever is envisioned."[13] Our constructions of student silence represent partial and interested accounts, ones that may offer useful theorizing into classroom dynamics but that ultimately fail to look outside of our own positions as teachers and theorists.

In my preliminary research, I was struck by how radically differently students view the dynamics of class discussions and oral participation than do their teachers. For example, I have encountered several students who saw themselves as highly vocal when I had unconsciously labeled them "silent students." And in my observations of a class populated by juniors and seniors who were Education majors, I was impressed by how vocal and comfortable the students appeared to be in discussing professional texts and their own writing. The professor concurred, arguing that they were some of the most skilled and sophisticated users of academic discourse she had encountered in her numerous years of teaching. However, more than three-quarters of these future teachers saw themselves as "quiet students," a label they understood to be problematic.

In addition, my preliminary research has suggested that students understand their own silences in far more complicated ways than we do, often seeing multiple causes and issues at play in a teacher's request for oral participation and their decisions to speak or not. Through the research that comprises this book, I have had the opportunity to explore these issues further. In the broadest terms, this data can be grouped around students' concern for teachers and their pedagogies, their sense of identity and community relationships, and their readings of silence that call into question our sense of classroom silence as inherently problematic.

Current pedagogy tends toward monolithic explanations of student silence: it is the failure to engage in empowering dialogue, or it is the product of political and cultural forces that makes *silence* an action. Both of these positions and their underlying principles strike me as valid and useful considerations of classroom dynamics. But I believe our classrooms and our students are too complex to be summarized in such assertions. As Mimi Orner claims in her critique of "calls for student voice," classrooms are the

> complex conjunctures of histories, identities, ideologies, local, national, and international events and relations. Those who would distill only singular, stable meanings from student silence ignore the profoundly contextual nature of all classroom interaction. Those who "read" student silence simply as resistance or ideological-impairment replicate forms of vanguardisms which construct students as knowable, malleable objects, rather than as complex contradictory subjects.[14]

Orner's critique is an important one, leading me to question our disciplinary construction of student silence as always negative. This critique is one that underlies my project: when we speak for quiet students in the ways we have, what might we be missing?

Study Design:
Collecting Silences and the
Roles of the Teacher and the Researcher

I collect silences.

—Heinrich Böll, "Murke's Collected Silences"

This study draws on the rich and varied traditions and practices of teacher-research that underlie essays such as Fishman and McCarthy's "Boundary Conversations: Conflicting Ways of Knowing in Philosophy and Interdisciplinary Research," Atwell's "Everyone Sits at a Big Desk," Curtis and Klem's "The Virtual Context: Ethnography in the Computer-Equipped Writing Classroom," and Faigley's "Subverting the Electronic Notebook: Teaching Writing Using Networked Computers,"[15] to name but a few.

Joy Ritchie argues, "Many feminist academicians continue to operate within a binary perspective, placing intellect against emotion, separating reason from experience, and ultimately setting theory against practice. As a result, important connections between feminist theory and practice are masked, and we lose sight of our common purposes."[16] I believe many researchers continue to see teaching and research in such an opposition. For example, E. David Wong argues that research and teaching have "distinct priorities. In brief, the primary goal of research is to understand; the primary goal of teaching is to help students understand."[17] Ultimately this dichotomy makes little sense to me in practice, as my teaching and research inform each other constantly. Owen van den Berg claims, "insiders research what they teach; they do not cease to teach in order to research. The goal of their research is to improve their practice; the goal of their teaching is to enhance the education of their students so that the students might become full democratic agents in the society."[18] To be both teacher and researcher requires "neither a split in attention nor a conflict in attention.[19] This particular research project formalized for me the kinds of evaluations and decisions inherent, even unconscious, in the process of teaching a composition class; in fact, I suspect I was a *better* teacher, as I documented the kinds of investigations and analyses one always makes as a teacher. Further, I was careful to vary course structures to allow my students and me to consider issues of voice and silence in a range of ways, and I was more rigorous in interrogating how and why I reached the conclusions I did about my own and my students' behaviors and responses. Jane Zeni believes that such research "opens the boundary between practice and research, because doing research becomes central to how one teaches."[20]

I believe this study proposes a way to coinvestigate a question with students, without radically altering the course structure and agenda to accommodate one's investigation; the class that became the subject of this study fundamentally remained a College Writing class, parallel to its sister sections. Along with Marian M. Mohr, I believe "Teacher-researchers are teachers first."[21] That is, while I designed my class to accommodate my research agenda, my questions could never dominate or obscure the primary objectives of the composition course I had been assigned to teach. I made the conscious commitment that if the occasion arose that experimentations with classroom design, and so on might benefit my research questions without advancing students' learning, then these questions would, out of necessity, be abandoned. (In the course of the research, however, pursuing my research questions did not conflict with students' learning, so neither objective was "compromised" by the "dual roles" I inhabited.[22]) My "minimally invasive" research agenda did not change the teaching and learning goals that the university Writing Program demanded. Further, and most important, this research design allowed students a maximum degree of control over their participation.

I chose to focus my research on the students in my own section of College Writing,[23] for several reasons. Because these issues of "voice" and "silence" are so loaded for both teachers and students, asking students to reveal themselves is also highly charged, requiring a high degree of trust and comfort that I do not believe I could have achieved as an observer in someone else's classroom. Of course, this raises important ethical objections: Did students make "unfettered decisions" about their participation in the study, without "fear of the consequences of not participating"?[24] Could my own students truly feel "safe" telling me what they really thought? Did their classroom relationships with me alter and limit what they could say? In order to account for those potential difficulties in the design of my study, I did not examine any data students offered until after the semester was over. Their written reflections were kept in sealed envelopes until their grades were submitted and students had the opportunity to renegotiate their participation. Interviews were conducted the following semester.

I also studied my own class because I would be able to engage my students, as research participants, in a wide range of classroom situations in which they might consider their decisions to speak or to be silent by varying the structures used to elicit their voices and to shape classroom conversation, deliberately building into the class opportunities for silence.

Finally, I was concerned that in another teacher's class, the focus of my investigation might have shifted away from the perspectives of students to account for the instructor's constructions in a substantive way and replicated the teacher-focused sort of theorizing and research that has characterized our discipline's thinking about student silence. To do so would have obscured the student-centered questions that prompted this research.

After the initial phase of research during the semester (explained later in "Sources"), I focused my research with students who self-identified as quiet students and who volunteered to continue their participation in the project. I did not deliberately pursue particular students I might have labeled "quiet." (From here on, I refer to them as "focal students" to distinguish them from the rest of the class.[25]) Because this label of "quiet student" often carries a stigma for those who understand it as a sign of deficiency or failure as a student, I believe that my labeling students this way would have been counterproductive to my larger objectives in this research. For me to have actively solicited students who otherwise might not have chosen to be interviewed would have, in a significant way, replicated what they already experienced when teachers try to "encourage" their oral participation. Doing so would have centered the investigation on *my* teacherly constructions.

Researching one's own class evokes a question about a conflict between the roles of teacher and researcher. I believe I was able to minimize this potential conflict through my study design. Students could choose not to participate in the project at all (although everyone did submit at least three of the four journal entries); because I did not read any of the written material until after the semester was over, students were assured that any (negative) reflections would not compromise their standing in the class. Periodically, students would prompt a discussion about my research, through direct questions about how I became interested in the topic, my perceptions of other teachers' interpretations of quiet students, and what I "hoped" to find through my research. Such questions seemed important to address in the forum in which they arose, whether in one-on-one conversations or in the full class. This seemed both a way to model intellectual inquiry and research (a focus of this composition course) and an important and ethical way to invite students to act as coinvestigators in this project.

Breaking the Silence about Silence?

When I was designing this project, a colleague asked if I might have difficulty obtaining data. How do you study silence? Would asking students to talk about their silence challenge the very premise of the project? My colleague's half-joking questions point to a larger, more complicated issue—the potentially skewing effect that speaking about silence might have on the data, a so-called "Hawthorne Effect," in which "behavior during the course of an experiment can be altered by a subject's awareness of participating in that experiment."[26] In other words, would participating in this project and *talking* about their decisions about speaking and silences change students' experiences of these, thereby invalidating the results of the study? Ultimately, Stephen R. G. Jones's rereadings of the initial Hawthorne experiments[27] that continue to influence the social sciences and research in the psychology of education were persuasive to me: while the received wisdom may be that participation in a research study skews the results, meta-analysis does not support this conclusion. Further, Gordon Diaper's examination of various studies, including those in education, leads him to conclude, "It would not be exaggerating to call the Hawthorne Effect a myth."[28] Thus talking about their decisions to speak or to be silent should not have affected how my students perceived these decisions or how they, in fact, acted in the classroom that formed the basis of this research.

This, however, led to another interesting question: what does it mean to *break the silence about silence?* Ultimately, in research methodology I loosely followed the lead of researchers interested in silence, such as Keith Basso, Cheryl Glenn, and Carol Gilligan, as well as Mary Field Belenky, Blythe McVicker Clinchy, Nancy Rule Goldberger, and Jill Mattuck Tarule.[29] Each draws on interviews, asking participants to name their experiences and to make meaning out of them. In this way, these researchers suggest that it is important to move beyond the traditional research paradigm in which "outsiders"—the researchers—investigate, name, and analyze to invite insider-participants to speak for themselves as coinvestigators whose voices must be heard. I wanted my research with quiet students to follow in this tradition, in the belief that such "qualitative research has to be collaborative arises from the recognition that participants hold multiple perspectives on what is occurring in social situations and what the meaning of those occurrences are. Educational innovation and research are socially complex phenomena that involve the 'process of coming to grips with the multiple of people who are the main participants.'"[30]

Furthermore, in American culture, to "break the silence" is often represented as a powerful political and social act. For example, in reviewing the first thirty Web sites that emerge in a Google search of the phrase, it becomes evident how powerful even this language is, as it is used in relation to therapy abuse, family violence, sexual assault, LGBT (lesbian, gay, bisexual, and trans-gender) issues, diabetes,

Palestinian refugee camps, HIV/AIDS, elder abuse, rape counseling, witnessing Christ, and colorectal cancer: the words "breaking the silence" themselves seem to have power. In class discussions of this project, in written reflections, and in various interview conversations, students seemed to understand the inherent weightiness of their participation in this project, even in very brief conversations about classroom silence—that to speak about silence is, in some ways, a political act, as it works, even in a very small way, as a corrective to the ways they have been named and misnamed by their teachers and the academy to which they seek membership.

Sources

1. Student journals. At several points during the semester, my students reflected informally on classroom silence by narrating a moment from the previous weeks when they or other students were (or were not) quiet and then commenting on why this struck them as remarkable. Like Madeline Grumet, I argue that "we are, at least partially, constituted by the stories we tell to others and to ourselves about experience."[31] What stories students tell themselves about their experiences of classroom silence[32] constitute—to some degree— their identities. These identities, I believe, shape students' interactions in and constructions of the classroom.

But I did not imagine these informal reflections as solipsistic exercises. That is, "autobiographical reflection [was] understood not just as an individual exercise but as a process that always takes place within a social context."[33] Thus I asked my students to consider each reflection in a larger context (of our class, of their educational histories) and to include their analysis of these observations. In their final reflections, I explicitly directed students to consider what connections they saw between the stories they told.

Students created these accounts as part of their journals, so my project imposed no additional requirements. Each student sealed her reflections in an envelope and signed across the seal to ensure this writing remained private until the end of the semester. Because of the complicated power dynamics that emerged through working with my own students (particularly centered around grading and evaluation), I was concerned that reading these accounts during the semester would radically alter my perception of these students and would inhibit what they chose to share. If students so chose, they were able to retract their consent after the semester was over.[34] Since many students did not perceive themselves as "quiet" or "silent," they were invited to explore their experiences in other classes or to examine the silences of others.[35]

2. My own teaching journal. I completed a teaching journal following each class that included the dynamics I established in a particular class (i.e., structures for interaction, particular requirements for discussions) and a narrative of what I saw happening in that class for both the students and me.

Later it proved useful to explore the connections between my interpretations of a particular class and those of my students in order to more fully understand the radical disjuncture between their perceptions and mine.

This commitment to self-reflection made me conscious of those reactions and constructions that would typically remain unexamined, even unarticulated, in the course of a semester. Such a self-consciousness and acknowledgment of the ways my own tacit values shape my work encouraged (in fact, forced) me to be more careful in both my teaching and my research.[36] As Anne Herrington argues:

> We should stop and reflect on our actions, trying to identify the be-liefs that guide us and reflect critically on them in light of alterna-tives. That reflection may reaffirm our commitment to how we have been acting or it may lead us to change. Regardless, if we engage in such reflection, we will be more likely to actually make choices and have a fuller understanding for our reasons for doing so.[37]

3. Follow-up interviews. These form the core of the project. I conducted a series of interviews with five focal students who volunteered to participate in this phase of my research; they identified themselves as "quiet" students, students un-likely (or less likely than their classmates) to choose to speak during class. Cer-tainly the perspectives of highly vocal students are critical in understanding the classroom dynamics of discussion and student interaction and merit further ex-tended exploration. (One brief example is that we often assume that vocal students are learning more, learning better through their oral participation. However, this explanation may not adequately account for their motives in "class participation," as several students in my study argue.) But in this present study, I was committed to working with those quiet students whose voices may rarely be heard, both in our classrooms and in our research. Teachers, researchers, and theorists have attempted to *speak for* quiet students by offering interpretations of their students' behaviors; this study asks us to listen more carefully to what these students themselves can tell us about their decisions, our assumptions, and our teaching.

My primary concern was to understand how students construct their own experiences and to explore what those insights can offer us about the class-room.[38] Therefore, I relied on a fundamental principle that links naturalistic re-search, in-depth interviewing, and feminist research—an interest in the everyday experiences of others, an assertion that the thoughts and feelings of others constitute valid research data, and the belief that the meaning they make of these experiences is able to be made explicit.[39] I chose interviews as one of my primary sources of data because, as I. E. Seidman claims, they are

> a powerful way to gain insight into educational issues through understanding the experience of the individuals whose lives constitute

education. As a method of inquiry, interviewing is most consistent with people's ability to make meaning through language. It affirms the importance of the individual without denigrating the possibility of community and collaboration.[40]

With each student, I conducted three open-ended interviews. In the first, I asked students to describe their experiences with oral class participation—the times it was successful or unsuccessful in their perspectives, moments they were vocal or silent, and moments that were particularly memorable for them. In the second interview, we explored the context of the students' history, particularly their history in school. I developed an Interview Guide,[41] a broad list of questions, to shape the second interviews. However, my objective was to elicit and explore those stories and issues that students suggested. These questions were revised to reflect the specific local issues and themes that emerged from the journals produced during the previous semester; I asked questions in an organic fashion, following the direction of students' reflections, rather than a rigid format. Indeed, as Ruth Ray argues, "Students are not merely subjects whom the teacher-researcher instructs and assesses; they are co-researchers, sources of knowledge whose insights help focus and provide new directions for the study."[42] In the third interview, I asked students to explore in more depth both the written accounts they produced and the interview transcripts. Students commented on their own narratives and considered the themes, patterns, and concerns they saw emerging in these texts.

4. Student essays. During the course of the semester, two students wrote essays that seemed particularly relevant to this research. With their permission, I have drawn on these works as well.

Listening to the Data

After a holistic analysis of the written reflections, I identified major trends in the data and several candidates for interviews during the second phase of the research. From the list of nineteen volunteers, I ultimately chose two men and three women to interview. Of these, one of the men identified himself as white, the other as Indian. Two of the women identified themselves as white, and the third—a citizen of Israel—was born of citizens of the United States living in Israel.[42]

When selecting these five students, I looked for students who seemed to express positions representative of the range of data in the written reflections.[44] I also looked for students who wrote at least an average quantity, both narrating and analyzing their experiences of silence to generate a depth of data during the second phase. Finally, I wanted the sample to represent the class demographics as accurately as possible. Given my skepticism about the generalizations that have emerged from much that has been written about student silence, I did not design this study to provide conclusive data about gender or race. Nor do I believe it is possible to do so. Looking for and believing we have found "the answer" to student silence lead us to view students reductively and to teach prescriptively. Instead, this study aims to ask new questions about student silence and to reframe interpretations in a conscientious, deliberate way by understanding the broad scope of students' concerns.

I was interested in exploring the frameworks that students themselves use to understand their own experiences. With both the student journals and interviews, I conducted inductive analysis in order to understand what themes and patterns would emerge from the data. What meanings do *they* construct for these experiences? What patterns and themes emerge from an extended consideration of the stories of so-called quiet students? In *Qualitative Evaluation and Research Methods*, Michael Quinn Patton argues that "inductive analysis means that the patterns, themes, and categories of analysis come from the data; they emerge from the data rather than being imposed on them prior to data collection and analysis."[45] Unlike Patton, I do not argue that such patterns exist without a pattern maker: the researcher herself is always implicated in constructing meaning through the categories and themes she identifies. In order to minimize those issues I might deem "important" to a discussion of silence (such as race, gender, class, "resistance," absence, silencing, etc.) and to emphasize quiet students' constructions, my coding and analysis began with what Patton calls "indigenous concepts,"[46] those terms participants use to describe their experiences. I first identified the terms and ideas that appeared repeatedly in students' reflections and then grouped related terms.[47] The nine major categories were: (1) "comfort" with other students; (2) "comfort" with teachers; (3) subject-related concerns; (4) classroom practices (inhibiting or encouraging speaking); (5) "internal" reasons; (6) alternate constructions of silence (including references and discussions where silence was not seen as problematic); (7) environmental factors (such as the time of day); (8) "difference"; and (9) references I could not otherwise categorize (including reflections that did not address the questions and issues of the study). Here it seems critical to acknowledge that those terms and categories I brought to the study (focusing on silencing, absence, hostility, etc.) emerged quite infrequently in students' accounts. The category "difference" appears in the accounts almost entirely as a result of specific questions I posed, generally during the final interviews with the focal students. Likewise, I anticipated a wealth of stories about resistance to teachers or texts prompting student silence, as much of our teacherly storytelling would suggest—these were conspicuously absent.

My analysis of the interviews initially took place through case studies. As Patton argues, "The [purpose of the] case study approach to qualitative analysis is to gather comprehensive, systematic, and in-depth information about each case of interest."[48] This structurally reinforced my commitment to listen to the particular voices that often get erased in teachers' and theorists' constructions of quiet students. Robert E. Stake delineates three types of case studies: the intrinsic, the instrumental, and the collective.[49] My analysis of the interviews was a hybrid of the first two variations, undertaken for a deeper understanding of the particular cases in order to provide further insight into the issue of student silence, theoretical constructions of the phenomenon, and pedagogical strategies as well.

However, my attention to these individual stories and particular constructions was not an end in itself. While I was concerned with investigating the experiences of each student, I also wanted to provide a more macro-view of the classroom. After a systematic exploration of the individual cases, I read thematically across the five case studies in order to offer a new (if not unified) perspective on student silence. How much time students spent on a particular theme, the richness and complexity of those reflections, and often students' conscious prompting highlighted the relative importance of particular issues in students' complex negotiations about speaking and silence.[50] To borrow a term from Peter Elbow and Pat Belanoff, "centers of gravity" and links between the categories emerged, and I began to hear student silence in a new way.

Finally, I returned to my teaching journal and to the written reflections of the entire class to consider any additional insights or reflections on what emerged as students' key issues or concerns. Ultimately I chose to include in this text not only the voices of the focal students but those of all students in the class in the ways they addressed the central questions I set out to explore.

Originally I had envisioned this book as a series of case studies. Each chapter would develop a portrait of an individual student as well as a distinct question or issue relating to the questions I posed about speaking and silence in the composition classroom. In this way, readers might come to see these students in the ways that I had known them. However, in looking at the data, this plan seemed less practicable. First, all students spoke at length about multiple issues they considered in the classroom, making it virtually impossible to select a single focus for each. Their reflections frequently overlapped, providing me with interesting avenues to explore in the subtle variations among their reflections. Simply put, case studies would prove reductive and repetitive, as my students' reflections were far more complicated and interrelated than I had anticipated. Further, on a philosophical level, I was concerned that case studies might lead to the conclusion that the concerns and reflections of these students were individual, isolated, and idiosyncratic, thus more easily dismissed. Instead of following a case study format, I centered my analysis on the questions students ask themselves when considering their decisions to speak or to be silent. In the following chapters, you will hear a profusion of voices, without necessarily developing a picture of individual students. Ultimately, I decided this slightly less satisfying exchange would have to suffice: while you might not see Edward, Catarina, Lucy, Sarah, and Sanjay with the clarity I do, you will hear the chorus their voices make—together.

Why Listen?

Brodkey argues, "The only way to fight a hegemonic discourse is to teach ourselves and others alternative ways of seeing the world."[51] It is in this assertion that I see the value and significance of my study. The critique raised by interrupting the authoritative stories we teachers and theorists tell through considering quiet students' experience of the classroom will, I hope, work to transform the theoretical and pedagogical understandings that underlie our disciplinary constructions of student silence. In Barney G. Glaser and Anselm L. Strauss's terms, I believe my project will help in the development of a "grounded theory" about our classrooms and our quiet students.

Chapter Outlines

In the next chapter, I examine a selection of teaching narratives and draw on a range of theorists for a discussion of how we in the field of composition have come to conceptualize student silence primarily in negative terms. In part, this will draw on the work of composition scholars. However, for a more fully articulated, more carefully nuanced understanding of silence, I also consider other discourses and other fields of study to complicate the picture we have drawn of classroom dialogue and student silence. My effort here is to establish what our shared interpretations of student silence are, as well as what issues and preoccupations in composition pedagogy these interpretations point to.

In chapter 3, I present an autoethnographic study of my own history of silences, particularly those academic silences that strike me now as both turning points personally and as crucial experiences shaping my perspectives as a teacher and a researcher. My own history as a student is marked by striking changes in relation to speaking and silence in the classroom: shifting from an eager, highly verbal student in my elementary school years, through many incarnations to my current position as someone who is most likely often perceived as "silent." In this chapter, I trace out what prompted each of these evolutions and the effects these had on my school life. I have several purposes here. First, I believe these experiences profoundly shape my current practices as a teacher and in turn shape my students' experiences. Likewise, I believe these constructions shape my agenda in this project: I find myself personally committed to fighting against the community wisdom about what it means to be a "quiet" student. As Gesa Kirsch claims in her exploration of feminist methodology:

> The goal of situating ourselves in our work and acknowledging our limited perspectives is not to overcome these limits—an impossible task—but to reveal to readers how our research agenda, political commitments, and personal motivations shape our observations in the field, the conclusions we draw, and the research reports we write.[52]

With Kirsch, I believe the exploration of my relationship to this research is an ethical decision. In this process, I acknowledge the ways that my own experiences and identity shape my work; likewise, I engage in the same sorts of reflections—which are often difficult—that I asked my participants for.

The very brief chapter 4 contextualizes the student reflections in the second half of the book. This chapter serves as a reference for readers—offering a profile of the student population where the study took place, introductions to the five focal students, and an overview of the College Writing course in which this study took place.

Chapters 5 and 6 investigate students' sense of classroom silence as problematic and consider the implications for writing (particularly in chapter 6). This interpretation generally centers on the sense that they are not meeting a teacher's requirements. Using the data from students' written reflections and the series of interviews with five students, I explore in chapter 5 my students' visions of the influence of teachers and particular pedagogies on their decisions to speak or to be silent. Often, teaching practices designed to "empower" students and invite their speaking (calling on students, requirements) are seen as problematic, intensifying the pressures that students experience. Students suggest that they are more encouraged to speak by what they perceive as "smaller gestures": the cultivation of teacher-student relationships, a teacher's presentation of "self," and focused attention on how questions are asked and responded to. For these students, such efforts positively alter the dynamics of power, knowledge, and authority in the classroom.

But there are limits to a teacher's influence on classroom dynamics. As I explore in chapter 6, more critical for many of these quiet students are the intersections between identity and community. For example, many cite the "openness" of the community and the ways that speaking invites public evaluation of one's response and intelligence, even one's identity. This is problematic, but not because these students fear conflict or want to avoid disagreement. (Indeed, several enjoy debate-style situations.) Rather, they perceive the interactions in classes as demanding risky self-revelation, often in anonymous communities that do not have "real" conversations. In composition classes where student writing is often a central text of the course, speaking is even more loaded. Thus these quiet students are very conscious of the lessons about voice and audience we try to teach in writing classes.

The final chapter investigates alternative constructions to understand classroom silence, both in our professional discourse and in these students' stories. Most significant in this chapter is the communal sense that silence is not necessarily problematic. As one student says, "It's not a crime to be quiet." For many, silence might be understood more accurately as a learning style, an opportunity for intellectual work through "internal dialogue." Silence can invite students to weigh competing positions, construct theories and arguments that reflect their values, and put into words that which does not feel already articulated. For one student I interviewed, silence allows her to consider how her responses might fit into the "academic conversation" and to translate from her home language, particularly for those concepts and ideas that have no direct translations. Thus for these students, silence is the space of engagement.

Throughout the text, I offer implications and considerations for a grounded theory of teaching. This research suggests several concrete pedagogical issues to consider: creating a range of speaking situations, including small groups and lower-stakes "real conversations"; devoting greater attention to the development of the classroom community; and providing more opportunities for reflective silence within our classes. But it also points to several areas for further investigation. It is not enough to say we will study *about* silence in classrooms; we must also explore it *with* our classes. Working alone, there is little opportunity for growth. Teachers create requirements, and students may comply or resist or resent or misunderstand these expectations. But a critical dialogue about a teacher's values and expectations and her students' experiences and perspectives invites a more complete vision—an expansion of the ways we think about each other, our classrooms, and the value of silence.

Chapter 2

Considering the
Problem of Silence

Silence's fame spread
throughout many lands.

—Heldris of Cornwall, *Silence: A Thirteenth-Century French Romance*

The Romance and the Classroom

Silence: A Thirteenth-Century French Romance tells the tale of Silence. Silence is
the extraordinarily beautiful daughter of Cador and Euphemie (whose name
translates as "Good Speech"). Because the king has decreed that no woman
shall inherit land or property, Silence's parents decide to hide their child's gender and raise her as a male. Silence becomes an exemplary boy who is "so
charming, handsome, and brave . . . the mirror of the world."[1] This instigates an
ongoing debate between Nature and Nurture, two human characters: which has
more power over the development and beauty of Silence?

Silence eventually runs away with two minstrels in search of adventure,
causing the people of his[2] homeland to deeply mourn his absence. Ultimately
Silence's companions become so jealous of his skills and the accolades he receives that they plot (unsuccessfully) to kill him. When Silence finally returns
home, King Evan makes him a retainer. Queen Eupheme (whose name translates as "Bad Speech") falls in love with Silence and attempts to seduce him.
Silence rejects these advances, and the queen threatens to disgrace him.

What Silence fears most is this disgrace and the loss of inheritance. A
complicated plot follows: Silence is sent to France, where Queen Eupheme
tries to have Silence killed. But without understanding the crimes of Silence,
the king of France finds himself unable to proceed with this plan. Silence ultimately becomes a highly skilled and brave knight. Nurture apparently triumphs

21

over Nature, as Silence is able to "overcome" the confines of gender to learn the arts and skills of men. When Silence returns home as a hero at King Evan's request, the truth about Silence is revealed through a trick of Merlin's. Queen Eupheme's duplicity is made known, and she is killed. Transforming from Silentium (the masculine form) to Silentia (the feminine form), Silence is made queen and King Evan revokes his proclamation about women's inheritance. Silence's many deceptions go unpunished, even unremarked, in the course of the romance, while other characters guilty of duplicity are punished.

There are a number of issues for analysis in this relatively unstudied text: the construction of gender roles; the theorizing about the relative influences of environment and heredity on one's abilities and behaviors; the political, national, and familial dynamics enacted; and the relationship between magical and realistic elements in the tale. However, what interests me in the context of this project is the role of Silence herself and the relationships created around her. While the character's name clearly seems to point to the silence about her gender, a literal reading of her tale offers broader questions that connect to this study. How do we know silence? What relationship do we have with silence? To what extent do we read our students' silences as "natural"? How is silence consciously or unconsciously fostered, and how does this affect our responses to it? What do we know about silence beyond the contextual and linguistic associations we have taken for granted? What assumptions do we make, what conclusions do we draw based on the outward appearances of silence?

In the romance, Silence in both her "natural" and "nurtured" roles, that is, in her incarnations as woman and man, is represented as the picture of *perfection*. In fact, Nature and Nurture argue endlessly about which can claim responsibility, and therefore praise, for Silence's beauty and accomplishments. Silence is the child of "Good Speech," who ironically speaks very little and is virtually powerless in the story. Silence is deeply attractive to "Bad Speech," who eventually threatens his very life and existence. It seems noteworthy that the names "Good Speech" and "Bad Speech"—Euphemie and Eupheme—are virtually identical, differing by a single letter. And the triumphant elevation and revelation of Silence's true self are dependent upon the destruction of seductive "Bad Speech." In both her masculine and feminine incarnations, Silence is celebrated for beauty, skill, and courage.

Unlike Cador's claim at the birth of his child, "silence relieves anxiety,"[3] silence has come to occupy a radically different place in the culture of American academic life. Certainly there are moments that require silence in the classroom: exams, writing exercises, or a teacher or student speaking will necessitate silence. These silences, initiated by teachers, are *good* silences. Such moments are generally an implicit part of the social contract of the classroom: teachers exert control over the voices of their students to foster a productive learning environment, and students typically share this understanding about when to maintain polite, respectful silences. While more attention needs to be paid to these and the productive silences of *listening*, as the work of Jacqueline Jones Royster and Krista Ratcliffe encourages us, the silences perceived as problematic tend to preoccupy us and populate our stories about our classrooms.

It is these other silences—initiated and controlled by students—that I explore here. Far from the world of the romance of *Silence*, we would not mourn the loss of this kind of silence; rarely do we see it as beautiful, heroic, or noble. Rather than celebrating student-initiated silence, typically we work to prevent its conception, preferring instead to center our energies on the tension between "good speech" and "bad speech" in the classroom, the exploration of the "good speech" of critical thinking, and (simplistically put) a debate about the "natural" or constructed quality of the silence of our students. Although it exerts a mighty influence over us, Silence occupies no heroic position in our classrooms, nor does it ensure any kind of equity. Instead, it is often constructed as the enemy of teaching, learning, and even teachers themselves. To extend the metaphor, in our imagination, silence might be born from "bad speech" (such as racist or sexist discourse), but "good speech" begets more speech, not silence.

So is there an analogy to be made between composition teachers and any of the characters in *Silence: A Thirteenth-Century French Romance*? Perhaps it is with the wandering minstrels who grow so envious and resentful of Silence's power that they try to rid themselves of him. And like the people of his homeland, we are accustomed to seeing Silence in one particular role, although we experience no joy, no celebration, when Silence's "true" nature is revealed. But I would suggest that if there are any characters in the romance we might productively emulate, it is the king of France and his advisors, who conclude that they cannot, in good conscience, kill Silence without a fuller understanding of his purported crimes. We might do well to remember that the deceptions Silence performs are legitimate, even just; Silence *can* be an active presence. Before trying to rid ourselves of the "crimes" of silence, I believe we need to understand it more fully, including our own (perhaps unconscious) participation in the perpetuation of silence and the complicated messages we send to our students about the value of speaking and silence.

The difficulty posed by student silence in our classrooms, I argue, is one of the most difficult, least easily reconciled challenges of composition pedagogies: the mismatch between theory and practice, between talking pedagogy and enacting it, ultimately calls these pedagogies into question. Put in the most basic terms, in dialogic education, student-initiated silence has often come to mean that something is not working. Of course, to see dialogue and silence as mutually exclusive entities is a reductionist binary. By definition, dialogue requires the silence of listeners in addition to the voices of speakers. And as some of the students in this study suggest, active listening demands engaged silence. Furthermore, many of us see classroom conversation and periods of silence in a sort of dialogue with each other, with "quiet" activities such as journal writing or drafting, leading to communal exploration, and conversation concluding in private writing and reflection. However, for many of us, these kinds of silences are seen as productive when a *teacher* initiates them; for students to choose silence may feel problematic, even antagonistic.

When we as teachers focus so intensely on *our* relationship to student silence and the relationship of silence to our pedagogies and goals, we can overlook students' relationship to their own voices and silences. It is this complex but underexplored dynamic that I investigate here. How do my students hear their own and other students' silences? Do they, like most teachers, read their silences negatively? What constructions do they offer to account for their silences, particularly in American school systems that place such a high premium on the highly vocal "good" student? If we take seriously our students' readings, then what do their constructions tell us about our own? Is it possible to read outside of the model of silence as lack, passivity, absence? As the indication of alienation or disempowerment? And ultimately, is it possible for us as teachers to maintain our concern for counteracting the mechanisms that work to silence students and still respect their right to silence?

As this book will suggest, I have many questions about much of the writing that has been done about silence and dialogue in the classroom from teachers' perspectives. I do ultimately find that it coincides with my own values about teaching and learning. Put rather reductively, I *do* think that learning generally takes place through dialogue, and that silence in our classrooms *may be* cause for concern. But I also believe that such constructions of the "problem" of student silence may further limit the roles we see for "good students," marginalizing quiet students even further by defining them as deviant from the supposed "center" of highly vocal students.

The Narrative and the Classroom

The eternal silence of these infinite spaces terrifies me.

—Blais Pascal, *Pensées*

Moving from the fantastic world of Silence in the French romance, I turn now to teaching narratives about silence in classrooms as a useful starting point for understanding our disciplinary constructions of student silence. Narratives are a useful research methodology, for several reasons. While it has been argued that narratives and narrative analysis are valuable because they are "closer to experience" than methodologies of observation and experimentation, I make a less problematic claim: narratives provide valid research data because they reflect the ways (or one of the ways) we construct our own experience. If, as Brodkey claims, "experience [is] the stories we tell about ourselves,"[4] then narrative writers gather for themselves and others the *data of experience*. Eleanor Kutz and Hepzibah Roskelly validate this sort of thinking:

> "Narrative knowing" accounts for a large part of the way we make sense of our world, and we use it in our must mundane conversations as well as our most significant texts. . . . When we select details from the flux of experience and shape them into a story, we're also engaged in naming, abstracting from, and restructuring the raw data of the physical world, and in finding its patterns of meaning.[5]

In other words, narrative offers a useful way of gathering and analyzing the data of lived experience in order to make sense of it. By structuring previous experience, narratives invite both reader and writer to "envision endings from the very beginning"[6] and to consider questions about the implicit interpretations and values that shape these stories. In this definition, active analysis is inherent in the process of narration.

These stories offer a variety of interpretations of silence in the classroom. It is important to note that teacher-authors have constructed these interpretations for themselves and for an audience of other teachers; one might legitimately wonder how the students represented might have narrated and interpreted these moments themselves.

As previously mentioned, I see two major kinds of silence in the classroom: those implemented by the teacher and those initiated by students. When teachers require silence, it is often for *pedagogical purposes*, for example, during tests, individual reading or writing, or while one person is speaking. In these situations, silence is seen as necessary for the intellectual work of the classroom to be done. When students are silent at these times, their behavior is interpreted (at least by the teacher) as respectful compliance (or, at the very least, the shrewd appearance of compliance). Perhaps less common is the use of silence as a *means of control*, even punishment, by a teacher. That is, as teachers we may not have our students put their heads down on their desks for misbehaving, but we certainly exert control to censor language, topics, or responses considered "inappropriate." In these ways, behaving appropriately—abiding by teacher-initiated silences—affords students citizenship in that classroom.

This chapter primarily investigates teachers' interpretations of those more complicated student-initiated silences perceived, by and large, negatively: the inability to speak, an unwillingness to "participate," resistance, hostility, lack of preparation or engagement, disempowerment or alienation, unwillingness to "go along" with the teacher. In the following chapters, I explore students' interpretations of silence that suggest definitions that challenge the resistance/ compliance or alienation/enculturation dichotomies upon which teachers' narratives often rely. When students do see silence negatively, this is premised on their sense of failing to meet teachers' expectations; their definitions rely on the negotiation of relationships with one's sense of self, with one's peer community, and with one's teacher.

Narrative Visions:
The Power of Speech

> When we were discussing Northampton [a local town] in class, I found myself wanting to be more involved. . . . When it was my turn to state my views, I really felt an urge to explain my own opinion, and try to let others know where I was coming from. I was actually excited to tell people. . . . Even after my turn was over, I found myself calling out comments to others. . . . After class I felt very satisfied that I had the chance to explain what I thought, even if the others didn't remember what I had said . . . I was definitely involved in participating aloud, [as] opposed to my normal commenting that remains in my head.
>
> —Jenna, student

Many teaching narratives position silence as an obstacle to be overcome; on the other side of this barrier is a richer, more vibrant promised land of dynamic classroom interactions. The goal is clear and unambiguous—get students talking, and make one's "reticent readers turn into nonstop talkers."[7] In Victor Villanueva's account, his students' collective ability to confront issues of race and class is represented as contingent upon the movement out of silence by particular students. And Patricia Shelley Fox's student who speaks out after a long silence is crucial for "our epiphanies . . . each has cleared the path ahead at the same time promising to make the journey more challenging, but finally richer and more fully our own."[8] However, it is in Kim Stafford's and Lynn Bloom's accounts that the most dramatic expressions of the need to move students out of their silences are found. In recounting his students' visit to a prison, Stafford reflects on the "forty faces made somehow mute by the fact of our confinement."[9] Here silence is conflated with the lack of mobility and the sense of guilt for wrongdoing symbolized by physical imprisonment. Bloom's account of her own history as a student and a teacher is one marked by silences and omissions—about the workings of sexism and power dynamics in various universities. She concludes that if our "commitment to teaching English is . . . for life," then we "will have to raise [our] voice[s]."[10]

What interests me in these accounts is the remarkable similarity between the representations of the transformative power of speech. The move out of silence is depicted as salvation, sometimes quite literally. In this dramatization, then, silence is much more significant than a decision *not* to speak: student silence is demonized. There is no space to see student silence as anything but an obstacle, the roadblock to a teacher's noble goals.

Not Complying:
The Power of Student Silence

> As a quiet student in class, I find myself troubled by the idea that teachers automatically assume that because a student is quiet, [she doesn't] understand what's going on or something is wrong.
>
> —Tracy, student

In seeking out the narratives I discuss in this chapter, I was struck by how frequently stories of classroom silence appear in our professional writing. For example, in the collection *Narration and Knowledge*, ten of the nineteen stories explicitly focus on student silence, despite another organizing principle for the volume. Nine of the seventeen essays in *Composition and Resistance*, edited by C. Mark Hurlbert and Michael Blitz, contain a narrative of classroom silence. The narratives in these two volumes, along with the many embedded narratives appearing in the pages of a journal such as *College English*, suggest a disciplinary fascination with this particular classroom phenomenon. Some of the themes that emerge in looking at a group of such narratives—resistance, disengagement, hostility—may help explain this preoccupation.

It is important to define the term *resistance* as I am using it here. Historians use it to denote struggles for liberation from an occupying power; psychologists employ it to describe unconscious opposition to recalling painful memories or repressed desires. In medicine, it describes the body's ability to withstand disease, toxins, or infection, while in critical pedagogy, it signifies the political act of asserting agency. In these discourses, resistance may be natural and self-protective or organized and liberatory. What is resisted is harmful, dangerous, limiting.

These are not the definitions of resistance I see at play in these teaching narratives: these students cannot (and implicitly should not) be automatically equated with the French underground, the ego, white blood cells, or composition's critical thinkers. These students are resisting their teachers who are, emphatically, not harmful or dangerous. Instead, in these narratives, an even more basic definition of resistance operates in their depictions of students. Their resistance is constructed as a refusal to comply, whether through deliberately oppositional behaviors, expressions of hostility, or passive noncompliance. In these teachers' narratives, they themselves become that which is resisted, a process that is often represented as illogical and counterproductive.

There is a virtually unanimous definition of students' speech as participation and the resulting equation of quietness to *nonparticipation* or absence from the classroom. Kutz and Roskelly's opening chapter of *An Unquiet Pedagogy* dramatizes this dynamic. They offer an admittedly generalized picture of the English classroom, one they expect teachers will find "disquieting[ly] familiar."[11] Of classroom interaction and dialogue, they note:

> Although the teacher may draw a particular student into the lesson, more often communication in the classroom takes familiar forms that both teacher and student know intuitively. . . . They [the students] give answers, and "they" are almost always the same ones who seem always to raise their hands. Every once in a while, the teacher surprises somebody by calling a name, but the selected student seldom responds with much more than a mumble, and she goes back to the familiar raised hand with a sigh of relief. Some students stay on the fringes of this "discussion"; they never respond and the teacher has learned never to call on them.
>
> [When students are doing individual work] there's silence in the room now, except for a few complaints. . . . Everyone is waiting for the bell to ring. She [the teacher] can also count on their lack of enthusiasm for any of the tasks they accomplish.[12]

Silence occupies two very different positions in this text. Initially it is a sign of resistance or, at the very least, patterned passivity in response to the class discussion and, therefore, the teacher. In the second half, silence, while perhaps marking disengagement ("everyone is waiting for the bell to ring"), also signifies compliance; students are obediently doing what the teacher requires. Silence equals control.

Another example of silence as nonparticipation comes from Elizabeth Chiseri-Strater's ethnographic study. She comments, "Anna earns her community membership by adding her point of view,"[13] as if this membership in a class must be earned, and that to be a "quiet" student may very well legitimately exclude one from that community. In a similar move, Villanueva notes of one quiet student, "He's not much of a participator in class. He won't be on this day either, though he'll end up playing a part in the drama."[14] And Sharon Hamilton recalls, "Tamla who, until this moment [when she made an oral comment], had not participated in the discussion."[15]

For a teacher who is seeking "class participation," speech may appear to be the only means of defining or eliciting that participation. But I wonder, is it possible to "participate" mentally or to "play a part in the drama" of the classroom without speaking? For a discussion to function effectively, yes, people must be willing to speak. From this point of view, the transitive meaning of "participate" seems to apply: students *take part in* a discussion. But it also is possible to argue that students who are active, engaged listeners also take part in the discussion. This suggests another broader way we might think about this slippery notion of "class participation." What if a student does not learn best by speaking? Can we say that she is *mentally participating* in the intransitive sense of the word—sharing in or partaking of the discussion?

Perhaps because silence is typically defined as lack or absence, and because it offers little data for interpretation, teachers have come to these common "truths" about silence as a sign of disengagement and/or hostility. At best, "Most of the faces register only politeness. A foot kicks the desk chair of the person in front of it. 'sorry.' Several rubberneck the clock. Nothing to make fun of. Not much to interpret, I suppose."[16] More typically, though, these students are "aggressively bored" and "distract [the rest of the class] ... they [are] responsible for the unproductive mood of the classroom"[17]; they show "their lack of enthusiasm for any of the tasks they accomplish"[18]; they are "aggressively apathetic."[19] And when silence is not explicitly connected to resistance and hostility, it is often linked to a student's withdrawal. Nancy Sommers remembers a student she could not "reach" as "announcing her presence by stretching her hand out on her seminar table, then spending most of our class time drawing intricate Escher-like worlds within worlds on the palms of her hands and in the webs of fingers ... for most of our assignments she struck a Bartleby pose of 'I prefer not to.'"[20] And Villanueva's "Silent Ones" are echoed in the noncommittal "Mona Lisa half-smile"[21] of Patricia Shelley Fox's student.

All of these textual representations of quiet students as "nonparticipating" grow out of composition's interest in collaborative learning and "student-centered pedagogies" that are driven by the presence of students' literal, audible voices. Certainly these form a central component of my own teaching. But I believe these narrative constructions of quiet students reveal how limited a model of the "good student" we have created. In fact, I would argue that the range of acceptable and appropriate student behavior becomes even further limited by these ideologies. This becomes even more problematic for me when I consider the ways that this model of the highly vocal student as "good student" is often gender-, class-, and culture-bound. As Brodkey claims about the denial of middle-class values implicit in educational discourse, "such a discursive practice reduces all who study and teach to one version of the good student and one version of the good teacher without benefit of discussion."[22]

I suspect, as well, that underlying these representations of silence is this concern: what we cannot see, we cannot evaluate. And if we cannot evaluate students, then how do we know that they are learning, that they are even thinking? Even within ostensibly student-centered pedagogies, I think there is a tension between what we would like our students to be (those we would most like to teach) and the students we see before us who do not meet that ideal.

Since student-talk is one of the ways we evaluate our success as teachers and the effectiveness of our pedagogies, student silence is more problematic than a lesson plan gone awry. If we are committed to pedagogies based on dialogue and the idea of socially constructed knowledge, then student silence forces us to ask this question: who is to blame for this pedagogy *not working?* Charles Moran, in his reflections on returning to teaching in a traditional classroom, says his class begins

> on an ominous note: I begin to feel I have to do more than I am doing, because I'm feeling that not much is happening. *"I'm thinking the class is pretty quiet—not sure how to bring them together in groups."*[23]

Such reflections are strikingly rare though; the breakdown in pedagogy is more typically represented as the failure of students.

In the narratives I have explored, student-initiated silence was interpreted—with a single exception—negatively, as the sign of a problem, the manifestation of students' resistance. Frankly, these Bartleby-like students are troubling; they can become a disruptive, less contained version of the passive resistance of the scrivener in their refusal to speak as we ask, in their silent "I would prefer not to." At the extreme (one I confess to have experienced), their "manner . . . nettled me. Not only did there seem to lurk in it a certain calm disdain, but his perverseness seemed ungrateful, considering the undeniable good usage and indulgence he had received from me."[24]

Writers such as Bonnie TuSmith read silence as an indication of students' willful hostility. She points to the racist dismissal she hears underlying her students' silence over the interpretation of texts that utilize Black English Vernacular: "A defensive 'yes' was the answer, and a dismissive 'end of discussion' attitude."[25] The accusatory tone I read in her recollection seems to have been heard by her students as well. She recounts that after a question she posed, "silence prevailed. Finally, one student challenged, 'Are you saying we're racist because we didn't like her reading?'"[26]

Not all of our accounts or our experiences are so extreme. For example, authors such as Ira Shor, Philip Brady, Cheryl Johnson, and Lad Tobin construct explanations that account for these resistances as reasonable responses to interpersonal dynamics, institutional alienation, and social constructions. While their students' silences are troubling, ultimately these resistances are seen as legitimate responses to the oppressive rhythms and routines of education. For example, in the opening chapters of *When Students Have Power* and *Empowering Education*, Ira Shor begins with a dramatic depiction of resolutely silent students. He recalls:

> My confidence was shaken a little that first day when I reached the open door of B-321 and heard not a sound. Was this the right

classroom? Had my room been changed at the last minute? I took a step forward, peeked in the doorway, and saw twenty-four students sitting dead silent in two long rows of fiberglass chairs. . . . They were waiting for the teacher to arrive and do education to them.[27]

He comments that they responded with "aggressive silence."[28] This "Siberian Syndrome . . . is a defensive reaction to the unequal power relations of schooling."[29]

While Shor focuses on the oppressive routines of schooling that lead to such pervasive silences, Brady, Johnson, and Tobin explore their own complicity in their students' silences by rereading their experiences within each narrative. Although silence is still, ultimately the sign of a problem in the classroom, these authors consider their own responsibility in creating these troubling dynamics. And self-critically, they investigate how their worldviews shape their readings of their students and themselves. The process of narration denaturalizes the events for both writers and readers as the perceived resistances and hostilities are reconsidered. It becomes clear that these narrative accounts *are* constructions, not simply the *truth* of the experiences, pointing out that they are "an *incomplete* and an *interested* account of whatever is envisioned."[30] In this process, we are asked to consider "the ordinarily tacit body of constructs (beliefs, metaphors, images, strategies, values, and the like) that inform practice"[31]: why do we read these silences as blameworthy resistance and hostility?

Part of the answer to this question lies in the value of speaking and silence in American culture. In this context, it is perhaps unsurprising that teachers pay such profound attention to the audible voices of our students, given the larger cultural understandings of the privilege and right to speak for oneself. In the history of the United States, freedom and speaking have been inextricably linked, even within the text of Declaration of Independence, which "declare[s] the causes which impel them to the separation." That is, it is not enough to be free and independent states, they "must publish and declare" this fact.[32]

The history of the United States reminds us that to have a voice, to be able to speak for oneself, is to have power. From Revolutionary War slogans about "taxation without representation," to the frequently invoked First Amendment right to free speech, to the suffrage movement and civil rights activism, and to voter registration drives in 2004 that instructed young voters "your vote is your voice,"[33] we are reminded of the power of speaking out as a means of self-definition in a democracy. As bell hooks argues,

Moving from silence to speech [i]s a revolutionary gesture. Once again, the idea of finding one's voice or having a voice assumes a primacy in talk, discourse, writing, and action. . . . Speaking becomes both a way to engage in active self-transformation and a right of passage where one moves from being object to being subject. Only as subjects can we speak. As objects we remain voiceless—our beings defined and interpreted by others.[34]

Likewise, the justice system of the United States relies on the individual citizen's right to speak. The accused have the right to tell their own version of their stories, to defend themselves against the charges against them. This is balanced by the awareness that speaking can be dangerous; as the Miranda warnings instruct, one's words can become the weapons of one's own incrimination.

Furthermore, I would argue that for many of us educated in American schools, a curious inverse of the axiom *actions speak louder than words* is lodged in our collective subconscious. Public speeches have come to be a means of understanding history: the Gettysburg Address, Martin Luther King's "I have a dream" speech, and John F. Kennedy's inaugural address have become a shorthand for capturing and reducing complex historical realities. In this way, *speaking* has emerged as symbolic action. This is enacted in our daily lives through communal prayer, in reciting the Pledge of Allegiance, and in swearing an oath in court: speaking is the means by which one's presence and participation are declared. To choose not to speak—in a classroom or elsewhere—is to symbolically reject one's legacy in a democracy, one's right to self-definition, and one's ability to act as a subject.

A Teacher's Silence as Power

Right after, he'll have read a passage or we'll have watched a really moving movie, everyone just kind of sits and thinks about it for little while. And the teacher never gets on our case to start talking right then. Because I think it's just kind of understood that we're thinking and gathering our thoughts.

—Catarina, student

The value of silence radically changes when it is initiated and controlled by the teacher. Several teaching narratives celebrate the productiveness marked by the silence initiated by a teacher:

The room is quiet except for the scrape of pen tips on paper. . . . I know the drama of this story, [Chopin's "The Story of An Hour"] and I don't want the outside noise to break the spell. . . . The class reads and writes in virtual silence.[35]

On day 2, I note the wonderful silence (*"there are sounds of people reading!"*).[36]

[After a particularly charged reading] there is silence. Charged, glorious silence. I let the class feel that power for a few seconds.[37]

People pick up their pens. The concentrated quiet in the room tells me that everyone is writing and the writing matters.[38]

Joseph Trimmer's celebration of the power of silence explores how his teacherly voice fills the gaps and silences in his classroom. His students "know" this pattern; they expect "teacher-talk" from him. After an unusually heated exchange with a student who has challenged his choice of texts and the interpretations offered, Trimmer refuses to fill that space. He "savor[s] the silence."[39] But the ultimate expression of this power to control silence comes in Toby Fulweiler's narrative "Telling Stories and Writing Truths," in which he explores his practice of conducting the first day of a seminar entirely in silence.

These representations, all centered on the *active* "engaged" student, reflect an ideology of learning-by-doing. Such classrooms are not structured around the lecturing voice of a teacher; rather, it is the activity and interaction of students that constitute "knowledge." It is important, though, to note that such "student-centeredness" does not include consulting with students about their perceptions of classroom dialogue and silence. In these representations, teacher-narrators do not question their authority or the legitimacy of that institutionally sanctioned authority to evoke the voices of students or to silence them.

In these instances, silence prompted by the teacher represents the smooth functioning of pedagogy. Passante's image of "charged, glorious silence" seems to underlie all of these representations in which what happens in silence *matters*. These two meanings of silence—as resistance and as the expression of powerful intellectual work—often exist within the same text (i.e., Trimmer, Moran, Perl, and Passante).

I believe that silence occupies a central place in our collective imagination because it is a virtually "dataless" phenomenon and because it is an ambiguous symbol dependent on context for interpretation. Those cues we use to interpret speech—inflection, pause, emphasis, volume, tone—are absent, thus the listener is often left to rely on the *feeling* of silence and his culturally constructed expectations to create both the text and the interpretation of silence. The listener is allowed to make of silence what he will, based on the context: the relationship of the participants, their location, the occasion, and a host of other factors, including his own history. The silence of a suspect being interrogated might certainly indicate guilt. This silence is unlikely to be confused with that of new parents staring at a newborn in a nursery, that of a young widow in a funeral home, or that of a priest kneeling at an altar. But are such silences unambiguous? Guilt, awe, grief, and meditation seem likely interpretations, but aren't language-barriers, fear, relief, and shame equally plausible? The silences in our classrooms may be even more difficult to read, despite the easy conclusions we reach in the stories we tell.

How does context affect my own claims about silence? Certainly the larger cultural context that connects speech with freedom and democracy and the more localized one of my life as a scholar and a teacher lead me to value speech and dialogue and to see student silence negatively, in much the same way the writers of these narratives do. However, my experiences as a student and my conversations with so-called quiet students situate the claims of this book in another context. However, I am not aiming to replace one reading with another, to privilege students' constructions above teachers', but to challenge the ways we read those silences that seem so problematic to teachers in order to reframe our discussion about quiet students and classroom dialogue.

Not Complying:
The Emotional Power of Silence

> Last week . . . my TA was getting very upset because she wasn't getting any feedback from the class. It wasn't that no one knew the answers to any of the questions, it was just that no one felt like answering. They weren't trying to be difficult, they simply didn't want to say anything. . . . There's too much pressure I guess. . . . I noticed how the teacher was affected by the students not talking. . . . This frustrated the teacher a lot.
>
> —Ben, student

While much academic writing and training strives for analytical "distance," teaching narratives collapse this posture, allowing for an exploration of how the act of teaching "acts on" us, what Hunter McEwan and Kieran Egan call "our affective orientation."[40] If all of our interpretations are partial and situated, than narration can make explicit the very situatedness and subjectivity of our teaching and our representations. Indeed, as Carol Witherall and Nel Noddings suggest, "Stories can join the worlds of thought and feeling, and they give special voice to . . . the power of emotion, intuition, and relationships in human lives."[41] I would argue that the exploration of emotional life is crucial to any critical understanding of the classroom; it shapes our teacherly "vision, our literal and figurative perception of reality, [which] is limited to what can be seen/'seen' from a particular vantage point."[42]

Several narratives point to the teacher-writer's positive emotions, the joy of some teaching moments. For example, I am struck by the conclusion of Villaneuva's tale. After relating his class's struggle with Silko's *Ceremony* and the resulting discussion that evoked the voices of even "the Silent Ones"[43] who challenged the consensus, he notes: *"I have never ever had such success confronting race, poverty, liberalism, the common saws that so many walked into the class with, confronted. Did it: the dialectic. Yes!"*[44] But these moments are few and far between; we seldom witness such a public celebration of the successes of our teaching lives. Trimmer's "Telling Stories About Stories" is structured, in part, around his emotional responses to his students' apparent contentment with silence. Like Villanueva, Trimmer focuses his essay around the "high point" of a particularly effective, engaged discussion. Through his narrative of this discussion and one student's passionate critique, Trimmer is able to reflect on his own position as a teacher:

> For once, I'm content with dead air. . . . I watch the rows of silent faces watch me squirm. They know—oh, how well they know— that eventually I will start talking. Teacher's talk. That's my job. I'm supposed to be in charge. And that's it. Or at least part of it. I'm tired of teacher talk, tired of hearing my own voice sort it out, nailing it down, slapping it with a label.[45]

In her book-length exploration, *A Life in School*, Jane Tompkins explicitly asks her readers to confront the emotional content of teaching. An "unsent letter" addresses,

> Dear Fellow Teachers,
> What do you do when silence breaks out in your class, the times when you suddenly forget what you were going to say, or you ask a question no one answers, and you sit there wishing you were dead, blush rising from the throat, face hot, throat clenched?
> Last semester when I tried to hand authority over to my students, we had many such moments. Often we just sat there looking at each other. I nearly died, and so did they.
> Yet living through those silences taught me something. They had a bonding effect, like living through a war. As a result of this experience I've come to think pain and embarrassment are not the worst things for a class.[46]

Tompkins's account of her embodied reaction to classroom failure is the most extensive I have discovered, the most explicit about the emotional consequences and the costs of teaching. But her profound discomfort over silence "breaking out"—as if it is a disease—is reflected in other narratives. Tobin admits to his own frustration with students who resist his classroom practices; Moran chronicles his growing anxiety with the sounds and silences of traditional classrooms; Hamilton reads that "we were all uncomfortable, they with the unfamiliar task and me with my growing sense of their discomfort."[47] And the narratives of new teachers collected by Elizabeth Rankin reveal how these teachers "take personally" the behaviors and perceived resistance of their students. Meredith (one of the new teachers in her study) sees a student's silence as assaultive: "'I couldn't look at her—it was like somebody was hitting me in the face or something.'"[48]

Here Meredith points to an often-unacknowledged issue underlying all of these representations. How do our emotional, "personal" responses to silent students affect our teaching? What difference does our discomfort with student silence—whether we represent it in physical, psychic, or political terms—make in our teaching and in our relationships with these students? Exploring the emotional context of teaching offered by narratives is not simply a "personal," therapeutic endeavor; rather, admitting to and exploring our affective orientations are an important part of the project of reflecting on our explicitly "political" orientations, given how our critical perceptions are shaped by our emotional lives.

In looking at this selection of narratives, several issues emerge. Silence holds incredible power, both in our classrooms and in our imaginations. I am struck by the profound discomfort running through these accounts. When silence is student-initiated, it is disruptive—the sign of a breakdown in the classroom or the failure of students to meet the standards and expectations we set. But when teachers control silence, it is productive. Student-initiated silence, however, connotes passivity and disengagement; at best, it is seen as resistance.

Why is there such universal agreement about the meaning of this phenomenon? Are we just repeating versions of Kutz and Roskelly's Everyclass, believing it to be our own story? If these stories are merely retellings of an "inherited script," then what are we missing? Are we open to hearing anything new in the story of student silence?

Critical Visions of Silence: Overview

While few of us in composition studies probably rely on texts such as *The Chicago Handbook for Teachers* (a practice-focused text for new college teachers that does not strive to "present a coherent theory of teaching or learning"[49]), I suspect the authors' assessment, that "leading a good discussion is the heart of effective teaching,"[50] strikes a chord for many of us as we measure ourselves, our teaching, and our students against an imagined ideal.

Contemporary pedagogy's concern for dialogue is rooted in the works of Dewey and Freire. Dewey's explication of "traditional education" and Freire's work provide the groundwork for a critique of top-down, teacher-centered, lecture-style education and for the elevation of "dialogue" as the fundamental means of learning and knowing. Freire concludes that "authentic thinking" can only take place through dialogue, and that "It is not our role [as educators] to speak to the people about our own view of the world, nor attempt to impose that view on them, but rather to dialogue with the people about their view and ours."[51] The methodology he proposes recalls Dewey's work and is premised on dialogic investigation.

Also central in our understanding of dialogue is Mikhail Bakhtin's notion that all language is *dialogic*, that is, the negotiation of outside discourses. The purpose of dialogue, according to Bakhtin, is not to synthesize or resolve these discourses into a singular vision but to hold many viewpoints at once, to see multiple, competing viewpoints without seeking resolution. Language can only be understood as always directed outside of the speaker; "Utterance . . . is wholly a product of social interaction."[52] Further, as he argues in *The Dialogic Imagination*, meaning is always collaboratively created in the process of interaction with and struggle between discourses. Within composition pedagogy, classroom interaction becomes a physical embodiment of that negotiation of discourses and meaning. This taps into what Katerina Clark and Michael Holquist see as liberatory in Bakhtin's understanding of dialogue that "insists that we are all necessarily involved in the making of meaning."[53]

Relying on these foundational concepts, composition scholars as diverse as Shor, hooks, O'Reilley, and Gradin claim the central importance of dialogue within education. Dialogue has come to represent all that is good and empowering and *right* in our pedagogies; it is a Burkean god-term.[54] For example, Shor asserts that education should be "dialogic" in character, allowing for "a meeting ground to reconcile students and teachers separated by the unilateral authority of the teacher in traditional education. Secondly, dialogue is a mutually created discourse which questions the existing canon of knowledge and challenges power relations in the classroom and society."[55] This theoretical grounding is present in hooks's assertion that through speaking, "everyone's presence is acknowledged . . . there must be an ongoing recognition that everyone influences the classroom dynamic, that everyone contributes."[56] O'Reilley sees discussion in the classroom "as the interplay between interiority and community . . . discussion is also vital to the dialogue between inner life and the outer world."[57] This, she maintains, is a "peacemaking strategy," one that values the individual while allowing her to see herself in light of that larger community. In proposing a "social-expressivist" pedagogy, Gradin challenges the myth of Romantic writers as isolated, solipsistic figures, in light of the active, interactive writing community to which they belonged.

In light of such diverse theoretical groundings that celebrate dialogue, how do we as compositionists understand the silence in our classrooms? What meanings of silence (and "quiet students") do we rely on to explain the observable phenomenon when we enact our theoretical visions? Are these explanations adequate? In her research for *Ways with Words*, Shirley Brice Heath found that in the average high school class, each student talks for less than two minutes.

But how does this account for *our* classrooms?

In my reading, I have been intrigued by the texts that explicitly point to the "problem" of silence. For example, in the preface to *Ways of Reading*, Bartholomae and Petrosky defend their selection of difficult texts by asserting that college students "want to believe they can strike out on their own." They conclude, "If a teacher is patient and forgiving—willing, that is, to let a student work out a reading of Percy, willing to keep from saying, 'No that's not it' and filling the silence with the 'right' reading—then students can, with care and assistance, learn to speak for themselves."[58] Whether one reads this metaphorically or literally, in this construction, one of the central tensions of teaching and learning is symbolized by the moment of *silence*. In other words, the most significant issue posed by the choice of texts is this silence. It marks the student's failure to comprehend; it is the teacher's responsibility to "forgive" this transgression and use her own authority to move the student out of the silence that results. Becky Ropers-Huilman, exploring silence in feminist classrooms, poses this dilemma in a more pragmatic way: "In and outside of educational environments, both silences and speech hold great potential for communicating and learning. Yet silences also confuse those who seek to implement 'liberatory' or 'empowering' pedagogy within traditional institutional arrangements. *How can students be evaluated for class participation if they are silent?*"[59]

Not Being Able to Speak, Not Knowing: Considering Feminist Theory

> It's probably more females [are quiet] than males . . . because females have always been quieted down, just, "no, men are the authorities." Nowadays . . . it's almost equal with race and gender. . . . We've all been taught to be self-conscious, just to have lots of self-esteem. . . . [My father] is kind of the authority. He's still kind of in the olden days and he doesn't like it when we all speak up. But my mom doesn't quite listen to him.
>
> —Sarah, student

While I believe composition's concern for classroom silence is rooted in the elevation of dialogue, feminist theory's focus on the silences of women offers useful insight into the negative construction of silence.[60] While I am particularly interested in audible silences and the oral texts that "break" them, silence can take many forms, including those in written and artistic texts or in the participation in specific communities (such as the sciences, government, religion, etc.). Here it seems important to acknowledge the ways that silence has traditionally been defined "as the absence of something else."[61] Likewise, many linguistic associations ("dead silent," "struck dumb," etc.) are also negative—connoting lack, absence, intellectual inadequacy. In essence, silence is defined only through opposition—perhaps not coincidentally correlating with notions of "feminine" as lack or absence. The common teacher-construction of "quiet" students as passive nonparticipants relies on a similar construction—these students are defined by what they are not.

The process of marginalization[62] depends upon defining as "other" what is presumed to deviate from a supposed "center." An important project of study in feminist theory has been an exploration of the ways women have historically, politically, and discursively been silenced in cultures "[in] which we have been materially central."[63] (A critical question to consider, then, is how might our constructions marginalize quiet students by defining them as deviant from an idealized—and imaginary—vocal student?) The feminist concern for silence has led to many explorations of how such a process of marginalization is effected. In literary criticism, foundational texts such as Gilbert and Gubar's *The Madwoman in the Attic* explore the ways women's voices that question patriarchal sensibilities have been textually marginalized, relegated to margins of social acceptability. And Olsen distinguishes between two types of silence: generative silences (a concept that is unfortunately often lost in discussions of Olsen's work) and those silences that are "the unnatural thwarting of what struggles to come into being, but cannot."[64] In our discourse about classroom silence, we use Olsen's second definition—of unnatural silences. In considering our pedagogies, does teacher-mandated "participation" radically alter what has contributed to the making of these silences?

In *Organizing Silence*, Clair relies on Antonio Gramsci for a theoretical discussion of how such unnatural silencing is effected through coercion, the exertion of force, and hegemony: the systems of control "'normalized' through institutions such as the family, education, religion, systems of law and law enforcement, medicine, and general administration."[65] The classroom research of Myra and David Sadker helps illuminate Clair's argument in concrete terms. Patterns of classroom discourse (turn-taking, interruptions, and the application of rules), learned assertiveness and passivity, and systems of validation and control are not gender-neutral. In schools, girls are held to a different set of standards and behaviors, a model of female studenthood that is essentially silent. The result of this, they found,

> is in a typical college class . . . while 80 percent of pupils in elementary and secondary classes contribute at least one comment in each of their classes, approximately half of the college class says nothing at all. One in two sits through an entire class without ever answering a question, asking one, or making a comment. Women's silence is loudest at college, with twice as many females voiceless.[66]

Through their observations, they found that male students at the college level are more likely to monopolize discussions, while women are twice as likely to remain silent. Men perform; women watch. The implications of this divide are further deepened by the pattern of women students prefacing their remarks with "self-put-downs" that neutralize the power of their speech and compromise their assertions, acknowledging, albeit silently, that their own voices are heard (and listened to) less frequently.

If the system of education does indeed work to marginalize female students, then how might we "denormalize" the silences of women students? Psychology and sociology research have added substantively to our understandings of the gendered nature of women's silence in and outside the classroom. Jill McLean Taylor, Carol Gilligan, and Amy M. Sullivan explore the observable phenomenon of girls' increasing silence as they move through adolescence. In *Between Voice and Silence: Women and Girls, Race and Relationships*, the researchers

> observe a fight for relationship that often became dispirited as girls experienced betrayal or neglectful behavior and felt driven into a psychological isolation they and others readily confused with independence . . . their increasing isolation and psychological distress, including their experience of having no affective voice, regularly preceded overt manifestations or symptoms of psychological trouble.[67]

These girls, then, were confronted with a decision between "the competing needs for self-expression and staying out of trouble."[68] This resulted, in most cases, in a public silence about their emotional lives or a process of dissociation, when girls "began to lose the knowledge of feelings and desires they had known before."[69] So *not being able to speak leads to not knowing*. Silence may be experienced as "safety" in the immediate context, but it carries long-term losses. Silencing becomes a systematic process.

In turning back to our classrooms, my concern is that it is easy to mistake a symptom—silence—for its underlying causes. That is, silence may (and often does) signify this process of silencing, but I suspect it cannot be "solved" merely by mandating the presence of women's voices in our classrooms. And we must not overlook how silence can be a legitimate, reasoned *choice*. Believing that we can "give voice" to students may confound our real intentions, as women students learn that they do not have control over (or even the right to control) their own voices. Rather than requiring students to speak, I think our concern for those who may be silenced is better served by working to actively create opportunities and conditions in which our women students feel their voices will be valued.

Women's Ways of Knowing: The Development of Self, Voice, and Mind has provided a useful matrix for many inquiries, including the exploration of women's behaviors in the classroom. By examining the intellectual development of women in relation to the ways that definitions of "self" intersect with "knowledge," Belenky and colleagues found that the women who were the least developed intellectually (and the most "socially, economically, and educationally deprived") were "silent"—viewing words as weapons, existing not "in dialogue with 'the self' . . . remain[ing] isolated from others and without the tools of representing experience."[70] This mapping of epistemologies, particularly the concept of "constructed knowledge," has proven extremely useful in many compositionists' attempts to define their pedagogies.

However, the danger in this schema, it seems to me, is in the conflation of silence with an undeveloped intellectual life characterizing the most alienated women in the study. These qualities may frequently correlate, but it is inaccurate and dangerous to assume that silence indicates intellectual disengagement (or "not knowing," as the system of labels implies). To make such an assumption in teaching may further disempower and alienate students struggling to negotiate the demands of the classroom. And while I am not suggesting any conscious classism in the study, the fact that the "silent" women were also the poorest troubles me. How are we to understand the correlation between silence, class, and intellect suggested by this study?

This feminist research and theoretical work lead to the conclusion that the silences in our classrooms are, in Olsen's terms, *unnatural* silences, and that our role as teachers must include actively eliciting women's talk. The cultural processes of devaluing women's voices and the resulting psychological dissociation point to the dramatic and sometimes traumatic consequences of the silencing of women students. However, it seems important to note that what this work calls for is not simply additional, more compelling strategies to "get them talking." These strategies may appear to positively alter what we can see—that is, more students, more female students, talking. But do these strategies address the underlying, systematic alienation of these students that is represented by their silences? Silence in our classrooms may be the manifestation of historical, cultural, economic, and linguistic marginalization, but simply filling the spaces of silence does little to address the conditions that constitute such alienation.

Not Being Able to Speak, Not Knowing: Theorizing Class, Race, and Culture

It's a totally different culture.

—Lucy, student

In addition to feminist theory's work on silence, the exploration of issues such as race, class, and culture provides an important framework for examining the patterns of discourse within our classrooms. Jean Anyon's research provides an important locus of consideration: the intersections of social class and the construction of "discussion" in the classroom. Her ethnographic study of five elementary schools reveals the range of discourses elicited in these schools as a function of social class. Oral discourse in "working-class"[71] schools was limited to repetition and rote behavior; in the "middle-class" schools, the emphasis on "getting it right" prompted explanations of how a student reached a particular answer; in "affluent professional" schools, students were asked to apply concepts; and in "executive elite" schools, students were encouraged toward "analytical [thinking], dealing with concrete social issues."[72] In short, students may come to college writing classrooms with divergent ideas about what role their voices should play in the classroom, having been taught a range of styles of "appropriate" interaction. In considering Anyon's class-based "ways of knowing," it is apparent that we in composition classes typically elicit the discourse of "executive elite" schools, which may be very different from the discourses encouraged in students' other classes. This consideration of the "hidden curriculum" is echoed implicitly in hooks's assertion that in

> privileged liberal arts colleges [such as Oberlin and Yale], it is acceptable for professors to respect the "voice" of any student who wants to make a point. Many students in those institutions feel they are entitled—that their voices deserve to be heard. But students in public institutions, mostly from working-class backgrounds, come to college assuming that professors see them as having nothing of value to say, no valuable contribution to make to a dialectical exchange of ideas.[73]

Thus it is not simply that working-class students do not have access to the privileged language of the college classroom. Rather, they have internalized the cultural and institutional devaluation of their voices, leaving them "not able to speak."

In *When Students Have Power*, Shor's metaphor of "Siberia" furthers this understanding of working-class students' responses and perceived resistance to dialogic education. Student silence is ensured by classroom design, traditional syllabi that present teacher-talk as disseminating knowledge, the perception of "real classes" as ones where teachers do most of the talking, and particular discursive patterns that are fundamentally "undemocratic."[74] School culture has alienated students—even from their own voices. For working-class students who construct themselves as "middle-class" (through their educational aspirations), the educational system's "structured silence" about the intersections of class and culture[75] leaves little alternative but for students to blame themselves for failing to meet the model of "good student behavior."

Shor remarks:

> Most of the students have learned socially to construct themselves as intellectual exiles as far from the center of the room as they can be ... the Siberian Syndrome is ... a defensive reaction to the unequal power relations of schooling which include unilateral authority for the

teacher and a curriculum evading critical thought about the history, language, and cultures of the students. Facing unilateral authority that disempowers them politically and disables them intellectually, most students position themselves in the Siberian corners . . . they construct themselves as subordinates who can't escape authority but won't fully cooperate with it either.[76]

For Shor, then, there appears to be little alternative for these students whose school life consists of both necessary compliance with authority and resistance to it, although he does not comment on the implications of this metaphor for the teacher in the Siberian classroom. Yes, students are isolated from the center of authority in traditional education, but within the classroom it is the teacher who experiences isolation and powerlessness in the scenario Shor describes. Students have formed a community, one that is implicitly structured around the exclusion of the teacher. Shor sees no distinctions between students; his analysis of the culture of school, while useful, does not take into account the ways that other factors (such as gender, ethnicity, success in school, family values about education) might be influencing and inflecting student behavior. In his account, all students are equally disempowered by these educational practices: these students occupy fixed, congruent positions of "studenthood." Although Shor identifies these students as members of the "urban ethnic working class," he does not acknowledge how those home cultures might offer competing or contradictory discourses about the meanings of voice and silence.

Sadker and Sadker's research findings call into question such an assertion of unilateral silencing. Coinciding with Shor's interpretation, they also see seating choices in a classroom as strategic, although they claim the distinction is gender-specific, with male students opting for front-row, attention-getting positions. And "those who want to hide, the silent students, who are more likely to be female, prize the corners, the unobtrusive areas, and the anonymity that grows with distance."[77] I do not wish to argue that either Shor or Sadker and Sadker is correct; in fact, it seems likely that both interpretations are valid in their own contexts. However, the contradiction between these visions offers an important caution: the lenses these authors chose predetermine their findings. When we look at the silences in our classrooms, what lens do we employ? How does that shape and limit what we see and hear?

Shor's explication of "silencing teacher-talk" is complemented by Chiseri-Strater's ethnographic research. She carefully examines how silence and silencing are enacted through the patterns of teacher-talk and validated forms of student interaction in the noncomposition classrooms she studies. In one class, a teacher-centered discourse of traditional lectures leaves students little space for interaction. Chiseri-Strater remarks that the professor "lectures brilliantly and we listen in fascinated silence."[78] In another, apparently more "democratic" classroom, "participation" is encouraged through a requirement listed on the syllabus and assigned "discussion leading," but the dynamics of these discussion-debates (the teacher interrupting and hijacking presentations, aggressive posturing, a model of performance) work against any democratic exchanges. These classes are contrasted to a Prose Writing class at the University of New Hampshire:

> Most students in this particular section of the Prose Writing course attest that they have not had another college class (except for Freshman Composition) where they were allowed to talk in an unstructured, conversational way. . . . [The] class provided many occasions for students to talk in small and large groups about their reading and writing processes. . . . These layers of narrative talk help shape students' ways of thinking and eventually shape what they will write. . . . With language as the center of this writing classroom, much of the learning comes through talk.[79]

Chiseri-Strater represents this "talk" as flowing seamlessly from theoretical grounding to implementation. "Quiet students" are remarkable in their literal absence from this class.

hooks, in *Teaching to Transgress*, confronts the intersections of race and gender through her own experiences as a black woman, as a feminist, and as an academic. On the question of student silence, she comments:

> The experience of professors who educate for critical consciousness indicates that many students, especially students of color, may not feel at all "safe" in what appears to be a neutral setting. It is the absence of a feeling of safety that often promotes prolonged silence or lack of student engagement. . . .
>
> Throughout my teaching career, white professors have often voiced concern to me about nonwhite students who do not talk . . . the politics of domination are often reproduced in the educational setting. For example, white male students continue to be the most vocal in our classes. Students of color and some white women express fear that they will be judged as intellectually inadequate by these peers . . . [students of color] express the feeling that they are less likely to suffer any kind of assault if they simply do not assert their subjectivity. . . . Who speaks? Who listens? And why?[80]

hooks's strategy of insisting that all students speak in class[81] appears to address this question of "engagement" by moderating the dynamic of who is authorized to speak in the classroom. Everyone does speak, therefore, everyone's presence is acknowledged. hooks's critique of well-meaning but misguided colleagues is a valid one—"safety" is *not* effected by asking students to remain distanced. However, hooks does not address the ways her own practices may, in fact, replicate the "politics of domination." The assumption that "silence" is absence/noncontribution and the binary opposition she sees between being an "active participant" (i.e., someone who speaks) and "passive consumer" offers little space for students' multiple and sometimes conflicting subjectivities and learning styles. Here I point to Bruffee's notion of *thought* as "internalized conversation,"[82] an active, *interactive* process. It seems a dangerous misreading to label as "passive consumers" those students who do not make the translation to external conversation in expected or desired ways. hooks's interpretation points, I think, to a central tension in composition pedagogy—we need (or feel we need) some way to measure students' "engagement," but classroom dialogue, while sometimes a viable measure, can never capture the complexity of our students' active and engaged internal lives.

Also, hooks's work does not address the question "Who's listening?," a question reminiscent of the "silenced dialogue" that Lisa Delpit evokes through the words of teachers of color and of the voices of the teenage girls in "The Understanding Adolescence Study."[83] Both these adolescent girls and the teachers Delpit quotes do not speak, because no one is listening, and therefore there is no motivation to speak. This leads me to consider the strategy that hooks proposes. Who benefits from this enforced talk? Particularly for those students who feel "no one is listening," what is gained? While we can devise strategies that encourage or require students to mark their "presence" through speech acts, it is much more difficult to enforce or evaluate engagement-through-listening. As Royster remarked in her 2000 4C's presentation, "The Other Side of Speaking: Claiming the Right to Response," perhaps we also need to develop for ourselves and for our students a rhetoric of *listening*.

Finally, Kay M. Losey explores the issue of student silence through multiple lenses in her study of Mexican American students in a Basic Writing class at a California university. Interestingly, this is the only extended research I have found that explicitly explores silence in college classrooms. She attempts to take into account the cultural, historical, linguistic, and economic silencing these students have faced in their local culture; the school culture that relegates them to an underfunded, undersupported satellite campus; and the effects of ethnicity and gender on student silence in the composition classroom. It is ironic and disappointing, however, that the voices of these marginalized students occupy a very small place in her text; only one chapter deals with students' perceptions of their classroom experiences.

Losey's work is striking in the extended exploration of men's written "silence," including behaviors that are typically read by teachers as resistance: late drafts, inadequate revising, failing to meet page limits. This framework suggests a substantial revision of the way that silence is typically constructed. Her other findings are at once startling and unsurprising: in class discussions, Mexican American women, while a majority in the class (47 percent), initiated discussion only 12.5 percent of the time and responded 8 percent of the time.[84] Losey's analysis takes into account "the complex practices and plurality of subject positions"[85] that enforce hegemony by considering the intersections of gender and race:

> Overall, males, regardless of ethnic background, interacted at rates higher than expected for their representation in the classroom . . . [the statistics] suggest an ethnic disadvantage in the Anglo American dominant culture and classroom, whereas, the gender differences reveal the prevalence of traditional gender roles in both ethnic groups but with greater effects for Mexican Americans, suggesting a stronger patriarchal hierarchy among Mexican Americans than among Anglo Americans . . . a cumulative effect, creating a hierarchy with Mexican American women at the bottom and Anglo American men at the top of interaction frequency.[86]

Losey's study, while minimal in its discussion of what these students have to say about their own experiences, raises several questions for further consideration. In what ways do the politics of the classroom replicate the patterns of marginalization and silencing that characterize larger cultural ideologies and the lived experiences of our students outside of the classroom? Do we need to redefine the terms we use—or perhaps use new terms—when we talk about silence? Are there pedagogical strategies that might significantly confront and transform these "normalized" patterns of discourse and marginalization? When we as researchers, theorists, and teachers talk *about* student silence, as Losey does, do we attempt to speak *for* students? What is lost in this appropriation?

Not Silent?
Cultural Studies' Response

There's always one opinion you can have on this; there's one right answer. And I never had it. Ever. [And what's the right answer?] More often than not, it's the opinion of the instructor.

—Sanjay, student

Many of the theorists discussed here connect their understanding of "the problem" of student silence to a particular teaching strategy or course of action in the classroom (e.g., Shor, hooks, Chiseri-Strater, Lewis, Gradin). That is, understanding the "problem" leads to pedagogical solutions. Many composition scholars committed to a cultural studies approach believe that the choice of texts addresses the problem of student silence (see Spellmeyer, Booth, Harris and Rosen, Berlin, and Walters). For example, in "Writing Teachers Writing and the Politics of Dissent," Frank D. Walters argues, "When difference is stressed . . . what emerges, often with difficulty, and not without anguish, is a profusion of voices, none of which claims authority over the others, but all of which claim a subjective space within the vacant statement of the classroom."[87] Such utopian visions imagine the cultural studies classroom *outside* of culture, exempt from the power relations and complex negotiations that students face in the decision to speak. This ignores

> the asymmetrical positions of difference and privilege . . . this [construction] fails to confront [the] dynamics of subordination present among classroom participants, and within classroom participants, in the form of multiple and contradictory subject positions. . . . Acting as if [the] classroom [is] a safe space in which democratic dialogue was possible and happening [does] not make it so.[88]

Like Walters, James Berlin posits the value of making students aware of the competing discourses that influence who they are, in the hope of encouraging students' "resistance" to such cultural codes. He believes with such leftist questioning that

> students can . . . disagree with the ideology forwarded by the teacher without fear of recrimination. Indeed one of the more notable features of the course is that students do feel free to resist their teachers, to disagree rather than simply conform. The class thus encourages open debate and confrontation in students who have been prevented from protesting about any feature of their experience. . . . The result, we hope, will be to encourage a more open and tolerant society, one in which the full possibilities of democracy might be openly explored.[89]

Engaging in what Elizabeth Ellsworth calls "the repressive fictions of classroom dialogue,"[90] Berlin overlooks the difficulty of resisting teacherly authority. He claims that disagreement is opposed to conformity, and that students "feel free" to resist in this climate of open debate. However, in doing so, he ignores the multiplicity of positions between "conformity" and "disagreement" and disregards the power relationships that make student resistance always tied to and limited by the politics of the classroom—teachers are teachers, with all of the authority and power this title conveys. I am struck particularly by Berlin's belief that students can "disagree with the ideology forwarded by the teacher" without fear.

Ideally, perhaps. But I suspect that most students see this quite differently. I am troubled too by what this classroom may feel like for those students who are not comfortable within or adequately prepared for a discourse of confrontation; this pedagogy carries the potential for further alienation and, yes, silence. Berlin revisits this class in his later work and concedes that "students and teachers are [at times] at odds with each other or, just as often, the students are themselves divided about the operation and effects of conflicting codes."[91] But even in this rendering, Berlin ignores the potential silencing in such classrooms, the silencing that he himself has participated in, both through his teaching and in such representations.

Outside the "Not" Stories: Other Possibilities

I think silence is a borderline thing.

—Catarina, student

Considering all of the political and emotional weight that student silence carries, it is perhaps unsurprising that teachers react so strongly to its unwelcome presence in their classrooms. It would be irresponsible *not* to be concerned about our quiet students. While much of the discussion in this chapter, and indeed in much of our professional writing, focuses on such negative constructions of classroom silence, I believe that more work needs to be done to actively understand and redefine student silence—for its generative and transformative potential.

The anxiety about student silence evidenced in our professional discourses is valid and important, both in its attempts to address difficult classroom situations and the unjust power relations that permeate our culture. I believe our sustained disciplinary attention to dialogue, constructed knowledge, and collaborative learning foregrounds the question of student silence in both theoretical and practical ways. And the work to understand silence as a mechanism of alienation and marginalization is imperative—politically, socially, and morally. I do not want to argue with these constructions; in general, they mirror many of my own concerns about students and their learning.

But while I believe we should be aware of the potential dangers of student silence, I also argue that our concerns should not deafen us to understanding other possibilities for silence as well.

We teachers want students to be engaged in their learning, and speaking is a way of being engaged. But it is *a* way, not the only way. And I suspect there is some slippage between our concern that students be actively engaged and that they demonstrate that engagement. Thus this issue of silence grows even murkier considering the growing institutional imperative for evaluation: do we "excuse" quiet students, or do we lower their grades for failing to meet class requirements because they do not speak (or speak often) in class?

It is critical to keep in mind that the pedagogies and theories explored in this chapter do not necessarily address the underlying issues and can replicate the patterns of domination and marginalization that they seek to subvert and transform. The notion that dialogue is central to a liberatory or an empowering education has profoundly dangerous consequences for those students who do not fit the model of studenthood that such pedagogies demand. As Orner argues:

> Educators concerned with changing unjust power relations must continually examine our assumptions about our own positions, those of our students, the meanings and uses of student voice, our power to call for students to speak, and our often unexamined power to legitimate and perpetuate unjust relations in the name of student empowerment.[92]

Our own desire to hear student voices should not deafen us to students' constructions and students' needs. The impulse toward pathologizing student silence as "the problem"—toward defining student silence in terms of "nots"—is strikingly counterproductive, particularly when it leads students to experience their silences only in terms of failure. Therefore, *our* constructions and definitions of silence should be complemented and complicated by an understanding of the terms students use. Chapters 5, 6, and 7 of this book begin to address this gap in our professional conversation about classroom dialogue. These chapters are propelled not by my interpretations and critiques of students' behaviors but by the voices of those quiet students. In the second half of the book, students' voices dominate the conversation, as I explore the ways in which the students in my study understand the silences they experience in classrooms, including the complex negotiations that lead them to silence, even when they know silence is perceived as problematic, the teaching strategies they perceive as encouraging them to speak, and their readings of classroom silence as positive, productive, and powerful. A small but growing body of writing suggests that there are alternative ways we might think about the silences in our classrooms. These alternate visions will be discussed in the concluding chapter in relation to my students' perceptions of silence as a generative space. Here I propose a "grounded theory"[93] of student silence that attempts to integrate our sometimes conflicting understandings of classroom interactions, a project I hope will ultimately contribute to a more complex understanding of student silence. To consider redefining silence is indeed a difficult, and at times mind-bending, feat: it takes seriously the notion that students' experiences (and silences) should critique and revise those pedagogies to which we are committed.

What possibilities emerge if we maintain multiple ways of hearing the silences in our classrooms?

Chapter 3

Locating Myself
Between Speaking and Silence

Silence can be a plan
rigorously executed

the blueprint of a life

It is a presence
it has a history a form

Do not confuse it
with any kind of absence

—Adrienne Cecile Rich, "Cartographies of Silence"

In the second half of this book, I explore the ways students perceive the silences they experience in classrooms. Included are the complex negotiations that lead them to silence, even when they know this may be interpreted as problematic, the teaching strategies and classroom situations that encourage them to speak, and their readings of classroom silence as positive, productive, even empowering. But before moving to my students' stories, I offer this autobiographical chapter as an exploration of my own silences that led, in part, to this study. These experiences— as much as the theory I have read and the research I have done—inflect how I read students' silence and shape what I think and believe, hear and know about the relationship between speaking and silence in my teaching life.

A young(ish) white woman. A former high school athlete from a modestly middle-class background. Educated first in private schools populated primarily by white students. A composition teacher, a college professor, and a department chair. What expectations about speaking and silence does this description conjure up? Almost none are borne out in my experiences, and the

51

stories I tell about my speaking and silence in school are not as simple as any of the labels I can use to identify myself.

Silence and Discipline, Speaking and Attention: Learning How to "Be Good"

I loved school. Or, more precisely, I loved the *idea* of school. Fueled by mornings of witnessing my sister and brothers gather their books and disappear for long stretches of time, I knew I would love school, long before I set foot into a room that always would smell faintly of chalk, wet wool, and stale milk.

Ironically, once I got to school, I was completely bored.

I had learned to read and write before I entered first grade, perhaps because I had felt left out when my siblings did their homework. But being "advanced" in this way did little to offset the pernicious boredom that regulated elementary school life: practicing row after row of letters; tracing a variety of shapes with military precision; dutifully coloring turkeys, snowmen, flags, and tulips as the season dictated. The most important thing in all of these tasks, we learned, was that good students were quiet students; "being good" demanded a Herculean self-discipline of silence.

I wanted to practice words and make my own sentences. I wanted to read stories, to tell stories. I did not see the point of reading silly little sentences that used the same words, rhyming words in predictable patterns: when would we get to *real* books? But I longed to be good, so I did as I was told. I craved those rare opportunities when we were allowed out of the silences into which we kept being compressed. When I silently finished my mimeographed classwork exercises before my classmates, I was told I must have been careless, so I began to pace myself dutifully but impatiently in silence, according to the other students' progress through a worksheet, across the lined paper on which we wrote. My teachers' penchant for seating students alphabetically or in height order meant that I sat in the back row of the class where I could surreptitiously check the clock, tracking how many hours, how many minutes until I could go home to read and think at my own pace.

The favorite punishment of the nuns at my school was *silence*. Discipline was meted out in periods of silence, with heads down on desks. To me, the worst possible fate was to be told I was not allowed to speak. I suspect this punishment bothered me, a perennial "good girl," more than it did those students who had provoked our teacher's anger. My anxiety ballooned as each painful moment ticked by. When would we be allowed to talk again? Would we be consigned to silence indefinitely? And why did we Good Kids get conscripted to silence along with those Bad Ones?

Thus it is probably no surprise that when we were allowed to speak and to answer questions in grade school, I was eager to the point of rudeness, my hand waving in the air before the teacher had finished her question. Times tables, spelling bees, state capitals—these were my chance to shine. I liked the attention, the validation: the sound of my own voice chased away the boredom that stalked me as I filled out math worksheets, practiced penmanship, demonstrated my reading comprehension by darkening in empty circles.

My grandmother's wisdom—that children, especially girls, should be seen and not heard—did not apply outside of her hearing. Her logic made no sense to me, a child in need of constant validation. Wasn't I more interesting when I recounted adventures, told jokes? Besides, the rules for school were different: answering a teacher's question earned one attention, maybe even praise. Eventually, though, I noticed teachers ignoring my frantic hand-waving, so I learned to ration out my hand-raising too, to hoard the joy of speaking.

At this point, no stigma was attached to being smart, to being the teacher's favorite. Speaking a lot, at the right times, made one almost iridescent. Other kids thought you were cool, and teachers just might praise you too. When you were quiet, you were "good," but teachers thought you were "good," too, if you learned to raise your hand just the right amount with the right answer. A delicate balance, certainly, but in my memory at least, so many of my classmates were so eager to please that we tried to parse the logic of these unspoken and sometimes mercurially changing rules.

I could never understand why other students would choose silence.

As I moved through elementary school, the rules governing student behavior subtly began to change. In the third, fourth, and fifth grades the silences in our classes slowly disappeared. Teachers seemed more interested in what we had to say, but suddenly there was less competition too. My female friends no longer seemed eager for airtime; they spent more time looking down at their desks, looking as if they wished, more than anything, not to be called on. During these years, I began to realize that attention from teachers and the visible display of "being smart" were something few other girls in my class sought anymore. As I look for some tangible explanation for this tectonic shift, I imagine some crucial conversation that I must have missed on the playground—the one in which my classmates agreed to stop trying in school or to stop caring or to stop *showing* they cared. This explanation, however far-fetched, feels infinitely more comforting than the idea of some more insidious process in which the subtle, repeated cultural messages led my classmates to silence themselves, believing a "good girl" could not also be a smart girl.

I wonder, as well, how I managed to escape this silencing. My parents did not take a particularly feminist stance toward child rearing. (I recall a dinnertime conversation during which my father patiently explained that I couldn't be an archeologist because I was a girl and wouldn't want to get dirty). And I had the same teachers my classmates did. Yet I also did not stop seeking the attention of speaking in class. So what accounts for the difference in my behavior?

Maybe I just identified more with teachers whose approval was easier to earn than I did with my peers whose tastes and preferences were mysterious to me, often shifting in ways that seemed inexplicable.

As I write this now, I find myself striving for coherence in the painful memories of becoming distinctly unpopular. Perhaps I was Weird because I continued to raise my hand, looking like a show-off and a "teacher's pet," making others feel badly. Or maybe I wanted to perform for teachers because the unpopularity with my peers left me longing for other kinds of approval. (And maybe I am using this external phenomenon to explain something I could not quite understand then and struggle to comprehend on some level still.)

I imagine the almost instantaneous frisson I felt when a teacher called on me: the eagerness and joy in speaking, in knowing things, in thinking an idea through emerging with the simultaneous anxiety that I was producing fodder for teasing, further evidence for my status as a geek. When I think back, the outright, outrageous hostility of my classmates *should* have shut me up. But it did not. Was I inordinately courageous? Simply stubborn? Lacking the basic defense mechanisms that would have led me to seek the protective coloration of the quiet background? Whatever the explanation for my unwillingness to be silenced, I find myself almost jealous of my gangly, uncomfortable twelve-year-old self who continued to speak up. Decades later, I doubt I have her tenacity.

With the illogic that structures much school life, within two years the social order changed in my school, as did the rules about speaking, and I somehow became close friends with three "popular" girls. I find myself, even now, idealizing these as halcyon days—it was somehow tolerable again to be smart and talkative; I had become popular too. The underlying anxiety comes back to me though, and I imagine what it must have felt like to be me at twelve, thirteen, fourteen—afraid that adolescent social opinion might shift again, afraid that "being smart" might become unfashionable again, afraid.

I think it was during this period of my life that I began to distinguish between kinds of silence and to understand that it has all kinds of values associated with it: silence always carries meaning. There was the soft, rich, full kind, indicative of a certain inner and outer peace. A transcendent, luminous quietness. I think I was supposed to find this in church, although more often than not, I would find myself fidgeting through an endless Catholic Mass, unable to concentrate during all that enforced silence. To this day, I associate this silence with the hushed solitude of my grandmother's house, where little was out of place and the surrounding pine trees seemed to cocoon her orderly world, crocheted doilies cushioning me in security. It is the feeling of a full afternoon of the guilty pleasure of reading a nonacademic book or the rare moments of a yoga class, when the busyness of perpetual activity—both internal and external—seems to cease, even for a single minute.

But I also became aware of a very different sort of silence during this time, one in which submerged tension masquerades as quietness, hiding sharp angles and jagged edges.

Silence can be pleasing. Or it may not. Silence can be reflexive, expansive, even generative. Or it may be something quite the opposite—insidious and destructive.

Changing Academic Rules and Roles: Can Students Choose Silence?

I was placed in the "A" track in high school: the honors, college-prep classes. We were designated the "smart kids." While outside of Honors English, Advanced Placement Physics, or College Calculus classes the rules might be different, within these classes it was acceptable, even expected, that we would flaunt what we knew, that we would engage in a certain amount of academic showmanship. (Those of us who have gone on to become career academics may recognize in these early performances shades of the identities we take on at conferences.)

But there existed another equally powerful, if unspoken, rule—we should not appear to have labored over assigned texts or chemistry problems. An odd competition emerged—we were supposed to be "smart," but we should not have to work at it. Geometry proofs and analyses of Shakespeare should just materialize, apparently, in extemporaneous discourse. My classmates perfected the art of the supposedly impromptu comment, and our teachers loved it.

I raised my hand much less frequently. Maybe these rules for speaking were too complicated for me. Maybe I cared less about teacher approval. Maybe I received enough validation elsewhere and I did not need to be the center of classroom attention anymore. Usually I spoke in class only when it seemed like no one else would and the teacher was drowning, silently pleading for anyone to raise a hand. The sad look a teacher would get as she shifted from foot to foot, repeating the same question would drag my hand up against my will. Even if I didn't know the answer she wanted, I would find myself talking to shatter that unpleasant silence. (I still find myself doing that in the strained, pained silences that sometimes blossom after a conference presentation, a student's question, or a colleague's comment at a depart-ment meeting.)

I think I became quieter outside of classrooms as well. Of my closest friends, I was probably the quietest. My friend Michelle remarked that I never seemed shallow when I was quiet, implying, I think, that *vacuous* was a legitimate synonym for *quiet*. She thought I "saved up" what I had to say, that my jokes were funnier because she "forgot" to expect my sense of irony, that my stories had more punch because I told them for a point, not for attention.

"Your Grade Is Based on Your Participation": Conflicting Messages about Speaking and Silence

I was startled by the attention my professors seemed to pay to students' voices; nearly every syllabus had some note of encouragement (or requirement) about speaking in class and an explanation of the value of a free exchange of ideas. But in reality, speaking in class rarely materialized as the idealized versions that syllabi and first-day lectures implied. Some professors never stopped lecturing long enough to allow for our voices; in other classes, there were simply too many people and an inconvenient classroom layout for anyone but students in the first three rows to speak. In still other classes, to say what one genuinely thought was a risky prospect indeed.

Early in college, I recognized a serious dilemma. Should I accept the rules others wanted to impose to govern my voice? Should I keep trying to "be good," according to my teachers' or my peers' definitions? Or should I, could I, find out how I learned best, how I could give texts and ideas my concentrated attention? In my first college classes, I decided to stop pleasing my teachers and doing what would make them happy, what would make them think I was a "good girl." I ignored my classmates' expectations about when, how, and how much I should speak that would make me a "cool girl." If, at the end of four years, I would have read tens of thousands of pages, written hundreds of others, foregone sleep on dozens of nights, and amassed student loans of paralyzing proportions, then I should try to understand my own ways of learning. If *speaking* was supposed to foster my thinking and learning, then I reasoned that I could choose *silence* if that suited me best. I stopped speaking and performing to soothe my ego, my teacher's, or my classmates and began to pay more attention to real learning—interacting in a meaningful way with texts and ideas. And that meant I often needed to be outwardly quiet. Luckily, large classes afforded me anonymity and a host of other students willing to perform as I had in high school to fill any uncomfortable silences.

It is not that I *never* chose to speak in classes. In several classes I spoke a great deal, sometimes dominating discussions. But I also recall classes in which I said very little, choosing when to speak quite carefully—that is, only when it really mattered to me. Looking back, I realize that those courses were the ones with which I was most deeply engaged. I do not know if I can construct a cohesive explanation that would account for this seeming paradox, but I suspect that in classes that fascinated me less, I engaged in a more shallow way with the material and responded to the professor's questions with any plausible, passing interpretation. As in my elementary school years, I would find myself speaking almost compulsively to chase away the boredom. When the material mattered less to me, the role of the good, active, engaged student came to me more easily, and I was able to approximate what teachers wanted. Class discussions were a game, one I had grown quite good at.

I recall what a graduate student at the University of Massachusetts said about being a quiet student: "Just because I'm not talking doesn't mean that there isn't a conversation happening inside my head." Her words help account for my silences in those classes that mattered most to me. The louder and more animated the conversation in my head, the less likely I was to participate in the audible classroom conversation.[1]

Some professors simply ignored me; I suspect now I became one of what Villanueva calls "The Silent Ones." For others, though, my silences were far more problematic. Soon enough I learned how dangerous my silences could be. In the Honors Program, I took a four-semester sequence that modestly attempted to cover the foundations of theology, philosophy, social science, and literature in Western culture. The twelve students in my sophomore class— three women and nine men—and Professor X met in the university's original library, complete with stained glass windows, cathedral ceilings, and dark wood bookcases that soared high above our heads.

In this movie-set stage of what a college classroom is supposed to be like, I spoke very little in this class. Overwhelmed by Big Ideas and theories and language, I found it difficult to quiet my internal conversation enough for audible speech. On the day we began discussing Freud, I slid into my seat as class was beginning. Before I had taken off my coat, Professor X said, "Mary, we don't hear very much from you. Do you have penis envy?"

I recall thinking very clearly, *I must have heard him wrong.* "No," hesitating. "I doubt it. I really don't think so." I suspect I was unsuccessful in my attempt to keep the sarcasm from my voice, and I heard a few nervous giggles from other students who were surprised at the question and my answer. They were relieved not to be me.

"Well, how do you know?"

My memory tells me the laughter faded as I stumbled around, trying to prove I had read and understood the assignment but respectfully disagreed with its basic premises. I can still feel my nineteen-year-old self failing, failing at language, failing to put together a cohesive argument, all the while I was thinking, *I know because this theory is bullshit.*

When I tell this story now, the question-and-answer exchange between Professor X and me drags on to epic proportions. To be honest, I cannot say how long it really was; I do know that as he pressed me for precise answers, I grew more flustered, less coherent. Even now, I can hear the growing coolness in his voice, see the narrowing of his eyes, feel the table vibrate under the insistent drumming of his fingers.

Finally he said, "You don't think so. But how do you know you're not just *repressing* your penis envy?" I said nothing more.

The conversation was over. I was, apparently, dismissed.

Now, years later, I can choose to read this interaction as a poorly executed attempt to *encourage* me to speak. I suspect this is how my former professor might tell it too. I imagine a somewhat self-deprecating tone, one that intimates his valiant efforts that came to naught in my stubborn, silent refusal to be drawn out, to give the answers I really should. Professor X's voice would betray his earnest desire to engage me and his disappointment in me. (I had failed him, hadn't I?) I can see the sympathetic nods that his colleagues would offer as they listened to his version of this story.

Since then I have heard effective and thoughtful teachers offer this argument. Quiet students need encouragement, need to be pushed to speak. Because they might get drowned out or because they are unsure of themselves, I call on them. I *have to* forcefully invite them into the conversation and give them a space that is all theirs. And yes, in theory, I suppose it can work this way.

In the weeks that followed the Freud discussion, I understood that Professor X disliked me because I had proven myself unworthy. I had not done enough, had not pulled my weight. Maybe I did not measure up to my classmates, or I just was not "being good." The grilling, the public humiliation, simply part of a logical demonstration of my inadequacy, *quod erat demonstrandum.* Professor X had named me and my silences; he had defined me by the contours and shades of what he imagined my silences to mean, so he was free to reshape me, fix me. Today this is what I see was the most devastating part: I allowed his definitions to replace my own. Unable to see how inappropriate this act was (no matter how well intentioned), I accepted his judgment of me as a failure. When I have told this story, people often ask with mild disbelief, "Did this *really* happen?," as if its absurdity and, yes, outright violence make the story suspect. For a long time, I would not speak of this day, this class even, taking on the shame of it as my own, the humiliation fresh.

My subsequent interactions with Professor X suggest a benevolence for which this story cannot account. When I became a graduate student at that school, he expressed pleasure I could only read as genuine, encouraged me to pursue a doctoral degree, and shared the praise of his other colleagues in the department.

So how am I to balance these two visions of the same professor? In less generous moments, I find the explanation of well-meaning but poorly executed intervention a bit hollow. No male students endured the kind of aggressive questioning I did. I like to fantasize that were this to happen today, I would be more prepared, less disoriented by the misogyny and hostility punctuating each of my professor's questions. I imagine snappy, smart, ironic comments that would reveal the weakness of both the theory and the questioner.

I am struck—still—by the effects of that classroom "conversation." It was the first time I wished I could become completely *invisible* in a classroom. And, yes, I admit to days of being completely unprepared or just simply out of my league in other courses. But it was this day that made me try to occupy as little space as possible in that class—taking no more risks in my writing, offering no interpretations that challenged others, drawing as little attention to myself as possible.

Silence was safer but far more dangerous.

Following that Honors Seminar, I obsessively dissected each professor's "requirements." Would she accept my respectful, active listening as *participation*? How much talking was enough to avoid humiliation? What did I have to do to get my A? My fledgling sense that I should focus on learning was sacrificed for a game, a complex ritual with arbitrary and fluctuating rules I had to discover. And I was going to win: the grade, the teacher's approval, the scholarship, acceptance to graduate school. What I had come to think of as "real learning" was often very different from what happened in class; it did not connect with the game I had to learn to play.

Professor X taught me that my learning patterns did not always coincide with those that professors preferred, and I had to figure out how to disguise that, often in preprepared comments I could offer at any second. (If I was going to be put on the spot, then I needed to be ready.) So I developed a student's version of sound-bites on Dickens and Dickinson, Lincoln's depression and the Great Depression. It wasn't learning, but it was a good show. And I am amazed at the accuracy of those evaluations: I perfected the role teachers had cast for me.

Escaping any other confrontations about my silence, I was rewarded, once again, for playing the part of the good student.

Confronting Teachers' Expectations: Breaking the Silence about Silence

When my mother was still hospitalized after a heart attack during my second semester of graduate school, I struggled to keep up with my coursework. To graduate in time, I was taking an extra course, trying to fulfill my language requirement, and training to teach for the first time. Maybe the wisest choice would have been to take the semester off, but I clutched on to routine and to the security of work in a stunned silence. It was a relief to take a class with a former professor who had seemed to like my writing in the past; he had offered to write me letters of recommendation for my applications to the Master's Program.

I have no excuses for my academic performance in that seminar. When I came to that graduate seminar of thirty-five students, most of whom became increasingly aggressive in the competition for airtime, I sat back. I simply could not muster the energy for it; it tired me out just to listen to the verbal jousting, let alone to engage in it. I was never unprepared, and I listened respectfully and completed every other requirement. The required class presentations became a site of hostile interrogation and minute flaw-finding, a practice I abhorred. And to shout over other students to hear myself speak seemed frivolous at best. Having seen that life and death could be a struggle on a visceral level, I just could not bring myself to push my way into this overdramatized "conversation" very frequently.

Like every other class I had taken since I was eighteen years old, the syllabus included an obligatory note about "class participation." Perhaps my extracurricular stress left me less attuned to the professor's real expectations and his apparent appreciation of the heated drama that unfolded in that room each week. Still, I was unprepared for the short, angry note at the bottom of my final paper:

> For your paper, I give you an A. But because of your *refusal* to speak
> in class, I am forced to lower your grade.

My relative quietness in this large class broke an unspoken rule, apparently projecting an active, hostile resistance I had not actually felt. (This seems particularly ironic, given that I was perhaps the most passive person in the room, not once given to histrionics over an interpretation of a poem.) My silence was more powerful than I had thought, powerful enough to make my teacher act against his will.

In seeing an overarching narrative that accounts for my decisions—about being a student, a teacher, even this study—this moment seems critical. It marks the moment I first began to consider actively and critically how people think about "class participation" and its seamless, almost universal, equation with speaking. It crystallized for me how personally teachers take this—and how personally I did as well. This was perhaps the first time I thought about student silence outside of my desire for attention or my need to please and without a sense of shame or contempt for a game I considered petty. And for the first time I let myself be angry at a professor—for employing such a limited definition of the "good student," for misdefining me, and for never talking about these student roles he held so sacred. Finally, I began to see that my silences *mattered* in some fundamental way that I could not fully fathom.

Since that class, I have never felt entirely safe in a classroom or professional space where someone has the power to command my speech: I began trying to anticipate where class discussions could go so I could be certain to have something "important" to say. Ultimately, I often could not genuinely engage in these conversations, because the sort of internal dialogue that comes most naturally to me would often leave me stumbling to articulate what I was thinking. I am disappointed to realize that being seen as successful as an academic meant I had to step away from the learning processes that are most productive to me so I could perform in the ways that others expect. I have told myself that everything requires compromise; this disengagement is mine.

What I regret most about my second semester in graduate school is this: I did not speak to my professor about his response to me. I would not argue the grade he ultimately gave me (my paper did not merit an A), but I still find myself disappointed in his failures to make explicit the requirement of "participation" or to tell me that I was not complying with his expectations. I am angry about his interpretation that my comparative silence marked me as willfully resistant. For someone whose academic career might be summarized as "the good girl," to be cast into the role of the disobedient child was disorienting and uncomfortable. I am angry about the narrow definitions prescribed for "good" students, how easily such labels are applied, and how damaging they can be. But still wanting to be the "good student," I took his critique to heart and read it as a valid criticism of my perceived nonperformance. I did not speak out.

Since then I have learned that it *is* possible to talk to others about how they interpret (and misinterpret) my silences. I think in particular about talking to another graduate professor who decided to call on me when I had not volunteered "enough," deviating from the more traditional seminar-style discussion of that class. I think about trying to explain that his gesture, while well-intentioned, felt like surveillance, warning, punishment. We politely acknowledged our differing interpretations—that we might each be right, in our own ways. His gesture to involve me in the discussion might be a legitimate gesture at inclusion, just as my own desire to choose the moments when I wanted to speak or be silent could be a choice, a powerful and thoughtful choice. And our interpretations of silences reflected our sense of power as well.

How different my college life would have been if I had been able to stand by the conviction that silence can be a valid choice in the classroom, one that does not signify laziness, disengagement, hostility.

I have also begun to pay attention to how we teachers talk about students who do not fit the model of the vocal student. Friends, even close friends, have said disparaging, angry things about students or colleagues they perceive as "quiet" or "too quiet." Passive, less intelligent, resistant, unprepared, disengaged, struggling, not keeping up, not contributing—these are but a few of the common descriptions. When I point out that I might well be described this way, they are quick to reassure me that *I am* the exception—the quiet one who is not like those others. *I* am clearly intelligent, well prepared, not shallow. Besides, *I* must have good reasons for preferring to be less vocal. (I am not sure how or when I made this transition.) When I ask what makes me different, they struggle for an explanation. Yet these same men and women worry that they "talk too much," that they may be perceived as pushy or dominating. Does this conflation of quietness and lower intelligence mean that being highly vocal makes one prone to show off how smart she is? How is that made troublesome too? Where, I wonder, is the fine line between vocal and too vocal? A thoughtful silence and one that is inherently problematic? And why are we willing to accept such constructions that place so many of us outside of what we perceive as the borders of acceptability? What is to be gained by seeing the classroom (and the world) this way?

Creating New Definitions for Myself?
Hearing My Own Students' Silences

The second composition class I taught consisted of twelve men and three women; they struck me as intelligent, thoughtful, willing to write and share intimate and highly charged essays. Anxious about my ability to challenge and engage students only five years younger than myself, I thought that these students were exceptional. After my first semester students, who were jubilantly, uncontrollably vocal, this class was their polar opposite. I insisted the class sit facing each other; they moved their chairs back to the walls in our miniature classroom, creating an odd, squared arrangement. By the time my colleague, Kate Dionne, visited the class, I had grown accustomed to this arrangement without realizing how very strange this was for a composition class. I suppose I saw it as a physical balance to the emotional vulnerability in the room.

After her first visit, Kate remarked not only on the physical arrangement of the students but also on their relative silence. Initially I was somewhat surprised that a group of eighteen-year-old men was so quiet, not competing for my or their classmates' attention, but I must have adjusted to that as well. She described this class's "quiet, humming energy" as one she would find disconcerting. And, indeed, when a question was asked, there would be a pause, often a long pause. Later, my faculty supervisor commented in her evaluation that I had an admirable ability to outwait student silence and not fill it in with my teacher-voice. Until other teachers noticed this apparently remarkable silence, I do not think it ever occurred to me to be anxious. My students' periodic silences struck me as productive, soothing white space where something *was* happening; it just was not made visible yet. The words that surrounded those silences were the way I measured them.

I have never again experienced this sense of calm when faced with other quiet students. Years later, when I first taught two sections of College Writing in one semester, one quickly became the "good class" and the other the "bad." A large part of what made those students "bad" was simply that they were quieter than their earlier counterparts. Rather than reading the dynamics of the two groups as different, I compared the classroom variable that seemed least complicated to quantify.

The first section met in a comfortable classroom and was full of many highly vocal students who said they were confident about writing. They made teaching easy. Workshops of student papers were a dream, and I often found myself cutting short discussions to move on to another student's draft. Then I would leave that room with a sense of dread, moving to a more industrial classroom filled with students who would not talk no matter what I did. Workshops of papers were painful, almost physically so, as I imagined the authors' dismay at the nonresponse of their classmates. I found myself resenting these quiet students and fantasizing about giving them Fs for their refusal to speak. (Yes, the irony of that statement is uncomfortably obvious to me.) The more I idealized the first class, the more loathsome the second became.

At the end of the semester, several students from the "bad class" commented in their course evaluation that I never seemed particularly happy. They were right. I wasn't happy. I resented their silences. But I wonder now how much of the discomfort, resistance, and silence I might have been responsible for, how much tension I invoked.

Stung by those perceptive student evaluations, since then I have struggled to become conscious of the interpretations I construct about my students' silences. *She's quiet because she's unprepared. He's quiet because he's hostile. They are resistant and know their silence will break me.* These readings sneak up on me, and I find myself taking personally the silences of my students, constructing explanations that position them as failures, unable or unwilling to comply with the simple requirements of the course. But if these students are not to blame for their silences, then who is? I must not ask the right questions, be the right teacher. Something, *someone*, has to be wrong.

When I taught for the first time in a computer lab, I fell into easy conclusions about the meanings of student silence. As I struggled to integrate community-building exercises with the presence of technology and a sterile environment that seemed to work against developing a productive class community, these conclusions about student silence afforded me a way to explain the culture shock I was experiencing.

In the first class, I asked each student to put a powerful song lyric on the board for a writing exercise as part of a writing exercise. One student refused. I encouraged her; any lyric was fine, something she liked or hated, a nursery rhyme, a religious song, an advertising jingle, whatever. She shook her head, sat down, and folded her arms. Looking back, I am certain that marks the beginning of my reading her as passive, almost aggressively so. Kelly often seemed to sit back from discussion, even in small groups, just as she had done with the song lyric exercise. She seemed to resist engaging—with me, with her classmates, with her own writing; I confess, I found myself resenting her for being "difficult." No one had ever, in my experience, refused to participate in so many class activities or not complied with such simple requests. When she revealed that she had suffered psychological difficulties the previous semester and had left school temporarily, I relented a bit. *That's the explanation*, I assumed.

When I received Kelly's final portfolio, she included several extra pieces of writing. A letter explained her crippling anxiety the first day of class—that she could not think of a song lyric if her "life depended on it," her embarrassment, her suspicion that she was not able to "do college," her determination to make up for her failure. After the first uncomfortable day of class, Kelly went to her dorm room, looked through her CDs, and constructed an elaborate collage of her favorite lyrics, one that covered several pages and incorporated detailed (and researched) interpretations far beyond the scope of the original assignments. It was only in her final portfolio that she had the courage to show it to me. I was ashamed of my easy assumptions about Kelly; my entrenched interpretations led, I am certain, to so many missed opportunities and unfair assessments of her work.

Since then I have tried to utilize teaching practices that ask students to think about the value of both speech and silence. With freewriting (and other low-stakes writing) and the opportunity to share this writing afterward, a routine quickly develops with the students who are willing to read. Often students who choose not to speak in full-class discussions will choose to read their work in this moment, suggesting that this ungraded space (yet not completely "free," as some argue) offers students a unique opportunity to think about the relationship between speaking and silence and to speak authoritatively inside the academy in less-guarded ways than they are usually afforded. Could this scarce classroom time be used for more traditionally "critical" activities? Certainly. And I suspect my colleagues from other departments would argue that I should spend this time reviewing sentence fragments and the intricacies of the semi-colon.

During the first semester of this study, my university witnessed a series of rapes and assaults on campus. One day, Jamie, perhaps the most lyrical and sophisticated writer in the class, a woman who almost never spoke in class, read a piece that explored her fear, her frustration, and her anger over the events on campus and the administration's inadequate response. The other students and I were struck by the weight of her words. Even those performative students who rarely missed the opportunity to speak remained silent in the wake of Jamie's reflections and careful analysis of the climate of fear that had developed. And I think it was apparent to all of us that this was a *good* silence, one of respect, reflection, and empathy.

So I find myself in an odd position, sympathizing with those students like Jamie who chose silence and fearing those like Kelly too. Is their silence a choice, reasoned and productive, or is it simple resistance, reflexive and hostile? Can I be a good—and fair—teacher to them both? It is made even more complicated when I realize that my responses to students are so deeply inflected by the kind of student I assume them to be. Perhaps I should not confess this, but "frat guys" and female students who are vocal about being in a sorority, students who gravitate toward each other to form a sociable clique, and the athletes often feel resistant, deliberately and thoughtlessly challenging my authority through their silences. Those students who fall outside of the mainstream— students who are not white, students who choose to dress in ways that are noticeably different, students who strike me as intellectual or artistic rather than social—evoke my empathy. I believe, by choice or by instinct, that they are *choosing* silence for good reasons. Are such assessments fair or accurate? Hardly. But even my consciousness of this cannot completely inoculate me from classifying students as "bad quiet" and "good quiet."

To Speak or Not:
Weighing My Silences as a Teacher

With all of these students, the Jamies, the Kellys, and the others, I wonder. Are they enough? Anything? Does their silence expose my failure as a teacher? If I was a different teacher, a better teacher, would they *want* to talk more?

I see an ideal class—a successful one—as one in which I say very little. Expanding on Bruffee's seminal work, almost all of my classes are designed around a workshop principle, in which I seldom lecture and I try to limit my participation to careful questions. And I worry about the power of my own voice to overwhelm my students': when I speak, I foreclose on many of the options through the authority of my institutionally validated voice.

When I tell other teachers of my interest in silence, they respond in now-predictable ways, ruefully offering to "give me" their quiet students for my research, as if I need to look for such students, as if such students are an unpleasant responsibility to be dispatched, as if my interest means I should relieve them of this burden. Others will (in varying tones of sympathy or annoyance) mention students' shyness or fear, echoing Irene Papoulis's account of her experiences as a student, in which she explores her "pathological fear . . . of opening her mouth. . . . I saw them [my ideas] instead as the potential expressions of a deep secret about myself that I did not want to tell."[2] Papoulis concludes that women students "isolate themselves from the academic conversation because of their fear of not being legitimate theorizers. Actively, albeit unconsciously, those women censor themselves, retreating behind the shield of their physical appearances."[3] This is certainly an important concern we must address, but I suspect if we stop there, we shortchange our students. First, this conclusion implies that silence is always the sign of a problem, one located within the student. And it forecloses on any other legitimate explanations for the silences in our classrooms. In her attempt to deconstruct Mike Rose's monolithic explanation of the class dynamics of schooling and marginalization, she and my colleagues create a new one that conflates silence and fear. We let our own voices explain students' silences.

My own professional choices work against such easy conclusions. Teaching is not a profession where one ever escapes the question of legitimacy as a thinker and theorist. (My own experiences and those of my full- and part-time colleagues suggest that these questions may be particularly weighty for young teachers, female teachers, teachers of color, and teachers without the institutional security of tenure.) No matter how decentered or student-centered a classroom may be, the teacher is always the focus of concentrated attention, struggling to maintain authority. In fact, as Susan Kirtley argues, such "decentered" classrooms may evoke more questions about a teacher's legitimacy than traditional ones for those of us with "already marginalized positions."[4] Indeed, as hooks argues, the equation of vocalness with confidence is a faulty one that ignores the lived experiences of both those who are seen and heard as "silent" and those who are not. When we assume that no one would *choose* to be silent, we unnecessarily narrow the range of possibilities for learning.

But often as a teacher, I do struggle with when to speak and when to remain silent. I recall a particular discussion in my honors section of College Writing in which I had brought in paired columns from the "Multicultural Affairs" page of the campus newspaper with the intention of discussing issues of audience and purpose, the assumptions the authors had been making about form, and the effectiveness of particular rhetorical strategies. However, the discussion quickly shifted to an exploration of the columns' "accuracy" in their depictions of white privilege on campus and the systematic alienation and disempowerment of black students. In retrospect, I can see this conversation was a crucial one, as students began to think more critically about how one comes to trust an author's voice.

At the time, it just seemed like a disaster.

My overwhelming urge was to quickly squelch the conversation and launch into a lecture on the generally tacit, but pervasive, racial issues that plagued the campus and the unacknowledged privilege of white skin in America to stem the flow of racist, offensive, and simply naive comments spilling forth. I wanted to interrupt my students so I could not find out what was in their heads. At the very least, I wanted to moderate the discussion very tightly, only allowing space for the comments of which I approved.

But I also knew I did not want to be that kind of teacher. Silencing students would not change who they were or what they thought. In reality, all I would be certain to accomplish would be the erosion of the fragile trust we had developed.

Instead the discussion proceeded much like the less-loaded ones of easier days, an exploration in which I would pull back the discussion to the central issue or reframe students' comments as questions in order to push their constructions and conclusions further. As usual, there were a few dominating voices. (Unfortunately, on this day, they were the angry, self-righteous ones who repeated weak assertions about the "end of racism" in the United States, bearing out Parker Palmer's claim that "speaking . . . is a way of buttressing our self-serving reconstructions of reality."[5]) Occasionally I stepped in to correct historical inaccuracies that were offered as *fact* in the course of the discussion. For example, Kevin, a student who had struck me as highly motivated and thoughtful, offered the "truth" (in his words) that women and minorities simply had not written anything worth publishing before the twentieth century, hence, a white, male literary canon. I was conscious that a lecture was likely to cause many students to shut down, to ignore me and the counterargument I wanted to raise. I recalled those undergraduate classes I endured—even those I fundamentally agreed with—in which my outward compliance masked my inner hostility at being an unwilling audience to a teacher's lecture. It seemed to me the worst kind of betrayal when a teacher said she wanted to hear what her students thought and then proceeded to correct (and admonish) our worldviews. We were tricked into revealing ourselves, then scolded for it. Rather than persuading us to interpret the world differently, those "interventions" animated in me a virtually unshakeable resistance to and mistrust of what the instructor preached. Even when I had initially agreed with her.

So in that uncomfortable composition class I sweated and on an embodied level finally began to understand the cliché about sailing between Scylla and Charybdis. Should I allow my students to keep speaking, even though it horrified me, even though I suspected it might affect how I saw their work? Should I respond as I wanted to, stop the conversation, and run the very real risk of alienating all of my students for saying what they thought? Perhaps a more skilled teacher could elegantly shut down this unexpected direction to an activity I thought I had planned so well without having completely antagonized her students; I still crave that kind of grace.

I sat tight and held my indignation in check, pushing where I could, asking open-ended questions rather than presenting the conclusions I had already held, intervening where it seemed most productive, and challenging everyone's beliefs (not just those with whom I disagreed). I wanted the angry, hostile voices to stop, but not just because I had outargued them and overtalked them, and not because I had used my institutionally powerful voice to silence them.

Most of all, I did not want these students to stop speaking because they had realized it was better to be silent than to be "wrong."

The few students whose politics resembled mine fought to find space in the discussion and were shrewd enough to accomplish this by asking provocative questions and offering their own "conversion experiences" ("I used to feel that way but now I realize . . ."). Perhaps they modeled their rhetorical style on mine, realizing that a frontal attack was likely to meet with stony resistance. Eventually, it seemed to me, the decibel level of angry, unthinking remarks declined a bit, as some students began to reconsider how their own behaviors and attitudes might be perceived as racist, contributing to the racial divide that they ardently wanted to believe "didn't really exist."

All the while, I was particularly conscious of the silences of the students of color in the room. If I thought the discussion and the attitudes revealed were offensive, then how could they not feel alienated? These offensive voices emerged from the students with whom they would work in peer feedback groups. How would they trust their writing to other students who so firmly believed and propagated such narrow-minded stereotypes? Before this class, Jon, an Asian-American man, had told me that he was very quiet in most of his classes, but he reassured me that it was not a sign of disengagement. With only a few minutes left in the class period, he asked: "Why are we only talking about race as if it's only a black and white thing?"

In my memory, the class that had been so raucous in nearly uncontrolled disruptiveness, with voices jockeying for airtime, stopped at that moment. I imagine that the seventeen other students in the room reconsidered their positions, confronting the narrowness of their own visions. Seconds passed, and people's expressions shifted as they processed Jon's question. In the next instant, the discussion erupted again—responding to the question that Jon had posed to us from his nearly complete, although clearly thoughtful and engaged, silence.

I am struck by the power of Jon's voice. His question was one to which several students returned later in the semester; it echoed in other contexts as students began to see that the division of the world into binaries is not always useful, as it masks more complicated relationships that should not be simplified into a silencing either/or. And I suspect that part of the power of Jon's question came from his relative silence. His question had more power and weight because he so rarely spoke, thus we knew it mattered a great deal. We listened.

I am also struck by the process of self-discovery that Kevin (defender of the white, male canon) reported at the end of that semester. In his final reflections, he commented that the semester marked a radical shift for him. Recognizing the insular privilege of his all-white hometown, he began to consider issues of politics and injustice through a composition class he had believed would be useless to him. He appreciated that I "let him figure things out" rather than asking him to parrot my views. I suppose I could see this as a success story, in praise of a teacher's silence: I *like* where Kevin ended up. I am proud of how much he grew, how much he *let* himself grow. For example, he wrote an essay bemoaning the pointlessness of grammar and eventually revised it to include his reflections on grammar as a class-based system of linguistic exclusion, focusing on the debate over Ebonics in schools.

But I cannot quite congratulate myself as thoroughly as I might like. Other students comment in their class evaluation that my holding back in the way Kevin praises prevents them from knowing "the truth"; I do not give them the answers. The narrative of Kevin's progress provides one conclusion. I suppose my students' discomfort in not knowing the "right answer" has become tolerable to me, a useful sort of growing pain, particularly because these same students frequently remark that the class is more challenging than they had expected since I force them to think for themselves.

I wish I could say I have learned in the years since how to gracefully handle situations such as the charged one I have described, that I could offer comprehensive advice to other teachers about effectively confronting students' racist, sexist, and offensive discourses. Certainly I have devised classroom management strategies that offer me some degree of comfort. I have taken away lessons about using highly charged texts more carefully (and less naively) by setting careful parameters for those conversations. After reading Ratcliffe's "Rhetorical Listening," I have also begun emphasizing the importance of *listening* to the texts and to each other as a means of

> *understanding* . . . listening to discourse not *for* intent, but *with* intent—with the intent to understand not just the claims, not just the cultural logics within which the claims function, but the rhetorical negotiations of understanding as well. To clarify this process of understanding we might best invert the term and define *understanding* as *standing under.* . . . Standing under the discourses of others means first acknowledging the existence of these discourses; second, listening for the (un)conscious presences, absences, unknowns; and third, consciously integrating this information into our world-views and decision-making.[6]

For example, asking students to explicitly connect their responses to another student's contribution or to the text itself, and to identify the points of both intersection and divergence in perspectives, would have kept that class from spiraling so far away from where we had begun. I see now that I missed an opportunity to deploy writing in a number of important ways. I could have asked students to reflect on the most important issue of the conversation to figure out what was at stake in their own positions and those of their classmates. I could have asked them to write a respectful response to the columnist who provoked their thinking and their emotions, outlining what they heard the text arguing, explicitly and implicitly. This might have resulted in a productive conversation about rhetorical strategies, using logical appeals, creating ethos, and addressing an audience who disagrees with one's beliefs. This would also have modeled how writing can be used as a productive means of thinking. Further, moving to writing might have refocused our energy and usefully slowed the momentum of the escalating emotional responses.

But none of these classroom management techniques are, in fact, the most critical thing I took away from this experience. I realized that the values I hold about classroom dialogue and students' voices are most important at the exact moment that I most want to abandon them and become the teacher who lectures. If I value students' voices, then I have to do so consistently, even when they are unpleasant, even when they reveal things I did not want to know. I have to remember the silencing power of a teacher's voice. Some might argue that this was a moment when my students *should* have been silenced. After much (painful) consideration, I disagree. To have cut off my students' conversation would have done little, if anything, to change their minds. Discoursing about my point of view to end the ordeal of that conversation would have driven their anger, hostility, and misunderstandings underground and betrayed the fragile contract that a teacher forges with her students in a collaborative learning environment.

Now I am working hard not to fear these moments too.

Finding a Middle Ground?
Hearing Silence in More Complex Ways

When we teachers talk about the discussions in our classrooms and the quality and quantity of student voices, usually there is no middle ground. Here is just one example. I attended a conference presentation during which one speaker reported on her work with a visually impaired student. The presentation focused on the teacher's complicated strategy of utilizing computers and the assistance of another student to facilitate this student's participation in class discussions. We explored strategies, considered options, and posed questions. The thing we did not discuss (because, apparently, it was not really a question) was why this student might have *chosen* not to speak during discussions. We worked under the assumption that this student should be talking, that his *silence was deviance*, and that we could and should find a method to correct it.

Another example. At another conference, a colleague of mine began his presentation with a brief pause. After being introduced by the panel chair, he did not speak immediately. Instead he made eye contact with many members of the audience. The silence did not last more than a minute or so. Later, he told me that he had planned to let the silence last longer, but he noticed the anxiety on people's faces and recognized the tension in their body language. As one of the other presenters in this session, I too could sense the mounting distress as people shifted in their seats, looked at each other, looked down, looked embarrassed. No more than ninety seconds of quiet in a professional arena made us so uncomfortable. Were they afraid he had forgotten what he was going to say? That he had been paralyzed by stage fright? As Palmer proposes, "In most places where people meet, silence is a threatening experience. It makes us self-conscious and awkward; it feels like some kind of failure . . . a silent space seems inhospitable at first to people who measure progress by noise."[7]

In our discourse, students and teachers evoke the scene from *Ferris Bueller's Day Off* in which the teacher drones on, unable to connect to students who are bored and apathetic, literally and metaphorically absent in their silences. Or the classroom resembles the most idealized version of classrooms in which the teacher prompts a "real" dialogue that in turn fosters her students reflective self-discovery and empowerment. Why do we see our students' silence as an all-or-nothing proposition? We talk about students' development of academic writing as learning to take part in an "academic conversation."[8] As such, we have the sense that this is, indeed, a process over time that responsible teachers demystify for their students. Instead, our stories about classroom conversation focus on the *failure* of students to have mastered this skill; they are deficient, resistant, or silenced. In the middle ground, perhaps we can come to see engaging in literal academic dialogues as part of a process that can be *learned*, like revision practices or the mastery of comma usage.

For all of the self-reflection and writing that has gone into this chapter and the other writing I have done about the silences in my life outside of school, I am left without tidy, definitive conclusions. Rather than clarifying, crystallizing, and purifying the issues of silence, this process has muddied the waters for me. I wrestle with this very project of "explaining" my own silences and my interest in this underexplored classroom phenomenon, as if I acknowledge these as something needing justification. I am left with the multiple meanings I hold for silence, the contradictions I have experienced and written myself into, and the powerful, even bodily, reactions I have to these memories. I am struck by the radical shifts I have experienced, and I want to believe that the narrative I have constructed represents the truth of these moments that feel critical in the development of my voice and silences in the classroom. But I know these stories might be told quite differently, highlighting other issues, offering alternate explanations for my own and others' behaviors and responses. Even while I resent those teachers who value the sound of student voices without asking why students might choose to be silent, I find myself, at times, becoming one of them. I am caught in a tension between valuing silence and dreading it too.

Chapter 4

Situating the Study

This brief chapter serves as an introduction to the study itself—to the university, to the students, and to the particular course in which the study took place. While I think the study ultimately raises important questions for us to consider about our perceptions of and conclusions about speaking and silence in the classroom in a more generalized way, it is important to understand the study in its localized context.

The University Population

This project took place at the University of Massachusetts at Amherst, a public, land-grant university with an enrollment of approximately 18,000 undergraduate and 6,000 graduate students from all fifty states and seventy foreign countries. According to the *UMass at a Glance* Web page, the school supported more than eighty majors at the time of the study. Approximately 73 percent of the incoming students were residents of Massachusetts; another 7 percent were from New England. (Anecdotally, many students cite the significantly lower tuition for in-state and regional students as a factor in their college decisions.) A vast majority (almost 86 percent) of the incoming class identified themselves as "White, Non-Hispanic." Their mean SAT score was 1127; the average high school GPA was 3.33.[1] The campus has more than thirty sororities and fraternities. The school is particularly proud of its NCAA-Division 1 athletic teams. Perhaps because of the size of the school, it "has one of the most unique and diversified student activities programs in the country," with well over 200 student-run organizations, including academic, religious, cultural, political, creative, and service groups.[2]

While such statistics may offer a useful touchstone for understanding the setting and demographics of this study, it is difficult for me to feel they do justice to the school or its students. For me, the stereotype this description conjures up does not adequately represent the "typical" class of first-year students. I suspect it might be easier to characterize their counterparts at one of the

73

neighboring, smaller, private colleges (Smith, Mount Holyoke, Hampshire, and Amherst).

I offer these additional, admittedly subjective, observations based on the anecdotes shared by my students and my own interpretations of what I witnessed in my seven years at the university. First, I find it virtually impossible to characterize a "typical" UMass undergraduate. While a portion of my students might have happily labeled themselves as middle class, suburban kids, as "average students," or as "frat boys," so many of them did not fit that mold. A great number of them work part time or even full time to help support themselves and their educations. Many were fairly successful in high school, as the previous entrance statistics suggest, but it often seemed that many of my students were not particularly confident about their academic abilities; many expressed concern over their ability to succeed in college.

At the risk of perpetuating even more stereotypes, I offer this generalized picture of a first-year composition course to provide a sense of the broad cross-section of students present in any given class. One is likely to find a student planning to stay at UMass for only a year or two before transferring to a more expensive private college, while several of his classmates have older siblings at the school as well. Those students who plan on rushing a fraternity or sorority tend to gravitate together, as do the various athletes on the varsity or intramural teams and the members of the Marching Band. At least one student plans to design his own cross-disciplinary major in the BDIC (Bachelor's Degree with Individual Concentration) program, and one or two may travel to a neighboring college for specific courses not offered on campus. A significant portion of the class may still be undecided about their majors, while a few have already been accepted to the School of Management. Still others are preparing their applications for the highly competitive School of Nursing. A couple students want to write for the daily campus newspaper or to work as a broadcaster on the local radio station, while some of their classmates are auditioning for one of the numerous campus productions. In any given class, at least one student has joined the Cannabis Reform group, and a few have visited the Stonewall Center.

Without idealizing these students, I was struck by both their diversity in interests, politics, and goals and their relative tolerance of these differences. That is, while it became relatively easy over time to see "types" of students based on their style of dress or extracurricular activities (and even to predict where they might choose to live on campus), as a teacher I never sensed significant antagonism—in the classroom or on campus—between students with diverging values and interests.

The Students in the Study

This study took place in the Orchard Hill section of the UMass Amherst campus; students in this particular class all lived in one of four dorms in this "cluster." Orchard Hill is a somewhat more rural setting and has an informal reputation for being a quieter, and perhaps slightly more academically focused, residential area on campus.

Since the majority of the data comes from the five "focal" students I interviewed, I thought it would be useful to identify them beyond what is revealed in their interview texts.

Two students chose to introduce themselves.

Edward D. Owen is presently a 19-year old sophomore History major at the University of Massachusetts-Amherst. Hailing from Southeastern Connecticut (yes, near Foxwoods . . . actually, the same town), he was drawn to the liberal character and the rustic overtones inherent in the Amherst/Northampton area. Edward spent all of his developmental years in SE Connecticut. He was diagnosed with Attention Deficit Disorder when he was in third grade, and in fourth grade, he started taking Ritalin for it. Often feeling very "controlled" by the Ritalin, he worked towards the goal of being able to exert self-control over himself, and when Edward was a freshman, he was taken off of Ritalin. For the rest of high school, he maintained a B–B+ average. Always somewhat of a closet extrovert, Edward participated in several theatrical productions in high school, and maintains that commitment in college, having done productions with the UMass Theatre Guild, as well as being a part of the UMass sketch comedy troupe, Casual Sketch.

My name is Sarah. I am the youngest of five girls, with a span of fourteen years between the oldest and me. I grew up with four older sisters that were very protective of me and did just about everything for me. Although I did not have to speak out on my account, I certainly was not quiet among the house or family members. I come from a Caucasian family which is composed of the following descents: Polish, Lithuanian, French, and Irish. I grew up in a small town setting for most of my life, until moving to our summer house on Cape Cod. Although these surrounding were completely different in many aspects, I still found the same type of treatment. Freshman year at the University of Massachusetts at Amherst I was nineteen years of age and accepted to the School of Management to work at my major, accounting.

The other focal students are:

Catarina identifies herself as a white woman. At the time of the study, she was an eighteen-year-old computer science major who lived in Orchard Hill. During her interviews she mentioned that she had one brother; her family is Baptist. She is an avid science fiction fan (reading, movies, and writing), an interest she saw as somewhat unusual for a woman. She considered joining the university's debate team, something she thought might be "good for her."

Sanjay is an Indian man, an eighteen-year-old computer science major, although at one time he considered pursing a medical career with his parents' strong encouragement. It was my impression that Sanjay was a comfortable and confident writer. He often chose challenging topics (such as the intolerance he perceived in a religious community he observed), and in his conferences with me, he frequently asked questions about the craft of writing. During the semester following this student, Sanjay asked me for a recommendation, as he was planning on transferring to another college.

Lucy identifies herself as a "proud female." Born and raised in Israel to American parents, she came to the United States when she was a junior in high school to live with her father and stepmother. Lucy frequently expressed concerns about the gaps in her previous education; having attended an art-focused high school in Israel, she worried that she did not have an academic background comparable to her classmates. In College Writing, she was concerned with developing her vocabulary, mastering the forms of essay writing, and attaining the kinds of cultural knowledge her classmates took for granted. After working in a small group with Brad and Allison, she quickly became friends with them and often studied with them. Also eighteen during the study, she had not yet declared a major.

Edward, Sarah, Catarina, and Lucy all chose their own pseudonyms; Sanjay expressed no preference.

An Overview of the Course

To get a sense of the College Writing class in which this study took place, perhaps the best overview comes from the standard course syllabus and guidelines established by the Writing Program and utilized by all new graduate Teaching Associates. Given my work with various aspects of the Writing Program (as a Graduate Mentor to new Teaching Associates, as a Writing Tutor, and as the Writing Placement Exam Coordinator), the syllabus excerpts that follow encapsulate the teaching philosophy with which I approached the course.

English 112: College Writing

Welcome! This syllabus introduces you to the aims, requirements, and structures of College Writing so please read it carefully and discuss it with your teacher.

Those of us who teach College Writing want to identify four central assumptions that define the course:

- You are writers and we are writers. We all have unique experiences and interesting insights that are worth writing about.

- We all learn and improve by doing: by writing to pursue our interests, by experimenting with new strategies, by having a receptive audience, by receiving feedback from others, and by reflecting on our own work.

- To improve as writers and as learners, we all need a respectful and supportive classroom community. We will respect and support you, and we expect you to respect and support each other—and us.

- As teachers, we will work with you to create a classroom community that helps us all grow as writers. Creating that community depends on each of us—teachers and students alike-fulfilling our individual responsibilities, offering mutual respect to one another, and being receptive readers of one another's writing.

Because we all learn to write best by writing and having a receptive audience, class sessions will be run as workshops rather than as lectures. It is therefore essential that you attend class consistently. In class we will ask you to write—often experimenting with new writing strategies; to share your writing in pairs, small groups, and even with the whole class; and often to give responses to each others' writing. Final drafts will be published regularly in class magazines.

Goals and Rationale

The goal of this course is to help you develop your writing abilities—not only for University writing assignments but also for using writing effectively in the rest of your life. We seek to improve your ability:

- to write for various audiences and purposes—for example, to explore a topic for yourself, to communicate with others (fellow students, teachers, general readers, etc.), and to create particular effects (persuading, explaining, etc).

(*continued*)

- to develop and extend your own thinking by questioning your own views and considering the views of others—and thus the ability to write essays which *move* through an extended train of thinking rather than just defend a static position.

- to use various kinds of thinking and discourse—for example, narrating, explaining, analyzing, interpreting, persuading, arguing, and using evidence or examples.

- to draw on various sources of thinking and information: your own experience and observations, conversation with others, and reading.

- to revise your writing in a substantive way by means of re-thinking and re-seeing, and also by means of playing with various forms and organizations.

- to take whatever steps are needed to copyedit your final drafts successfully.

- to be a constructive reader of your own and others' writing, and to give constructive and helpful feedback.

- to understand and manage your own writing processes.

Required Writing

1. Six essays (each at least 750 to 1,000 words). With each finished essay, you must turn in all preliminary drafts, including exploratory and mid-process drafts, as well as any written peer and teacher response.

2. Journal writing.

3. Other shorter assignments written in class and at home.

You will be doing a wide range of writing that will include the following major essays:

The Documented Essay

In this essay, we are asking you to advance your thinking about a topic that interests you by entering into dialogue with published writers who have written about it. The goal is not so much to summarize what others have written but rather to use their thinking to help you work out *your thinking.* Don't think of this as a "gathering-and-presenting-information" essay, but rather a chance for you to figure something out and support it with outside sources. A secondary aim for the documented essay is to gain more facility using a standard form of academic documentation. (You'll receive more information about this essay from your teacher.)

The Text-Wrestling Essays

For these essays you will be asked to read two texts by published writers and scholars and to write about them. The goal is to practice reading closely and carefully and to *engage* with the ideas and thinking presented in the text. There are many ways to engage a text and with your teacher you will explore and experiment with various ways to do so. In writing your essays you won't be asked to summarize the text but rather to work out your own train of thought.

The Case Study Review

For the final essay you will be asked to review all the writing you have done this semester. This is a chance for you to reflect on the development and progress that you have made over the course of the semester. In many ways writing is about choices and this is your opportunity to reflect, articulate, and evaluate the choices you have made in your writing. This is also an opportunity for you to take stock of yourself as a writer, to evaluate where you have been and where you are going. This is not just a report of the work you have done this semester, but rather it is a developed essay working out a hypothesis, developing a train of thought and/or figuring something out about yourself as a writer and your writing.

A part of the process of developing this essay will be the review of a classmate's portfolio. This is your chance to get valuable feedback on the body of your work as well as to gain experience reviewing the work of another.

Drafts and the Writing Process

Sometimes people write papers all in one draft—sometimes even the night before the deadline. Sometimes this process can produce good writing. Nevertheless, a central aim of our course is to teach you a longer and more thoughtful writing process that invites more development and evolution in your thinking. We will require you to write multiple drafts for each essay. This process will permit you to be more exploratory and adventuresome in early drafts and more disciplined in later drafts. As you work from one draft to the next, you'll have the chance to assess it yourself and also to receive some feedback from classmates and/or your teacher. Note that when we ask you to revise, we are asking you to make substantive changes, not just edit, correct, or touch up. You might do well to think of different "drafts" as different "versions" of a paper.

(continued)

Exploratory Draft. An exploratory draft is where you get down on paper all the ideas and information that come to mind. You can try out different approaches—even in the same paper. Don't be concerned with organization or how the draft will work for readers, but do be concerned with opening up your thinking, exploring possibilities, and getting down lots of writing that you can work with.

Mid-process Draft. Since your first draft was an exploratory attempt to get down as much thinking as possible, now is the time to work on reorganizing, adding and cutting sections, and other kinds of rewriting. You'll be trying to think about your readers, focus your purpose, clarify your thinking, and convey a particular point of view and tone of voice. But even a mid-process draft can benefit from remaining still a bit unsettled—from having a bit too much in it—so that when you do a final revision, you will still have some choice of direction or emphasis.

Concluding Revision Draft. This is your chance to make substantive changes again after getting feedback from your teacher and classmates. Since this is your last draft except for copyediting, you need to work on crafting the wording, style, and voice.

Final or Publication Draft. Your only job here is to copyedit well—to remove all remaining mistakes in spelling, grammar, or punctuation. It is fine to get help in copyediting, indeed, it is desirable to do so: from the handbook, from a dictionary, from friends, and even from a paid typist or editor. You need to learn to take whatever steps are necessary for successful copyediting, because your final draft will not be acceptable if there are still mistakes.

When you submit your mid-process, concluding revision, and final drafts, always include all preliminary work: all notes, drafts, process writing, peer-responses, and teacher responses—everything. Drafts are not acceptable without this supplementary material.

Your Journal

Your journal is for informal, personal writing and reflection. Use it as you wish, however, there may be times when your teacher will give you a specific assignment. We ask you to keep it because we want you to write regularly, experiment with your writing, and develop a writer's habit of observing and reflecting. You can use it to play with language too. Plan to write for at least one hour a week—at least three or four pages. Try to make entries three or four times each week. Your teacher will check your journal periodically but will not read any passages you mark as private.

Your Portfolio

Don't throw anything away! As you move throughout the semester, you will be creating a portfolio of all your written work. The portfolio will include the major essays, all the drafts and preliminary work that accompany the final draft, process writing, the additional in-class and out-of-class writing exercises you do, the written feedback from your teacher, and the written feedback you give to classmates about their writing. You'll need a big folder and/or an accordion type file.

Conferences and Office Hours

At least twice during the semester, you will have individual conferences with your teacher. These conferences are a time to discuss your writing more fully and your progress in the course. Your teacher will also have regularly scheduled office hours. That time is set aside for you, so we encourage you to use it.

Final Conferences

A third conference will be scheduled during final examination week. This will be your chance to meet with your teacher to go over your portfolio and to discuss the progress you made during the semester. Final conferences are mandatory, so be sure to include them when making your plans for the end of the semester.

While the syllabus lays out the expectations of the course, several features seem particularly notable in light of the data generated in my study. This writing course, as laid out in the department syllabus, presupposes students' *identities as writers*—a position that students may find difficult, even uncomfortable, to take on. In my own section of the course, I foregrounded this writerly identity in a low-stakes writing assignment, entitled "Seeing Yourself as a Writer," which asks students to explore their histories, experiences, and perceptions of writing as a grounding point for the work of the course. Students were also asked to complete brief "author's notes" after each draft, reflecting on their writing processes, authorial intention, and assessment of their work. Such consistent self-reflection trains students to become more skilled managers of their own writing process. That is, I believe this reflexive self-awareness helps students' writing improve, not just on that particular draft of that particular essay but in developing strategies and behaviors for other writing situations. This component of the course carries through in the "Case Study Review," an examination of the student's growing portfolio of writing throughout the semester.

The syllabus reveals the strong *process basis* of the course, as laid out in the rigorous four-draft sequencing of the assignments. Teaching Associates were encouraged to hold students to high standards for revising as a means of re-thinking and revisiting an idea or a question; inadequate or minimal revision was unacceptable, even for highly skilled writers. To further the idea that one can *re-see* through writing, I encouraged students to revisit topics of interest in subsequent assignments, to draw on journal entries as a viable source of essay topics, and to develop and extend their thinking from a project by addressing a new audience or by using a different kind of discourse to address a related question in a later piece. (For example, one student wrote an argument-driven piece about the issues of religious tolerance and respect that emerged for him after completing his ethnographic research on a religious community; another student researched a local drug intervention program for teens after writing about her friend's unsuccessful battles with drug addiction.) For me, this focus on process and revision is not merely about revising papers for excellence. What I hope is that students come to see writing as a conversation of sorts, a way of investigating, of thinking, on paper.

Careful student readers of this syllabus might discern an unspoken "participation" requirement. Teachers are not lecturers in College Writing; the language about forming a *"respectful and supportive classroom community"* positions students quite differently than, say, a Psychology 100 lecture, where a student is one of 500. In College Writing, students are writing for real audiences—including other students in the class who will be sharing drafts, reading each other's work, and providing feedback. Student writing becomes public in peer feedback groups and class publications; it is itself one of the primary course texts for examination and discussion. In our initial discussion of the syllabus, students questioned the "requirements" for speaking. I explained that we would work in a variety of arrangements, including individual work, collaborative writing, pairs, small groups, student-led discussions, peer feedback groups, full-class writing activities, and full-class discussions. While I hoped to see students participating in as many classroom forums as possible, I was unlikely to simply call on students. Ultimately, the pattern that was most common was a combination of individual writing, small group work—peer feedback, a collaborative writing exercise, or discussion—and a shorter, full-class summary. Given students' skill at working in small groups, this quickly became the most frequent use of class time.

In the English 112 syllabus, the *teacher-student relationship* is constructed perhaps quite differently than in other courses. First, the rhetorical stance of the syllabus makes this document not simply the communication between one teacher and his students ("I require . . .") or the more typical third-person diction ("The requirements of the course are . . ."). This syllabus sets up a relationship with a larger collective of teachers—the "we" who teach the many sections of the course who have agreed on the shaping values, rationales, and objectives of the course. In addition, the syllabus draws attention to development of the teacher-student relationship, mediated through the one-on-one contact of conferences. In this way, communication about student writing is not relegated to marginalia or the justification of a grade. I extended this by scheduling one conference per paper; I have found that discussions during conferences often produce stronger and more extensive revisions than my written comments do.

Finally, the syllabus indicates a concern for the student-writer's personal growth. Consider the descriptions of the Documented Essay and the Text-Wrestling Essay, the two most traditionally "academic" components of the course, at least as described in the syllabus. Students learn that they will have the "chance . . . to figure something out and support it with outside sources" and "*engage* with the ideas and thinking presented in the text. . . . work out your own train of thought." In this way, while students are learning the skills of critical thinking and academic citation, it is cast in the light of students' own development *and* a dialogue with the ideas of others. Students are not receivers of knowledge or outsiders to the culture of the academy; instead, they come to their own conclusions through conversation with the texts and ideas of others.

Chapter 5

"What Teachers Want"
Exploring Teaching Practices

I think each teacher would ideally have a class full of smart people knowing what they're talking about, willing to participate. That's the utopia for any one teacher. And no teacher is going to get . . . I think the teacher has to try with every student. That's what their job is—to try to reach every student. The student's not willing to respond . . . but that doesn't mean the teacher is not, shouldn't be, willing to try anymore.

—Edward O., student

"Anyone? Anyone?"

—*Ferris Bueller's Day Off*

I wish I did not see myself in both of these quotes. I wish I did not crave that utopia that Edward describes, eager for those "smart people" who "know what they're talking about" (and cannot wait to share those ideas); I wish his subtle critique of the teacher who is too dismissive of those students who do not fit the model of the "good student" did not sting so much. I wish I did not see myself with that teacherly desperation, plaintively begging for anyone to say anything. I wish I did not cringe over how easily I find myself falling into the easy position of thinking that good students talk and resistant students do not. But I am not alone in drawing this equation: it underlies many of the teaching narratives I explored in chapter 2. For example, Tobin's quiet students are accountable, at least initially, for the "unproductive mood of the classroom."[1] TuSmith reads overt racism and defensiveness in her students' silence.[2] The few students who raise their hands are met with "relief" in the classrooms that Kutz and Roskelly describe,[3] and the silence of students is depicted as a violent attack against one's teacher.[4]

85

How tempting (and comforting) these explanations. But beyond the simplistic conflation of silence with resistance—to the demands of education in general, to a required writing course, to the content of a particular class, to my pedagogy, to me—my students suggest a far more complicated set of relationships mediated by teachers and their practices that will either encourage or limit their voices in discussions and in writing.

This chapter was, by far, the hardest to write, although not for a lack of rich and provocative material. Overwhelmingly, my students told rich stories about their teachers, duplicating, echoing, and complicating the themes in their classmates' reflections. Honestly, some of this was heartwarming and validating: I could feel good about myself for what I was doing *right* as a teacher. But other reflections were far more difficult to hear, as they questioned my practices and challenged my interpretations. I suspect that some readers will share this tension as their values are nakedly confronted. Many times during the interviews, in analyzing the data and in writing this chapter, I found myself wanting to argue, "You're not getting it right; that's not how it is in *my* classroom."

But . . .

My commitment was to try to understand students' perspectives on speaking and silence, no matter how challenging it might be to hear what their constructions could tell me about the classroom, about the negotiations of silence, and ultimately, about my own teaching. Accepting students' praise means I have to listen to their critiques as well. If I am committed to dialogue as a means of learning, then I need to consider my responsibility for the dynamics that students face and the tensions they may feel in speaking.

It might be possible to read their comments as dictating the sorts of teachers we should be. But I do not think that is a particularly useful way to frame these reflections. Often one student's contributions complicate, even contradict, another's. Further, students' views, like our own, are limited and partial; they are no more *the truth* about the classroom than our versions are. But they do offer us important—if difficult—considerations (about the purposes of discussion, our personae and the teacher-student relationships we foster, our responses to students' contributions, practices of grading and requirements, the models we develop for speaking and silence, and the student relationships we foster) as we think about who we are, the work we do in our classrooms, and why our students choose speaking or silence.

Why Discussion, Anyway?

As chapter 2 suggests, we often have multiple objectives in fostering classroom dialogue; for many of us, it has become the logical embodiment of collaborative learning and dialogic education so deeply entwined with composition pedagogy. However, these values may not always be so transparent to students, who may perceive our requests for "participation" as a means of surveillance, testing, and subtle control. These (mis)understandings explain, at least in part, the discomfort, anxiety, and tension that both we and our students may experience in classroom discussions.

So what do students think their teachers want to "happen" through student interaction? Of the five focal students I interviewed, only one imagines that classroom discussion might be a way of constructing meaning. Edward reasons:

> The goal is perhaps—well I'm not a teacher so I don't know—but I think part of it is [that] teachers want students to learn from each other . . . to be able to offer those opinions to others so they can take it in. . . . Being able to have students almost teach each other and offer those points of view and interpret those points of view. You take that point of view and interpret it, and you turn right around and put it back out. When you put what you had out for people to sample and you see what they think about that.

First I am struck that the purpose of discussion is not clear: "I'm not a teacher so I don't know," a gap that may help explain many of the differences between teachers' and students' experiences. Edward goes on to explain that discussions can be a dynamic process during which opinions are available for interpretation, perhaps changing how one thinks. His metaphor for the interaction is "sampling": try out a bit of the view of another, reject it if it seems unsuitable; accept it and look for more if it is compelling. This process feels interactive (at least between the students), calling to mind Joseph Harris's metaphor of the classroom as a *city*, where "competing beliefs and practices intersect with and confront one another. . . . The classroom [functions] as a public space rather than as a kind of entry point into some imagined community of academic discourse."[5] (Of all the students in this study, Edward's dynamic and interactive vision most closely parallels my own.)

On the other hand, for Sanjay, teachers have two possible objectives in asking students to speak: the first, for younger teachers, is to "achieve some interest in [the subject]. . . . Like if you talk about this maybe you'll actually enjoy what you're talking about. With the older teachers, it's like they have to make sure you're still awake." Catarina echoes this, assessing discussion's supervisory and disciplinary function: to "make sure everyone's paying [attention]. . . . I guess they kind of want to see where the students are . . . [to] know if they're understanding the material or make sure they're not just doing the whole gaze-into-the-wall thing." In this formulation, teachers assume students' subtle disobedience; classroom discussion allows teachers access to what is happening inside of students' heads, ensuring their overt compliance. Catarina's vision is shaped by her high school experience, where the school-wide model

for classes was to have forty-five minutes of a fifty-minute class spent in
lectures, and

> the teacher would spend maybe five minutes at the end of class ask-
> ing the class questions. But it was never something where you were
> expected to say . . . "I think this." It was just "know what the teacher
> wants to know and say it." In history class it was . . . "Why did World
> War II happen?" And you were expected to . . . know exactly what
> the teacher wants to hear. . . . You don't say, "Well, I *think* this hap-
> pened." It was, "No, the Nazis did it." . . . But it wasn't, "I thought it
> was the population," or "I thought it was environmental issues." It
> was a very "*know what I'm going to say*" thing. (emphasis added)

In this way, Catarina and her classmates have become accustomed to seeing speech as an examination, "a normalizing gaze, a surveillance that makes it
possible to qualify, to classify, and to punish"[6] as they are transformed into visible objects of the invisible disciplinary power[7] of the teacher. Students learn
not to hypothesize or speculate but to give the "right answer" in order to avoid
a very public sort of punishment, thus creating a particularly limited view of
what counts as "knowledge" and appropriate classroom conversation. In the
context of writing, this view of knowledge may lead to short essays that summarize the text read or the teacher's point of view, with little development of
the student's own critical thinking. In this way, essay writing is reduced to a
search for "what the teacher wants" and is no longer seen as a process of making meaning, developing ideas, or testing one's own thinking. Writing becomes
a process of hunting down and transcribing the elusive "right answer."

Catarina's comments (and the nonverbal stress she demonstrated while
speaking about these experiences) suggest how complicated the invitation (or
requirement) to speak in a College Writing class may be. For students who perceive this as another way that teachers subtly but publicly test them and ensure
their compliance, the practice may feel intrusive, even manipulative. Indeed,
two focal students spoke at length in their interviews of their resistance to the
types of questions they felt were designed to track student comprehension.
Therefore, for students like Catarina, a classroom based on student dialogue
breaks the rules students have come to accept about *how classrooms are supposed
to run.* This paradigm shift, often not fully explained, may seem mysterious,
with a set of alternate rules that are rarely articulated. How do you speak (or
know what to say) when you do not understand these rules for interacting?

These reflections suggest strategies we might usefully employ to help our
students become the "nonstop talkers"[8] we might yearn for in our classrooms.
Clarifying our sense of the purposes of discussion *in a particular class* and ex-
plicating the local rules, expectations, and rationales for dialogue will demystify

this practice that is so baffling to many students. In doing so, we must acknowledge that our expectations may be very different from what students have experienced in previous (and sometimes concurrent) classes or will confront in the future. We do our students a disservice to act as if one classroom discourse style can simply supplant another because it is somehow superior. And if we want students to see dialogue as the practice of *making meaning*, then how we pose questions or frame issues must actively reflect this orientation. So we must also be explicit about those situations for which there is a "right" answer and avoid surveillance-style questions that test students' faith in this form of communication we propose. Finally, and perhaps most importantly, students may be persuaded to think of dialogue, to use Edward's metaphor, as "sampling" if we can model ways of speaking reflectively (not performing mastery over the subject) and being transformed by the words of others.

Teachers' Personae and Teacher-Student Relationships

Students adjust their behaviors and attitudes based on their perceptions of the interpersonal dynamics, focusing on the cues a teacher provides about her sense of the teacher-student relationship. As Erica Scott concludes in her article "Composing as a Person," "Who students are in the classroom depends upon how teachers define them."[9] How we as teachers construct our students inflects their participation in classroom dialogue. When we use terms such as *conversation* and *dialogue* in composition pedagogy, we imply a relative equality between participants. However, if that relationship feels unbalanced, when teachers are perceived as the embodiments of Authority and Knowledge (not as coparticipants), they are likely to produce anxiety in their students, often resulting in uncomfortable silences. If a teacher's identity and the relationship she establishes with her students are limited in these ways, then students may be unable to imagine themselves in a position other than novice, supplicant, and unequal.

Beyond the teacher-defined purpose of discussion, the perceived personality of a teacher often affects students' willingness or capacity to respond. For example, Sanjay recalls a not particularly skilled high school teacher who was "a good guy" and generated a great deal of discussion, in contrast to another very knowledgeable instructor who was not respected and was met with silence. So silence may indeed be a form of resistance in which students can exert power over a teacher, as the accounts of TuSmith and Tobin suggest.[10] But in the reflections of my students, this was far less common than teachers' stories would suggest; it was mentioned only briefly by two students.

Catarina finds classes "less stressful [when] you're not expected to just sit there and kind of know what the teacher wants to hear." She found that our class was "more comfortable with speaking what they really thought, not like, what they were expected to say," concluding that our class "had a better—it sounds kind of strange—rapport with the teacher, well you." Part of what created this rapport for her was our conferences during which I consciously strove to talk primarily about the students' writing, but which inevitably included brief references to the *material subject* of the students' writing, their lives outside of College Writing, other classes, jobs, families, recent movies, the prints in my office, what we were each currently reading, my own academic life, and campus. These conferences made our relationship, in Catarina's view, "less formal," and in mine, the space of "mutual engagement."[11] Some of my colleagues (and some of my readers, no doubt) find this kind of student endorsement suspect. Does the kind of teacher-student relationship to which Catarina alludes mean a class is too "touchy-feely"? Does rapport replace rigor? Along with hooks, I believe "engaged pedagogy is really the only type of teaching that truly generates excitement in the classroom, that enables students and professors to feel the joy of learning."[12]

The relationships students perceive between teacher and student can also contribute to students' decision to speak or to be silent. Catarina recalls that meeting me in conferences was initially frightening because she had never experienced a teacher-student situation such as this before. "Scared stiff" to come to my office, she said very little, uncertain in this situation that had different rules of interaction than she had previously encountered. (From my perspective, this early meeting seemed a bit painful: I asked questions, and she seemed to answer in as few words as possible.) What I had asked her to do—meet me to talk about what she saw going on in her paper—contradicted the relationships between teachers and students she had come to expect through her years of very successful schooling. And Lucy comments that professors

> just seem so smart and they just seem like they have so much knowledge. . . . My Women's Studies professor, at first I was so intimidated by her because she's so powerful . . . and she's the kind of woman you look at and say, "Wow I want to be like that." She talks with so much confidence and she knows so much. . . . I said to myself, "How could I say anything in this class? . . . NO way, I'm just going to sit here and listen."
> *I guess because of who they are or what they represent, I kind of feel like I have to be at this certain point or level to communicate with them.*
> (emphasis added)

So it is not a teacher's particular action or individual identity that silences Lucy. The asymmetrical relationship of power between teacher and student, even the category "professor"—with the knowledge, power, and presence it implies—becomes problematic as it highlights Lucy's own perceived lack of authority in comparison and leaves her silent.

While much of our academic training has taught us the value of being distanced, critical, and uninvolved, students seemed to value the opposite: three of the five focal students suggested that an explicit acknowledgment of the teacher's identity can make the classroom a more comfortable and, ultimately, a more productive space in which to speak and write, echoing O'Reilley's calls that we "free ourselves . . . to operat[e] from the center of our real personalities rather than from wearisome social facades."[13] Says Catarina, "There were a couple of teachers, the first class they would either start lecturing or they would just kind of *talk* to students the first class. And um, just kind of getting to know the teacher was different than the classes," where there was little personal interaction between the teacher and her students. A teacher who revealed her interest in snowboarding "let the kids, the students in the class, know who she was and that she actually had a life outside of class. She also kind of made the students understand that inside and outside of class she was two different people." So Catarina's decision to speak is inflected by a teacher's acknowledging the gap between classroom identities and out-of-class identities. Whether or not we are persuaded by O'Reilley's arguments or Catarina's reflections, both ask us to consider this question: what model do we provide our students of academic thinking and academic life? If our self-presentation and our "critical" stance make us appear unapproachably distant, then we may, by our own example, devalue the work that can be done in the university. Indeed, as Kirtley argues, "We should not be afraid to address our desires and emotions, the feelings that inspire and limit us. . . . [Eros] will guide us to traverse us to boundaries coming to a place where desire leads to wisdom."[14]

At stake for some students is an acknowledgment of the essential *humanness* of the teacher. For example, Lucy finds that she responds most productively to a teacher's actively breaking down that distinction in his identities, thus if a teacher "presents himself as a person and not as 'Professor Whatever' . . . it's easier for me to talk to them . . . 'Academic Professor blah blah blah' [is] just more intimidating." She is especially struck by a Sociology teacher who is

> very down to earth and he gives examples from real life, from his life, from our lives, and it makes things a lot easier to understand . . . he's more approachable, I think. I feel like I understand more because it's more personal, and I think when you know that it's more personal, you kind of want to learn more.

In this way, Lucy's learning (and perhaps even more crucially her motivation to learn) depends on the relationship permitted by the instructor's self-presentation and vulnerability to her students. As hooks argues, "To teach in a manner that respects and cares for the souls of our students is essential if we are to provide the necessary conditions where learning can most deeply and intimately begin . . . professors must practice being vulnerable in the classroom, being wholly present in mind, body, and spirit."[15]

For Lucy, the way a teacher positions herself in very practical ways illuminates her attitudes about education and her students. As she notes,

> If they [say] "Call me Ed . . . let's do this, it's going to be great, you're going learn a lot and have fun with it." And some [say], "this is how it is. Call me Professor This. It's going to be very hard . . ." It's totally different. *They just represent themselves differently.* . . . If they kind of present themselves on the first day of class or near the beginning as, "I'm here to share knowledge with you, to teach you," rather than "[I'll] just tell you what this is and don't ask any stupid questions." It's very different. (emphasis added)

So Lucy sees that how the teacher-student-knowledge relationship is configured by the teacher is an important factor in determining the presence of her voice in a classroom. (I suspect this relationship affects her writing in much the same way.)

Catarina links the teacher-student relationship to particular practices or ways of being in the classroom; the teacher's position in classroom interactions shapes her own feelings about classroom interactions. She speaks appreciatively of one teacher who "acts more friendly, to be honest . . . he interacts *with* the class, he doesn't just sit there and ask questions . . . . It's not like there's a professor in the room . . . it's not as stressful as a regular class, because you're not expected to just sit there and kind of know what the teacher wants to hear" (emphasis added).

These students seem to be seeking a more equitable relationship—one based on *sharing* knowledge rather than *telling* it, one based on the teacher's acting as a full participant in the class discussion rather than metaphorically (or literally) sitting outside of it in order to oversee, direct, evaluate. I think it is important to note that students are not asking teachers to give up their authority or to ignore it. Indeed, Lucy and Catarina are well aware of the power and authority their instructors hold by virtue of their knowledge, the way they carry themselves, and their institutionally inscribed positions. What they are seeking are instructors who both acknowledge their authority and define themselves beyond, outside, and in addition to it; as Lucy notes, "Sometimes it's hard to look beyond the fact that they're more than just a professor, they're a person too." She finds herself most comfortable when she is allowed to think of the interactions with an instructor as "a person-conversation, not a professor-student conversation." Catarina echoes this, narrating a particularly effective class discussion as one in which "it's not like there's a teacher in the room."

One student notes that a teacher's plan for the first day of class is a telling one, indelibly setting the tone for the rest of the year. For example, the decision to lecture or to engage in a conversation reveals for her the instructor's attitude toward the students and the possibilities for future interaction with the teacher and other students. Is the teacher "this huge ogre that stood in front of the class and taught, or more of like, an actual person"? She notes that on the first day of College Writing, when I asked students to interview a partner and introduce her to the rest of the class, "You made a point that everyone had to pair up. I think there was one person left over and you paired up with her. And even that was kind of nice because you got involved and you didn't just stand in front and read a book or something."[16]

I know that it might be possible to read this data as a prescriptive list of particular practices to make students such as Catarina, Lucy, and Sarah "comfortable" with their teachers. Ask students to call you by your first name. Spend the first day of class in a low-key conversation with students rather than plunging into a lesson on effective thesis statements. Draw on material from your own experience; incorporate bits of your life into lessons. Conduct discussions in a particular way.

Many of these ideas resonate with me, with the teacher-persona I strive to create, with the relationship I work to develop with my students. On the other hand, I know that such practices are not comfortable or productive for all teachers. And any self-satisfied, self-serving conclusions I might reach are limited by the realization that no strategy works for all students. Just as no teaching persona fits all teachers, it will not serve all students. What encourages one student may feel frivolous or, worse, alienating to others. So I clearly cannot and am not arguing that we can (or should try to) please all students all of the time. Instead, I argue that we need to teach—thoughtfully, consistently, and mindfully—in light of the persona one wants to project and consider the ways this can and does affect students and their decisions about speaking and writing. As O'Reilley muses, "Maybe you'll teach them, not by what you say, but by who you are."[17] For me, I hope this is a teacher who demonstrates that she values student voices, by backgrounding her own by asking more questions rather than lecturing, by listening generously to all voices without "correcting," and by actively modeling how students' voices influence her own thinking. Rather than implying that a certain kind of teacher is the *right* kind of teacher, I want to make a more modest argument: our students are well aware of the authority we carry, as Freire and Shor remind us. Indeed, for some students, the title "teacher" bears a certain unquestionable authority. Perhaps it is not necessary to remind students of this power at every opportunity; in doing so, teachers will only increase the distance between themselves and students, a gap that may seem unbridgeable for some.

And the way we present ourselves—as teachers, as people—is carefully read by our students, giving them important cues about how we feel about them as individuals, about students in the collective, about the processes and aims of education, and about how we see our roles as educators. I would argue that presenting ourselves as *more than* what fits in the institutionally defined subject position "teacher" may be especially important in a composition class, where we continuously ask students to reveal, explore, and question their own identities in public ways.

Teachers' Perceptions and Teacher-Student Relationships

Students valued—and felt nurtured by—teachers who strove to see students as individuals, as people with lives separate from their classroom selves, with personalities extending beyond "studenthood." There is, as hooks argues, "such desperate need in students—their fear that no one really cares whether they learn or develop intellectually."[18]

Related to the issue of a teacher's self-presentation (sometimes embedded within it) was the issue of how teachers view their students. Lucy dismisses classes where "the professor doesn't know your name," and she "could be there and just write letters or . . . do something totally different and he never seemed to care." She finds herself more likely to speak in classes where "the professor probably knows you or something about you." This helps her avoid feeling "like just a number" and to view the instructor as someone she "can have a conversation with."

Sarah believes that to develop this feeling there needs to be repeated, direct interaction between a teacher and a student. One possible way she sees to achieve this is "conferences where we can actually talk with you and you can see what level we're on and . . . it kind of gave you a sense that, 'Yeah the teacher does know who I am and that she does actually read my paper and know what I'm writing about.'" Here she points to a theme that underlies many of her classmates' reflections: this relationship with one's teacher will not only change one's classroom behavior, it is likely to influence what one can achieve in writing as well. Stressing the importance of this kind of connection between teacher and student, Sanjay remembers one teacher who would

> actually talk *with* us. Two of my friends at the time were having a little difficulty at home and she would stay after class with them and talk to them. And I thought that was cool. There are a lot of teachers that just would not pick up on things like that. . . . For a teacher to actually realize that something's going on, that says a lot about [her]. (emphasis added)

While some teachers (and students) may resist the relationship that Sanjay proposes here, the underlying sentiment is reflected in many of his peers' reflections: students want to be seen as individuals, with identities separate from the generic category "student." As Edward argues in the quote that opens this chapter,

"The teacher has to try with every student. That's what their job is—to try to reach every student." What is important to these students (and I would argue that this is particularly relevant in a writing class) is for the teacher to see students as *people*, separate from their general category of student, outside of the globalizing trends and patterns that teachers often use to explain the observable behaviors of their students. Neither students nor teachers can be seen as "disembodied spirits."[19]

For Edward, this means that a teacher must allow him to express his distinctive identity. He sees himself as "kind of goofy and kind of a smart-ass . . . the kind of guy who makes jokes," a student I might describe as highly (even overly) performative. He notes that to express such an identity is to "tak[e] that risk by flying in your face."

Edward has to determine the

> vibe from a teacher, like where the line is, and where you should go, and how far you can push the envelope with them. And if I'm a smart-ass in class it just means I'm comfortable with people and I'm not like worried about putting anything on the line or anything like that. . . . That's just my personality. . . . I could kind of tell that you could take it in stride . . . as long as I did that sparingly and just had fun but did my work and tried to focus on everything, I pretty much thought you wouldn't care that much. . . . I was comfortable with the people, I was comfortable with you as the teacher, so I mean, I didn't mind making a fool of myself, I took that risk. . . .
>
> It's just this feeling that I get. It's the attitude of the teacher, and how they interact with the class, and how they teach, and it's just a whole bunch of different factors that I eventually develop a feel for.

Actually, I am surprised that Edward saw me as a teacher who allowed him to be "who he is" and to express this identity. In my teaching journal, I noted that he asked "a ridiculous question," was "off-task, *again*," and "doesn't take a hint." While I think I tended to diffuse my discomfort and irritation through sarcasm, I recall feeling like I spent a lot of time reining in Edward, redirecting his attention to the tasks at hand, and quieting down his distracting and "off-task" talk. So I wonder: how much space is there in my class for students' differing identities that do not fit into my narrow mental model of the "good student"? And how much should there be?[20] Edward and I clearly saw this dynamic differently: he felt more freedom than I wished he had. Ultimately, though, this freedom Edward felt to express his identity affected his writing as he began to take more risks with it—tackling more challenging topics and less practiced approaches, utilizing the "experimentation" drafting process outlined in the syllabus. Knowing that it was safe to "make a fool of himself" in early drafts ultimately made Edward a stronger, more versatile writer.

Reading Teachers' Responses

Our oral (and sometimes visible) responses to our students' voices provide a space for evaluating the "mutual engagement" in the classroom and negotiating the teacher-student-knowledge relationship. Every student in this study spoke of a teacher's potential to encourage—but far more frequently deployed capacity to debilitate or silence—her students' voices through her immediate responses. I found it surprising and a bit distressing that my students could offer very few examples of *positive classroom interaction* with their instructors; they simply could not recall feeling encouraged or supported by their teachers during classroom discussions. In fact, there was a single example of a teacher's response that was unqualifiedly encouraging. Sarah tells this story:

> At the beginning of the [History] class, he comes in with a quote . . . everyone's just asked, "Who do you think this quote is from?" And one of the times, people just kept guessing, and finally I . . . [said] "I think I know who it is." And I actually raised my hand and I actually got it right. . . . He said, "Good job. Wow." . . . It was really great.

Sparse praise indeed.

Far more common were examples of feedback and responses from teachers who discouraged students' voices. Catarina remembers how a teacher's visible lack of response silenced a student who had previously been highly vocal: "The teacher kind of took a step back and was trying to figure out whether or not he even agreed with what she was saying. She didn't raise her hand after that." This teacher's atypical silence was read by the speaker, by Catarina, and presumably by their classmates, who were also less willing to volunteer as the silence of unspeakable disapproval. The depth of students' responses suggests how powerful our voices and our silences can be. No matter how we would like to think of ourselves—as coaches, mentors, collaborators, guides—we seem, inevitably, to be constructed by our students as evaluators.

The fear of evaluation frequently shaped students' motivations and ability to speak. Lucy is afraid that "teachers will say or even think, 'What are you talking about?' and make me feel even more discouraged to talk next time." Similar to this are Edward's and Sanjay's experiences:

> Being openly evaluated in majors' classes [makes me feel dumb] . . . and makes me think "OK, maybe I shouldn't try anymore."
>
> The teacher would [say], "That's not exactly the answer that I was thinking of. That's not entirely correct," and then pick apart the student's answer, which is kind of belittling.

The language used to describe a teacher's response is striking: being "shot down" (a phrase that surfaced repeatedly), leaving students feeling "devastated," "dumb," or "belittled." Such accounts suggest to me that it is not simply being told that a response is incorrect that troubles these students, it is *how* this disagreement is enacted. Clearly the opinion of the instructor and her evaluation matter a great deal to these students; they are eager to comply with what is expected of them and to have their contributions taken seriously. If they cannot, then they prefer to remain silent.

Such reflections on speaking have an obvious parallel to writing and the limitations students consciously or unconsciously perceive through their readings of teacher feedback. The focal students in this study seemed to me exceptionally careful readers of the responses I gave to their writing. Catarina, while initially uncertain about conferences ("frightened to death" in her words), began to schedule additional meetings with me. And Lucy, particularly concerned with "catching up" to her peers, often asked for clarification of my feedback and reported that she spoke to her other professors about their assessments of her writing. I do not believe that these stories indicate a desire to be told that their oral and written responses are "fine," no matter what. Rather, these students gauge their ability to speak and write well upon careful readings of teacher feedback, ones sensitive to the nuances of their teachers' attitudes. For Lucy,

> If the professor seems like someone who would accept your answer, even if it's wrong, but would, you know, want to hear it and just be open to what you had to say, then it's different. When you feel like the professor . . . is looking for one answer, and if you don't have that one answer, then it's horrible to try and even answer.

Again, she chooses silence.

Equally troubling for many students was a teacher's practice of eliciting students' responses and then dismissing them. Sanjay explicitly connects a teacher's response to practices of evaluation:

> You know, he'll ask us a question as to what is our opinion on it. And then he'll say, "Well this is my opinion." He'll neither validate nor invalidate our opinion on it. Um, it kind of becomes clear that you'd probably be better off with . . . his opinion. Not to say that he wouldn't accept a different answer, but that's an incredibly unsafe risk to take.

In such a scenario, I suspect there is little incentive to offer one's thoughts, speculations, or questions either in class discussions or in writing. The teacher's authority, disguised as an opinion, inevitably trumps a student's perspectives, and silence feels like the wisest option. In writing, this can lead to temporary writer's block, as students try to conjure up the right answer, stilted, empty prose, or, worse, the conclusion that it is simply "unsafe" to write what one thinks.

And for Lucy a particular concern surfaces about a teacher's response that might "put her on the spot." She tells this story about an instructor who "drilled" her about her resistance to a film on Rasputin and his violent intimidation of a woman. When she interrupts the screening to offer her objection that the film was making her uncomfortable,

> he said, "Well, why did you get so defensive?" And I said, "Because I'm a woman in this society and I think guys often feel they can do this—use their power over you. And we don't say anything. *And I want to say something because I think it's wrong.*" And he said, "He [Rasputin] wasn't forcing her to do anything." He was going on and on. And I was like, "What is his [the professor's] problem? Does he not see this? Doesn't anyone else see this?" And then finally, I was getting really emotional, because he kept saying, "What in your life makes you feel this way? . . . And he just kept going on and digging and digging. It was enough already. It was getting me really upset.
>
> And then he just stopped and said, "I'm not saying that what you're saying is wrong." And this is the first time he responded to what I said. Before he was just trying to get me to talk. He said, "I just want you to come up with a clear answer." He said, "We often just throw these lines as responses but they don't really mean anything. In order for you to talk in class and have it be clear you have to have a good answer, and to be clear and explain yourself, and that's what I was trying to get you to do. To really explain what you were feeling and not just say this and that." So that was an interesting experience. [Lucy laughed after a minute.] (emphasis added)

While Lucy did not make this point explicitly, it is interesting to see how her teacher's behavior replicates the interaction in the film she protested. He has the power; he asks questions; he makes demands of her. In this situation—or any classroom situation—it would be unthinkable for Lucy to ask her teacher, "What is making *you* feel the way you do?"

Through her professor's series of pointed questions, Lucy is left feeling that her response is inadequate, that it "doesn't mean anything." The professor's aggressive response certainly makes the point (for her and the other students) that speaking is indeed a dangerous undertaking. Who would want to be subjected to the types of questions she faces, particularly about a subject that is intellectually and emotionally important? Who is brave enough, in those circumstances, to speak when she may be told her answer is not good enough?

Note as well that Lucy chose to speak first; she was not forced to speak. This "interesting experience," one that leaves her powerless, is the consequence of *wanting* to speak up.

Lucy reflects on this incident again. She recalls:

> I kind of felt like, "What do you want from me? Just stop. Forget it. Never mind. I just wanted to say that. I didn't want you to ask me anything." . . . He wanted me to say what exactly it was, in one sentence that's bothering me. And I didn't know really what it was. . . . I didn't have an answer for him, because I didn't have an answer for myself. . . . *I almost wanted him to tell me what my answer was because I felt like he had something in mind that he wanted me to say, that he wasn't going to leave me alone with it.* So I said, "I don't know," but it really bothers me. (emphasis added)

As the narrative progresses, Lucy suggests a loss of control—even over her own reactions. If she is not allowed to raise her objections for which she does not have an already articulated frame of reference to contextualize her response, then she eventually wants her instructor to tell her what her own answer is, that is, what it is *he* wants her to say. Unfortunately for Lucy, her desire for "self-expression"—in this case, to raise important political questions in the historic framework of the film and the social context of her classmates' polite, school-regulated reactions—has been replaced by the need for "staying out of trouble."[21] Rather than giving Lucy more of a sense of power over language, her reactions, a troubling text, and the underlying cultural issues, she ultimately feels she has far less.

My point here is not to suggest that Lucy's professor is a bad teacher, although I certainly empathize with her growing uneasiness throughout this story. But in a seemingly contradictory way, I feel an uncomfortable kinship with Lucy's teacher who, I believe, desperately tried to capitalize on this eminently teachable moment. I suspect he had the best of intentions but failed spectacularly (at least with Lucy), because the patterns of interaction to which we have grown accustomed as part of the culture of the academy are counterproductive to our larger goals. For Lucy and her classmates, this discussion could have provided an opportunity for learning, for examining difficult issues, for connecting personal and academic knowledges, and for critiquing culturally inscribed patterns of gendered interaction. However, I suspect what Lucy and her classmates may have learned was very different than what their professor had intended: it can be profoundly unsettling, even dangerous, to choose to speak. Silence is safer.

These stories, particularly Lucy's, raise profoundly challenging questions about the effects of our pedagogies. Those teachers' responses that students experience as negative, critical, and even silencing grow out of the desire to develop students' critical thinking, to encourage more sophisticated articulation both orally and in writing. But how are students to understand us when we "begin by being dismissive,"[22] when we try to get students "to come up with a clear answer," when we respond to their writing or their speaking with our gentle "no, that's not it," as Bartholomae and Petrosky suggest? I want to be clear here: I am not arguing against critical pedagogy. As Ellsworth argues, "Critical pedagogues are always implicated in the very structures they are trying to change."[23] Thus I suggest that, with our best intentions, we need to think more carefully and realistically about the methods we use and how we may subtly, but emphatically, be silencing students such as Catarina, Sanjay, and Lucy.

"The Failure to Speak": Students' Responses to Requirements and Grading

Many students do not experience Lucy's *choice* to speak. They have been in the classrooms of thoughtful teachers who have concluded that it is logical, even *fairer*, to call on quiet students. As Elbow argues, in the *University of Massachusetts Writing Program Newsletter*, to call on students is a humane alternative, in its attempt to "bring the real world of human discourse into the classroom."[24] However, students often see the practice of "requiring participation" as problematic, prompting their concerns about speaking frequently enough to meet a teacher's expectations, giving the right answer, and being evaluated for *how they speak*. As Lucy's narrative might suggest, students are unlikely to experience forced participation as consensual or productive. When the invitation and opportunity to speak becomes a syllabus-mandated requirement with the attendant threat of "being called on," students in this study find themselves increasingly anxious, even angry at times. In these measures—almost universally seen as coercive—students' intrinsic motivation to speak declines as they focus on grading and evaluation of all sorts rather than on the more noble goals we profess to find in discussion.

Catarina summarizes common sentiments about required "student participation": "I always disliked it when teachers would force us to talk. . . . That only made people more and more nervous about it."

In Sarah's case, a lower grade resulted from her "failure" to speak. She says, "If you go up and ask them 'Why did I get a B?' they [say], 'Well you don't participate.' And I [object], 'Yeah, but I got just about the same grades on all the papers as an A student.' And they [say], 'Well part of the requirement on the syllabus is that you participate a certain amount.'" What is troubling to me here is that *participation* is defined solely as speaking: Sarah's attention in class and investment in her work emphatically do not "count" for her teacher in the accounting of her accomplishments. This seems particularly problematic in a course whose objectives relate to reading and writing; shouldn't these learning behaviors be the primary means of evaluation?

Also compelling to me is the prevailing idea in teaching discourses that speaking in class must be mandated, as if students will not choose to speak if it is not required. Edward points out that he himself may be "motivated" to speak through concern for his grade, but requiring him to speak will not change the quality of his answers. He further argues, "There's also something to be said for classes where you say, 'What's the answer?' . . . And someone will raise their hand without being picked on." Edward makes an important distinction: going through the motions of speaking in class is not contiguous with intrinsic motivation or the genuine learning we want to believe results from dialogue.

For some students, even the explicit requirement for speaking in class can cause anxiety. Catarina notes that in our College Writing class, "I think there was an aura of dread when we figured out we had to talk in class a lot. But that lessened over time. . . . I think people look at that as frightening—that what they say in class is graded and whether or not they say something is going to affect their grade." For Sarah, "When I am called on the spot or we are told that we must participate, my mind becomes blank. Not a word worth saying will come out of my mouth." Lucy echoes this idea, using almost identical language:

> I don't like [when teachers call on students] because for me I just feel like I'm put on the spot. And that makes me really nervous and my mind just goes blank. . . . I'm so nervous that I can't think of the answer or of anything besides "Oh My God, I'm going to die," because it just makes me really nervous.

Catarina and Lucy are not alone. How closely their words reiterate O'Reilley's: "You come to class, frozen with terror, for the teacher can ask you any question about any part of the text at any moment. What do you know . . . ? That will not satisfy the professor."[25] I am not convinced that it is worth producing the kinds of anxiety that Sarah and Lucy describe. Nor does it seem likely that being called on repeatedly will help them develop the rhetorical flexibility for which we hope, if students are focused on teacher-pleasing behaviors.

Sanjay takes into account the issue of motivation and the ways it can alter the teacher-student relationship. He thinks,

> It's kind of bad if the instructor has to call on you. If it's a sufficiently motivated class, you'd have the students participating by themselves. I don't think you really had to call on anyone in our English class in order to get them to say something. If the students are interested enough, they should be participating on their own. Calling on them is just going to make them mad, pissed. . . .

[Students] want to answer on their own terms. It doesn't even matter if I have the answer, there's probably a reason I haven't offered it. Maybe I think it's wrong, or there could be any number of reasons. But I definitely don't want to be called on and forced to give it.

What links this series of reflections is the question of control over one's voice and one's silence. Students experience an internal lack of control that echoes the external one when a teacher forces them to speak. Lucy recognizes that there may be consequences in a lower grade, but she asks that teachers allow students to make that decision for themselves. And as Sanjay implies, the reasons for a student not speaking may be more complicated than teachers can recognize—a teacher who intervenes will rob a student of a sense of autonomy as an independent thinker. Letting students speak "on their own terms" grants them some measure of authority and control. It seems contradictory that we ask our students to see themselves as critical thinkers, yet we do not see them as capable of deciding when to speak.

I am struck here by the questions Orner asks: "Whose interests are served when students speak . . . [?] What happens to students who refuse the solicitation of student voice?"[26] Can we conclude that students are best served by being called on? While some may find this structure comfortable (if only because it has become a predictable school pattern), for other students, such as Lucy and Sarah, it is tremendously alienating. These practices designed to foster equal participation are ultimately repressive and fundamentally undemocratic. For these students, being "put on the spot" is decidedly not the same as being part of a conversation, a discussion, a dialogue; coerced behaviors should not be represented to students as consensual. Further, it is, I think, dangerous to assume that our students will feel able to resist "teacherly authority," as Berlin suggests, or authority of any sort, if they are not able to choose when and how they speak.

For many students, the issue of whether to speak or not was linked to having the "right answer." Sanjay says:

The worst possible question an English teacher can ask you is "What does this passage mean?" . . . or "What did this represent?" or "What is it symbolic of?" And the English teacher always has only one idea in her head. At least in high school that was true for all my English teachers. There's always, there's one opinion you can have on this, there's one right answer. And I never had it. Ever.

Thus even in classes that "should be opinion classes," Sanjay finds himself in a complicated position. There *is* a right answer, one that is impossible to arrive at:

Because you're never going to be thinking about the same thing the English teacher is. . . . They went to school, they've studied all this. . . . You'll never have the same reasoning as the teacher. Or like, because obviously the teacher has read through and decided this passage means this. . . . So whenever they ask you, no matter what you do, you're going to get the answer wrong.

For Sanjay, then, I would suspect that such "discussions" feel disingenuous: a teacher asks for a student's opinion, even emphasizes that any sufficiently grounded opinion is acceptable, but then corrects the student. Perhaps it is an "opinion" question, but in Sanjay's view, there are always right and wrong opinions in a classroom. In this way, the discussion practices that we teachers might see as liberatory, aimed at examining the multiplicity of interpretations, may feel very different to students—a scavenger hunt for the elusive answer the teacher wants.

The anxieties that my students describe might seem to suggest an argument for the kinds of student-centered pedagogies of circled-chairs, quasi-therapeutic personal writing, and "sharing" for which expressivists are often critiqued. These reflections hint at some of the inherent problems with the models of teaching that many of us are most comfortable with, no matter how democratic we believe our classrooms to be. When we are the center of classroom discussions because we ask the questions, when we assign essays that appear (at least to our students) to have a "right answer," we are likely to evoke and encounter defensive reactions such as Sanjay's. To effectively counter this, we need to radically alter what our classrooms look and feel like. Some possibilities include smaller group discussions during which students endeavor not to come up with the "right" interpretation of the text sanctioned by the teacher but with a reading that is plausible to one's peers. (In doing so, we can capitalize on the less authoritative, potentially more generative presence of peers.) Likewise, our work as a class might shift productively from more traditional textual analysis (codified in many composition readers in the "discussion questions" that follow readings) *toward* the mechanics of building and supporting effective arguments. (In this way we may, in fact, be able to take on that mentor/coach/guide role we desire.) In writing, we might productively integrate more low-stakes writing into our class, beyond the reasons Elbow and others have already articulated. That is, low-stakes writing might be utilized as a tool for more genuine dialogue—between teacher and student, a student and her peers, and a student and herself.

Even a teacher's *absence* from a discussion can evoke a sense of being watched and evaluated. For example, when a teacher chooses to be "outside" of a discussion—to present an issue for discussion and then to step back—can be "a little more nerve-wracking . . . it makes me nervous. . . . When the teacher sits back and doesn't say anything, it makes a mood like they're looking over your shoulder at what you're saying." Instead Catarina would prefer the omnipresent evaluation be made overt so that she could understand the "rules." And for her, the issue of *offering an opinion* creates a different complication. So indoctrinated by her previous education about education, in classes such as ours, where she perceived that there was not a "right answer" expected, it was more difficult "because I couldn't go, 'She wants to hear this, this, this, and this. And this is how I'm going to say it. And I'll be done and I can be quiet again.' I guess that kind of made it a little more difficult for me." This change in expectations ultimately proved fruitful as Catarina became more accustomed to a different kind of classroom discourse, partially through her conversations with me about her confusion over what constituted "good answers." Had she not been able to approach me about her initial discomfort, I confess, I do not think I would have been able to read her early silences as positively as I do now. Ultimately this shift made her "talk up a little more . . . just say what *I* meant more and not what was *supposed* to be said."

Students spoke of the perception that any contribution to a class discussion "has to be very well said and specific in order to actually [be] a real comment." This becomes particularly complicated for Lucy when she is asked to respond directly to what her teachers have said. She wonders, "Who am I to make a comment on what they're saying? What do I know?" She further notes, "Sometimes I just want to say, 'Hey yeah, I know what you're talking about.' But I feel like you don't really do that in class because it's more of an intellectual kind of conversation, so you can't just say that." Lucy astutely recognized what some of her less successful classmates have not—that one's "mother tongue" often holds little currency in the academy.[27]

Two issues are at play here—the specific directives and responses that limit the range of acceptable answers and a school ethos that dictates an "intellectual kind of conversation" of which Lucy believes she cannot be a part. She undercuts the supremacy of this conversation, calling this sort of talk demanded by school and by individual teachers "bullshit. I feel like sometimes with professors I feel like I have to bullshit to get this elaborate, this 'really good' answer," perhaps not unlike what Shor calls "teacher-talk." Even while wanting to master this kind of discourse, Lucy sometimes resists it, commenting that she does not always

> want to go on and on about something. I just want to say what's on my mind and not have to explain, not have to come up with this really wonderful answer, and I feel like maybe sometimes in a smaller group or in a student-led discussion, I can just say something and not have to explain it or not have it be something good, or something good enough. . . .

[If] it's just the students, [there is a] feeling of whatever I have
to say doesn't have to be that sophisticated. You know, it's just like,
"Let's really talk about this and not have to bullshit."

How one speaks is particularly loaded for students who perceive a distance
between their home and school languages. I suspect that for students such as
Lucy, the mandate not only to speak, but to speak in a particular way that is "sophisticated," "elaborate," or "well said," might itself become silencing. This is
not limited to the students who speak English as a second language; it affects
any student who does not perceive herself as possessing academic authority,
"the written [or spoken] language of power and prestige."[28] The issue is not
simply that students do not *value* academic language (although that may certainly accrete this tension). As Bartholomae reminds us, we are asking students
to take on a discourse that feels foreign, elitist, or unnecessarily abstract.

While I think it is impossible for teachers to "give authority" to our students and deceptive to pretend we do not have institutionally sanctioned authority of our own (including the power to command students' speech), I
wonder if we might find more productive ways to reframe the issues of students' speaking or silence. Within the classroom, I suspect our efforts to encourage students' speech by requiring it may, in fact, have the opposite result we
intend. As several of the students in this study report, being compelled to speak
or being told there is a price for their silence increases anxiety, produces tension,
or makes them "go blank." And, indeed, in what other situations (other than on
a witness stand) do adults feel compelled to speak in this way?

How can we expect students to understand themselves as authorities, to
respect their own knowledge, and to see themselves as constructing knowledge
when they are not allowed to mediate their own voices and silences? Within an
institutional context that often leads students to understand dialogue as a
process of finding the "right answer," our efforts at a different type of interaction may prove difficult. For dialogic education to work in any meaningful way,
it is paramount that we understand how students interpret this context. If students are baffled that they are being asked to share their opinions rather than to
simply recite the "right answer," or if their previous experience suggests that
there is one "right opinion"—the teacher's—then the dialogic classroom may
seem like a complicated, even dangerous, place indeed.

Perhaps one possibility is to have more "lower-stakes" discussions of the
types Lucy suggests. Whatever shape these discussions ultimately take, the most
crucial step in creating classrooms that promote genuine dialogue is to clarify both
the expectations for students' performance and the rationales for these. Without a
clear understanding of what they are expected to do and why these requirements
are in place, some students may simply opt out of speaking because they perceive
the rules to be arbitrary. Others who misinterpret the rules and expectations may

respond to our "invitations" or requirements in ways that seem inexplicable, even inappropriate, because of our vagueness and their misperceptions.

What I have learned from observing other teachers and experimenting with the strategies they propose is that *more* limitations can be generative for classroom conversations. The caveat is that these limitations must be clearly explained and fairly deployed so that no student is singled out. For example, asking all students to contribute one question or comment to guide a discussion after a brief period of writing may feel like a more genuinely "opinion-based," low-stakes way for students to speak in classes. Asking students to report in after small group discussions about the most profound (or useful or thought-provoking) insights that their partners said can be confidence-building, in that speakers do not have to share their own ideas, and group members receive subtle validation by their peers. Finally, artificially imposed limitations to discussions—such as having students call on each other, or requiring *and* limiting all students to speak a certain number of times per discussion—can lower the stakes of discussions by breaking the traditional routines and encouraging voices that might not otherwise be heard in more typical teacher-centered classroom conversations.

Developing Models of Speaking: Introductory Exercises and Freewriting

For the students in this study, their initial impressions of the classroom dynamic established by the teacher, particularly activities designed to promote student interaction and to develop classroom relationships had a profound (and sometimes the most significant) effect on their decisions to speak or to be silent. How might we plan our classes to make students feel like the space of engagement and interaction that *we* want them to be? Several students emphasize the importance of the first days of class as indicating the types of interactions expected during the semester. For Catarina, being told immediately that "participation is required" is intimidating. She proposes instead a "low-key, model discussion" that would set a useful precedent; afterward, the teacher might say something "to the effect of 'that's what's expected that the year will run like.'" Likewise, Allison argues that the most productive environment that encourages her to speak comes from "developing good, casual conversation early on." She explains her thinking this way:

> I find that in the classes that I don't talk in the first class, I wouldn't talk for the rest of the year, or I would be very hesitant to do so. In classes in which I did speak or participate on the first day, on the other hand, I would tend to continue participating throughout the year.
>
> This has led me to what I think is an important conclusion. If you, as a teacher, get everyone talking to each other as a group

in the first day or two of class, they will most likely continue . . . talking to each other.

Many students point to activities I asked the class to do during the early days of the semester—primarily those activities that were less formal, designed to get students interacting with each other. For example, on the first day of class, I asked students to compose a set of "interview questions," to pair up for a brief conversation with a partner, and then to introduce that partner to the rest of the class. Several students reported that this activity ultimately lowered any anxiety about having to speak to the entire class. Christina spoke appreciatively, because "in doing this activity a student meets the whole class and becomes a little closer with a classmate. In one of my other classes, we did not do any exercises in getting to know each other. As you might guess, I do not express my thoughts as I might do in other classes." Other activities included investigations of criteria for "good writing," how these overlapped with or differed from students' sense of "school" definitions, and activities related to the drafts students composed about "seeing themselves as writers." In each of these activities, I hoped students might begin to break out of the right/wrong dichotomies that many carry with them, both about the "rules" for writing and for classroom conversation. Many of these exercises took place in pairs or small groups, with the idea that students might feel more able, even eager, to actively engage in exploring questions and directions of their own if they did not feel overly directed by my teacherly micromanagement.

A practice that met with surprisingly positive results was a "test" I gave early in the semester. After three separate sets of introductions, I told the class there would be an oral quiz on students' names. Students spent the remaining minutes of class and some time afterward reminding each other of their names, coming up with mnemonic devices and other strategies for passing the test. My objective was this: students would remember at least a few names to make the upcoming peer feedback sessions more comfortable and a little less anonymous if I could pair "familiar" students. I also wanted to emphasize how important it would be for students to develop working relationships with their writing community. The quiz was modest—consisting of students volunteering to name at least five other students. (Those who were successful earned a lollipop.) But for Meg, this exercise proved a pivotal moment with far-reaching consequences. She tells this story:

> I feel that it was the first time we worked together as a class . . . this, for me, marked the first time we would ever work as a whole. I remember how frantically we all attempted to cram each other's names, and work up mnemonic devices to simplify things. It was more than merely getting to know names then. We worked to get to

know each other as classmates. I truly think that was an important step in the introduction process. . . . It was time in class set aside for us to get to know each other, critical to our involvement in class. Outside of class we most likely would have continued to pass each other by. . . . *I think that as our relations evolve our writing shall to,* for we'll be able to share our reflections with people we know will not criticize. *This whole event was striking to me because for the first time it wasn't just about coming to class. It became more than that, about coming to a class of familiar faces, where you could strive to improve your work based on the positive feedback of others.* I think, too, at this moment we stopped being just about class that met between 11:15–12:30, that this introduction brought it beyond that, into our lives outside of campus, to a personal level. At that moment we took the time to get to know each other and be more than fellow students. I think that with this event we made a great deal of progress, both in our relationships and our writing. (emphasis added)

I feel a sense of accomplishment that these small exercises worked well in creating an environment where speaking felt "safe." Meg articulates what I had been assuming—that students need to feel something more than that coincidental enrollment in a College Writing class entitles them to read and respond to each other's work. Familiarity and connection are, in her words, "critical," predicting the growth of students' writing. (See chapter 6 for an extended exploration of student and community relationships.) Such relationships, it seems, are unlikely to develop without some deliberate intervention on the part of the teacher to create a working community of writers.

Not everyone celebrated my choices. For example, in her reflections, Tracy notes:

I don't go to class to socialize, I just want to learn and pay attention to the work. In smaller classes, such as my English class, the teacher makes you sit in a circle and learn each other's names. If I wanted to know someone's name, I'd ask them. I don't like working in groups. I want the teacher to teach, students listen . . . and learn. . . . When teachers make you work in small groups or call on you a lot because you're quiet, it just makes me not want to go to class. I sometimes dread English class because I hate groups so much.

While I suspect—based on these comments and others—that my conception of "good teaching" and the process approach in general is probably incompatible with Tracy's vision of education, I do take her comments seriously. Is it possible to reach, please, or empower all students? To create classrooms that feel like productive and comfortable spaces for everyone? Probably not. So can I simply write Tracy off, dismiss her as a black sheep in the happy process family, and ignore her complaints? Had I read Tracy's comments during the semester, I admit I would have tried to persuade her to see the value of my approach. (I suspect I would have met with little success.) So what is my point in the Tracy story? That the choices we make in our classes—while productive for some students—may alienate others. Had I known how she felt, would I have traded Tracy's happiness for what I consider the success and comfort of the rest of the class? Yes, probably. Would that have felt like a good decision? No.

By nurturing new social structures and "ways of seeing the world"[29] in the classroom, I believe we can offer our students new locations from which to speak. No longer are students performing solely for the teacher, seeking her "right answer," if they can actively perceive themselves in relation to a classroom community beyond the dynamics of competition. What I want to suggest is this: by creating changes, even small changes, in how students relate to each other and to their teacher and by offering alternate ways of speaking in the classroom that do not replicate familiar dynamics, we are able to dramatically influence our students' decisions to speak or to be silent. Low-stakes conversations between classmates and freewriting routines are two relatively small structures that connect to the larger goals and values of the course. Indeed, as Lucy reported, sitting in a circle in two of her classes "opens the lines of communication rather than sitting in rows. Because everyone's looking at everyone. You don't have your back towards anyone, so I think it just makes it more of a conversation environment." At the very least, I hope my students learn to see that there are indeed "new lines of communication."

Students reflected on other practices that offered them different ways of hearing their own voices in the classroom, most notably our daily freewrites, with students supplying prompts. During the semester of this study, students frequently chose to bring in visual objects that required some sort of explanation (a photo album recording a student's recovery from cancer; a script from one student's theatre experience; a poster from a recent protest on campus; etc.). Students wrote for a brief period (five to ten minutes) at the beginning of each class. The only "rule" was that we would all write nonstop for the allotted time, trying to generate as much text as possible. (For many, this meant relaxing their attention to grammar and proofreading.) Freewrites were kept as part of students' journals. After several minutes of private writing, students could share what they had written, either by reading or talking about it. My goals were fairly simple: to get students focused on writing and to provide material for their weekly journals and possible essay topics. Several students said that this freewriting practice had other effects on the classroom climate and on their decisions to speak in particular as well. Lucy said the class eventually felt more "open" to her, because in presenting a prompt you were in front of the class, and you had to talk about something. And it's usually something that meant something to you . . . sharing something of your personality. And I think mostly people understood that . . . the things I shared meant something to me. I just felt like that was putting yourself on a stand in front of these people and having to share. So that kind of opened it for me.

For Jodie, the space of freewrite prompts and the knowledge that everyone would take a turn ultimately altered how she felt about talking in class:

I think that having freewrites, which each student has to bring and talk about an object gives each of us a chance to speak and voice opinions on the topics which are on their mind or issues that really matter to them. I have found it easier to talk in class just by [the] free-writes. Because I know everyone in our class is given the chance to speak so I am comfortable talking in front of everyone.

Sarah claims that even while she never spoke, she appreciated that option, because "it kind of broke the class in together."

The sense of fairness (all students knew they had to participate at some point during the semester), predictability (this was a daily routine from the first day of class), and flexibility (students could choose the day to present and if they would read anything after writing) proved to be a workable formula. Students were able to choose what and how much of themselves they wanted to share. I could provide both structure *and* freedom for students to feel safe, adventurous (some students, it seemed to me, took incredible risks in the prompts they brought in and in the pieces they read), and challenged—as some students turned freewrites into full essays. Ultimately, it seems to me that this is the balance we need to strive for: between a more genuine equality, consistency, and student choice if we genuinely want to empower our students and encourage their voices in our classroom conversations.

Developing Models of Speaking and Fostering Student Relationships: Peer Feedback, Small Groups, and Student-Led Discussions

Peer feedback,[30] small groups, and student-led discussions also fostered productive spaces that encouraged students to speak. Catarina suggests that the forms of discussion that a teacher implements for student interaction can have a profound effect on how students feel about speaking in the classroom. In considering the high degree of student conversation and interactivity in our class, she says, "I think it was the way people were *allowed* to interact in class. We did a lot of

discussion and small-group stuff, and people had a lot of opportunity to discuss."
I want to note here what Catarina mentioned during the course: this was a
welcome—albeit, novel—opportunity for her. Unlike the stories we teachers tell
about students' apparent contentment with silence, in Catarina's representations
she and her classmates do not want to be "dumb enough, dead enough . . . to train
the teacher to leave you in peace. Hating the silence as she does, she will fall into
lecturing."[31] Instead, Catarina believes they want the opportunity and the invitation to speak, while still maintaining the right to choose silence.

Peer feedback was one such opportunity for the student interaction Catarina describes, a classroom practice that carried both unique possibilities and
obscured dangers that we should not ignore. For Lucy, peer feedback and its inherent connotation of evaluation left her feeling exposed. She narrates the
process like this:

> By correcting other people's papers . . . *you criticize other people . . .*
> [and] you're kind of in a vulnerable position because someone is
> criticizing you . . . you both have to understand that there's a certain
> way you do it, even though it's not such a big deal, it's just a paper,
> but there's still criticizing going on. So I feel like that kind of
> opened another level of talking to each other and explaining and
> being accepting of what that person has to say about you in writing.
> (emphasis added)

Such a perspective suggests several things to me. First, peer feedback, despite my frequent reminders, carried with it the onus of evaluation. While I
thought I created an environment based on *response*—reactions and analysis—my
students read this process as one about *fixing* and *criticizing*. And there is a further
(dangerous) conflation: as Lester Faigley argues, criticizing writing is criticizing
the author.[32] For the typical eighteen-year-old student, this is not an interesting
theoretical exercise; it is felt on a visceral level. So is it possible for us to alter that
dynamic that equates feedback with judgment and evaluation? Elbow and Belanoff's *Sharing and Responding* poses a broad spectrum of possibilities for non-
evaluative feedback. But after hearing many variations on Lucy's theme, I am not
sure we can reasonably expect our students to see feedback as anything but evaluative. In less optimistic moments, I am tempted to say no, that years of schooling
have led students to stubbornly believe that any response is directed toward what
Lucy calls "correcting." While I am not ready to give up on the possibilities for
peer feedback, I think there is another dilemma beyond changing our students'
views that we teachers must address. Without adequately addressing the perils of
peer feedback, I do not think we will convince students of its benefits. If students
feel vulnerable—exposed—in the process of peer feedback, then I believe (perhaps
unlike hooks) that it *is* our responsibility to make the process as comfortable as

possible. This might mean allowing students to pick their own feedback groups and to construct their own questions to receive the kinds of feedback they believe they most need. It may even mean, on occasion, allowing students to opt out of receiving feedback—to shut out the voices of others when they are too limiting or disabling, furthering the argument Elbow makes in "Closing My Eyes as I Speak." That is, if we are essentially forcing a kind of intimacy, then perhaps our goals would be best served by allowing students to choose the conditions of that exposure. The "good for you" approach to peer feedback is far less persuasive than genuine discussion and reflection, with students making their own informed choices about what will best serve their writing needs.

In Lucy's example, her experience with peer feedback changed for her the dynamics of the rest of the class. It "opened a new level of talking" for her, particularly as she developed a good working relationship with partners she frequently chose. (My teaching journal records this too, as I noted Lucy's increased vocalness after working several times with Allison and Brad.) Thus I am reminded to see peer feedback not as a discrete unit of class time but as part of a larger continuum, affected by, and in turn inflecting, students' other interactions.

I was surprised at the difference in the language used to describe interactions in small and large groups. Small groups were seen by my students in terms reminiscent of Bruffee's theorizing about collaborative learning: "coming to a consensus," "very focused," and a "synthesis and a combination of what everybody thinks," where you "would remember more or consider more things." For those of us who fear small groups for their potential to get derailed and off-task,[33] such student descriptions paint small groups as a surprisingly focused and thoughtful space, where students collaboratively negotiate meaning. Contrast this to the description of full-class discussions as a space

> where everybody is just throwing out what they have to say . . . it's almost like a debate . . . you can throw out these points, and somebody will say, "Well, I don't know about that, because whatever." And someone else can go, "If you look at this, it says . . ."

With this description, it is not surprising that Sandra—who says she voluntarily spoke very seldom throughout her high school career—was excited that during a full-class discussion she "even retaliated when people spoke against my opinions." Such descriptions suggest that students see large groups as a competitive, rather than a generative, space, connecting to a feminist critique of classroom discourse. As Catherine Lamb argues:

> We need . . . to consider a feminist response to conflict, at the very least to recast the terms so that "argumentation" is opposed . . . to "mediation." . . . Negotiation and mediation are *cooperative*

approaches to resolving conflicts that increase the chances of the goals occurring. . . . A win-lose orientation encourages narrowness and a wish to use resources only for the goal one has already identified. . . . Negotiation and mediation are also *collaborative*, with both parties using the process to identify interest and outcomes they share.[34]

Considering the different purposes students see for small- and large-group discussions, my point here is not to argue for small groups instead of large ones but to suggest that these different formations ask students to take on quite different rhetorical roles. The combative language used to describe large group discussions and the more fluid descriptions of small groups would imply that students act and think differently in each. It is important to consider what we want students to get out of a particular discussion, and what roles we hope they take on when we are planning a class. Likewise, it seems important to consider the ways some students may be naturally drawn to one type of interaction without a solid understanding of how to perform appropriately or adequately in the other. A student confident with synthesizing and collaborating may find the directive to take on an argumentative role uncomfortable, even impossible. Again, I think it is important for students to see not that one rhetorical model is "better" than another but that each has particular uses in specific contexts. In order to do so, students need more than exposure to collaborative learning environments and assignments that ask them to negotiate between seemingly conflicting positions. They need to understand *why* we make the pedagogical choices we do. Given the prevalence of competitive/argument/debate-style discussions in and outside the academy, rhetorical practices that foster mediation and negotiation may require particular attention.

While I asked my class to do a substantial amount of small-group work (at least half of the class time was spent in small-group discussions or peer feedback groups, with the other half divided between private writing, exercises in which the whole class participated, and, least frequently, full-class discussions that I led), the students I interviewed identified only one "student-led discussion," one that took place on the last day of class after everyone had read the final publication. (I participated in the discussion, but on a seemingly more equal footing with other students; I was not "leading" the discussion.) So it seems for these students that discussions in small groups appear not to *count* as student-led discussions. I am left with many questions. While these conversations may have "lower stakes," do they also have a lower status for students because the teacher is not present to guide the discussion, ask questions, and evaluate responses? If students seemed to value the conversations that take place in small groups, then why did these simultaneously seem to matter less in their overall view of the class? Why did these not "count" as student-led discussions? Does the work done in small groups seem less valuable than that done in more traditional, teacher-dominated structures? How can I validate these alternate models of learning as valid, viable forms of education without using assessment?

Edward offers this analysis of the distinctions between "teacher-led" and "student-led" discussions:

> A teacher-led discussion if she has a list of questions . . . it's almost like a script . . . they have a map almost, "we have to start off with this and we will end up with this because I'm going to lead them in that direction." While a student-led discussion is a little more free-form, it's off the cuff, it's what you think at that moment, there's no direction in it per se. It ends up where it ends up. So I think that's different in that respect . . . when it's more open, I'm a little more apt to participate, maybe contribute.

A student discussion allows for more exploration, while a teacher's agenda is rigidly predetermined: the teacher is trying to make a point, and it will be made, regardless of the student's participation. What the student thinks is of little consequence. Perhaps, like Lucy, the student can "be there, without really *being* there." I think Edward is misreading many teachers' intentions (including mine, in most instances). To evoke that common binary in composition studies: Edward sees the emphasis on the product—the conclusion, the "point"—rather than the process of interaction and negotiating competing interpretations. But because I think Edward "gets it wrong" does not make his position and implicit criticism any less valid. Thus it seems to me that an important challenge is to think about how to emphasize the sense of openness and exploration of small-group work in full-class discussions. Is it possible as a teacher to have an agenda without the class feeling scripted and predetermined? Is there possibility for *possibility*?

Culture Shifts: The Rules of School

Moving for the moment outside of the individual classroom, I consider an institutional and a social dynamic that mirrors other issues raised in this chapter: an unfamiliarity with the "rules" of college, evoking Mike Rose's analysis:

> To live your early life on the streets of South L.A.—or Homewood or Spanish Harlem or Chicago's South Side or any one of hundreds of other depressed communities—and to journey up through the top levels of the American education system will call for support and guidance at many, many points along the way. You'll need people to guide you in conversations that seem foreign and threatening. You'll need models, lots of them, to show you how to get at

what you don't know. You'll need people to help you center yourself in your developing ideas. You'll need people to watch out for you.[35]

While the students in this study might disavow any connection to those Rose describes—because of race, perceived economic status, or degree of success in high school—they still construct themselves as outsiders, unfamiliar with the rules of college. This unfamiliarity was silencing for some, as it was for Rose's students. Several students also spoke of the enormity of coming to college as a major transition for them, marking a shift in their speaking or silence. Michael comments that while he is usually "outspoken," since he came to college, "It's weird . . . I haven't participated much at all." Kurt remarks, "It's not like I've been intentionally trying to be quieter. It just sort of happened." Jenna finds that her "hand was one of the first to shoot up" in high school, but now her "outlook has changed." Such comments make the sudden silences of these students seem like a mysterious process.

The high school that Lucy attended in her home country of Israel was an art-focused high school, prioritizing different subjects than high schools in the United States typically do. The profound differences in her education ranged from the texts studied to the teacher-student relationships to the structure of the buildings. These numerous differences left her feeling like she did not know "what to do with myself in classes." During our interviews in the second semester, she reflects that now "I don't feel completely unfamiliar with the whole school system. I feel like, 'I'm here, it's my second semester; I know what's going on,' and I'm not totally shocked by everything. So that's definitely a big change. I mean it's pretty overwhelming at first." Lucy's account, while perhaps more extreme because of the language and culture gap she describes, highlights the first year of college as a time of incredible upheaval and acclimation, particularly in students' sense of what it means to be a student. There are echoes of Lucy's story in her classmates' reflections. This sense of alienation—uncertainty about teachers' expectations and unfamiliarity with the rules that govern interaction—may be more profound at a school such as the University of Massachusetts, where many students do not come from financially or academically privileged backgrounds. That is, I suspect that many students may have an unarticulated, unacknowledged feeling of "not knowing what to do with myself in classes."

How much of our students' discomfort and silence comes from this feeling of profound dislocation, where even their behaviors change inexplicably without their conscious decision or control? For many students, I imagine the feeling that Lucy describes so eloquently may itself be temporarily crippling. Depending on students' educational background, the types of interactions expected in college classes may seem baffling with their new—and virtually aways tacit—rules. It is not a developmental model for students that I am proposing— that second-semester students will be better able to "discuss" in the ways we think appropriate. Instead, I think we as teachers should shoulder the responsibility of making explicit what assumptions we hold about classroom discussion and what rules we see in place about how those discussions should take place. Merely exposing students to classroom discussion is not enough. Just as we would not expect our students to understand Modern Language Association (MLA) citations without explicit directions, we should not expect them to simply absorb the climate and culture of our classrooms. They need people to guide them in conversations; they need models; they need people to watch out for them. If not us, then who?

Implications: What Do I Do Now?

When considering these reflections on teachers, teaching practices, and the culture of school, I resist any easy conclusions about how I or other teachers should alter teaching practices to elicit "good" discussions. Rather than a collection of maxims for good teachers who generate discussion or a list of perfect practices that will help me achieve that utopia Edward describes in the epigraph for this chapter, I am left with the following considerations:

- If the people who participated in my study are in any way representative of their classmates, then students generally seek to understand and comply with their teachers' requests. The sorts of resistances described in our literature and our lore are far less common than our stories would lead one to expect.
- Teachers and teaching practices *do* have an effect on students' willingness and ability to speak. Seeing the "problem" solely as a student issue that is solved when students "do what I want" offers me little that is productive.
- There is often an enormous gap between what teachers and students (and between student themselves) see happening in the very same interaction. What we see as "knowledge" or the purpose of discussion may be widely divergent, resulting in puzzling, unsuccessful, or unsatisfying classroom conversations.
- Just as students want to be seen as individuals, separate from a generic identity, they see teachers as individuals too. There are no magic solutions, no perfect practices that "work" with all students. In fact, as I learned in several stories, what feels liberating to one student may have a very different effect on another. Perhaps one solution to this dilemma is for me to be more explicit about my values and to ask for more frequent feedback from my students.
- On the other hand, I am but one of the dozens of teachers my students will have. I am one small part of an educational system that has taught

my students lessons about what it means to be a teacher, a student, a citizen of school. They will try to fit me into the structures they already know and understand. Sometimes that means they will misread me; sometimes my intentions or actions will seem baffling or troubling in how they contradict the embodied knowledge my students carry.

- Many students carefully read the persona a teacher creates and the relationships she fosters with and between students. Even very small decisions may have a big impact on those relationships. I do not mean to place too much emphasis on this point so that every teacherly decision is fraught with anxiety. Rather, I would suggest as a teacher that I need to be reflective about what my practices and my persona might suggest to students about how I see them and how I understand "knowledge."

- Teachers' strategies to "fix" the problem are not necessarily productive. It seems like I often see the problem of silence as a "me versus them" dynamic. *I* have to find the solution; I am the wizard behind the curtain who makes discussions run smoothly. Through the process of this research, I have learned that I need to give up that posture. I cannot "give" students authority, but I can work to create conditions where it feels safer to speak. As a teacher, I have a responsibility to do more than simply "require" students to speak. Explaining my goals, motives, and values may go a long way toward alleviating some of those tensions and misconceptions my students carry with them into the classroom. But it's not all about me. That is, while I cannot conduct the sorts of in-depth research that I did for this project, I can ask students to reflect on and share their perspectives about their speaking and silence. Together, I believe this will help foster productive practices and deconstruct what is often left unspoken about discussions in our classrooms.

Chapter 6

Identity and Community
Negotiating
Ethos and Audience

> When I went to kindergarten and had to speak English for the first time,
> I became silent.... During the first silent year I spoke to no one at school,
> did not ask before going to the lavatory, and flunked kindergarten. My sis-
> ter also said nothing for three years, silent in the playground and silent at
> lunch. There were other quiet Chinese girls not of our family but most of
> them got over it sooner than we did. I enjoyed the silence. At first it did
> not occur to me I was supposed to talk or to pass kindergarten. I talked at
> home and to one or two of the Chinese kids in class ... it was when I
> found out I had to talk that school became a misery, that the silence
> became a misery. I did not speak and felt bad each time that I did not
> speak. I read aloud in first grade, though, and heard the barest whisper
> with a little squeak coming out of my throat. "Louder," said the teacher,
> who scared the voice away again. The other Chinese girls did not talk
> either, so I knew the silence had to do with being a Chinese girl.
>
> —Maxine Hong Kingston, *The Woman Warrior*

Soon after I began elementary school, one of my favorite games quickly became
playing school. I was the teacher, naturally; dolls and stuffed animals sat in orderly rows as my students. The joy I experienced as a good student could only
be surpassed, I assumed, by the powerful pleasures my teachers *must* feel. These
pretend classrooms always revolved around the exercise of that teacherly authority. When I gave directions, my perfect, imaginary students would comply
eagerly. When I asked questions, they raised their hands (or paws) enthusiasti-
cally to answer respectfully. I was in complete, masterful control of that classroom, of the students devoted to pleasing me.

I loved being in charge.

119

In my little imaginary kingdom, students rarely acknowledged each other and had no desire other than to please the teacher. Rarely, if ever, did I consider what my hypothetical students would be thinking about themselves or their classmates. I was the center of their universe. Perhaps not surprisingly, this was usually a solitary game for me; the flesh-and-blood presence of others made my perfect classroom too messy, too complicated. The powerful teacher, with her eager, compliant students, was a far more satisfying relationship to consider.

While my visions of the classroom have become more complex than those early dress rehearsals, I confess I still love the kinds of control I did as a child—over the classroom agenda, over pedagogical decisions. I plan lessons, choose texts, and assign essays. Usually students seek to understand and comply. The system works.

In reading many of our professional stories about the classroom, I am struck by how many are more sophisticated versions of the narratives I told in my childhood play. That is, while we often see silence in terms of the effects of cultural forces (for example, ingrained, unconscious perceptions of gender or race), generally we see the problem of silence as inevitably embedded in the teacher-student relationship. Think of Moran's worries that he should be "doing more" than he is, Sommers's reflections on the Bartleby-ish student she could not "reach," Shor's depiction of students sitting quietly, "waiting for the professor to do education to them."[1] Consider the student-teacher in Rankin's study, who felt like one student's silence "was hitting me in the face."[2] Think of Villanueva's triumph: "*I have never had such success . . . did it!*"[3] In such stories, teachers are constructed as the center of students' concerns.

In light of the student reflections discussed in the last chapter, these teachers' narratives and my childhood image of the classroom are justified: teachers' identities and self-presentations, their relationships with students, responses, evaluations, and particular practices, *do* influence students in their decisions to speak or to be silent. And like my fairy-tale classroom, these stories may overlook the fundamental importance of how students see themselves, how they perceive other students, and how these profoundly shape their decisions to speak or to be silent.

In the brief excerpt from *The Woman Warrior* that opens this chapter, several issues seem particularly relevant: the narrator marking her silence in the transition to an unfamiliar environment; her response to the silence that results; the realization that silence is problematic only when her teachers tell her so; and the intersections of identity—individual or community—and silence. Many of these concerns are reflected in the stories my students tell about speaking or being silent in classrooms. In this chapter, I explore issues of identity[4] (including their perception of "natural" characteristics, the radical alteration of identity when faced with the unfamiliar, and self-evaluation) and the community dynamics of conflict, intimacy, self-revelation, and group size. Ultimately I argue that these so-called silent students are wrestling with many of the issues we hope to teach in composition classes. Conscious of their own ethos and authority, and the demands of the audience as it invites, shapes, or limits their voices, these students make active, conscious choices about speaking and silence in the oral and written texts they produce. Reconsidering student silence in this way will help teachers understand the complexities that students face in their decisions to speak or to be silent. Further, I believe the kinds of questions that these quiet students reflexively ask provide a more concrete rhetorical model that we can utilize with all of our students: we can encourage students to bring this experiential knowledge back to their writing to more fully understand the slippery concepts of ethos, authority, and audience.

Seeing Yourself:
"Natural" Identities

Many students represented being quiet as inevitable, often linked to another aspect of identity. For example, the issue of self-confidence came up quite frequently and will be discussed at length in relation to community dynamics. On an even more fundamental level, many students assert the "naturalness" of one's speaking or silence, the presence of an inherent tendency disposing a person toward either the pole of being quiet or highly vocal (a tendency present in many teachers' narratives as well—think of Villanueva's classroom of "Quiet Ones" and "Outspoken"). Many spoke of "normally," "naturally," or "always" being quiet and the sudden disruption of those long-standing patterns a person had come to identify as her typical way of being. Brad concludes, "The fact of the matter is, there are quiet people and there are loud people," as if this is an inarguable identity category independent of situational factors or other influences. Jenna discovers that although her "hand was the first to shoot up in high school . . . [now] her outlook has totally changed." Michael, who sees himself as "outspoken," thinks it "odd" that he rarely speaks in his college classes. In these examples, the move to college —an unfamiliar setting with different rules—is the catalyst that affects typical behavior.[5] In this way, identity and one's tendency to speak or to be silent are understood as malleable, responsive to one's environment. What I want to emphasize here are two things: (1) the perception these students have of a natural, innate style or identity, and (2) the notion that the external world may alter that identity, a process the students themselves do not control. This blending of Romantic individualism and elements of a postmodern sensibility shapes many students' classroom interactions. As Kurt says, "[Becoming silent in classrooms] just sort of happened."

A more extended exploration of this reasoning comes from the research paper Sarah produced during the course. Given the assignment to investigate any topic she wished through library and nontraditional sources, she explored the causes of "shyness," a characteristic she sees correlating strongly to being quiet.

Her research revealed two strains of thought. The first was that shyness or quietness is due to a lack of social skills or self-confidence and may be the product of negative experiences. Testing this theory, Sarah identifies in herself "a loss for words . . . not knowing what to do or say" that results in nervous, habitual actions. She also explores the theory that shyness is "an inherited trait." This biological basis helps her understand the shyness "trait" she sees permeating her whole family. As she asserts in one of her written reflections, "I have the gene for shyness. That is something I cannot control." She concludes in a paper that

> the cause of shyness is most abundantly caused by both a genetic trait and "situational factors" (Zimbardo 248). . . . I feel I have discovered why I am shy. I believe it is a combination of both an inherited trait and also the lack of social skills. I do not feel I have a lack of self-confidence, although it could be caused by negative feedback I have received from elders. I have also realized shyness is something that is learned, as well as inherited. *Consequently it is not the shy person's fault for being shy.* (emphasis added)

Thus it would seem that one motive for Sarah's investigation is a need to diagnose the "problem" of her shyness and quietness and to find someone or something to blame for it. Whether quietness is a biological consequence or the product of socialization, Sarah sees it, in some sense, redeemed—she is not to blame for what is beyond her control.

I suspect that Sarah's anxiety about being shy or quiet may result from being left back in kindergarten because she "wasn't social enough." (Ironically, Sarah remains one of the most academically sophisticated students I have encountered in my teaching career at three institutions.) She recalls that she seldom asked questions and was one of several students who repeated kindergarten. These students were paired with "buddies" on many activities, encouraging them to socialize and to get used to working with peers. The idea that a student might be *held back* in school for her silence strikes for me a curious parallel to *Women's Ways of Knowing*. Sarah's silences were perceived as evidence of her *not knowing*, intellectual deficiency, and social ineptitude; only when her behavior was remediated was she promoted with her classmates. Such a practice, while intended to ameliorate anticipated difficulties, seems dangerous: how can a student interpret the behavior that receives such administrative and parental action except as a "problem"? Like Kingston's narrator, Sarah has heard the emphatic message that she is "supposed to talk," without (as she perceives it) supplying her the necessary tools to make that task any less formidable or an adequate explanation for her "failure." (And given that Sarah still describes herself as "painfully quiet," it seems that those early lessons have fallen somewhat short of expectations.) A parallel might be to return a draft of Sarah's with a failing grade and the directive to "develop and expand," without any explanation of why this grade was given, how such revisions might be undertaken, or the value of this further work.

Similarly, Catarina hypothesizes that one's tendency to speak (or not) has much broader implications. She compares herself to a friend who is a Theater major, and therefore, "very, very apt to speak in class . . . she just likes being the center of attention." (Edward, a regular performer in campus Theater productions, might disagree with this assessment.) Catarina notes that this style is very different from students in her own major, Computer Science, who do not "tend to jump up in front of everyone else and give a lecture on their latest computer language." In this way, as students perceive it, speaking or being silent can define identity. So while students' identity categories might differ from our own—relying on markers such as majors, membership in fraternities, campus clubs, or sports teams, and even the area of campus in which one chooses to live as an indication of one's "type" and propensity to speak or to be silent— students also analyze other students' behaviors, search for discernable patterns, and ascribe meaning to the visible phenomenon of the classroom.

These students are aware that perceptions of themselves as "quiet" students are likely to chance over time, in response to external influences, just as the move to college revealed or created a new identity for many. But as Shor argues, "Students generally need time and a reason to speak up, and some will not manage to do so inside the confines of a semester."[6] Others in this study experienced the transition more rapidly. If a student finds herself quiet at the beginning of a semester, she may not necessarily be so throughout the duration of the course. One woman discussed the difficulty she experienced when moving to a new atmosphere and the effects this had on her self-perception and, consequently, her silence in class. She tells this story about coming to college: "It sounds kind of odd, but when I first came here, I felt like a total weird person. Everyone else knew where they were going, and knew what was going on, and I had no idea what to do." However, this self-perception changed during the early weeks of the fall, with her increasing familiarity and sense of "belonging" on the campus:

> I think it started to change for me about a month into the semester and I started to get some friends on campus and I started to feel like a college student and less like the person who came to school and has no idea what's going on.

Many students also explore the development of their own and the class's collective identity over the course of the semester:

> Everyone seems to be more comfortable with the other classmates and seemed to have "opened up" now from the beginning of the

semester, which was only three months ago. I noticed that everyone has become more familiar with the class. Even the students that I thought of as "shy" and "quiet" have begun to come out of their shell.

People who seemed really shy in the beginning . . . began to open up and take part in the class.

This developmental model is most clearly shown in Lucy's reflections on speaking more frequently in her classes during the second semester. She has *"gotten a lot better"* because of her conscious effort to speak more frequently, again emphasizing the notion that to be silent is inherently problematic.

What is remarkable to me about these accounts is the implicit progress narrative: at the beginning, I (or the class, collectively) was inadequate; now I (or the class) am performing better. This seems particularly striking because I (believe I) was careful not to represent silence as a problem. On occasion, I prompted the continuation of a discussion by asking follow-up questions or rephrasing a question. When discussions appeared to be reaching some sort of natural end, I tried to respect that and move on. If a small group finished a task sooner than I anticipated, then I checked that the group had covered all aspects of the assignment. Yet my students seem to collectively see their silences as problematic. This suggests two possibilities. Either I transmitted the message that their silences were an issue of concern without directly verbalizing it, or the school-based rhetoric of "speaking equals participation" is so ubiquitous that it need not ever be directly said. While this message has a particular urgency in classrooms (in the need to systematically quantify and evaluate), it also connects to the notion of a democratic society in which each citizen has not just the right but also the obligation to make his voice heard.[7] This seems an especially powerful and dangerous message for students who see their identities in conflict with this "requirement." For students who see themselves as "naturally quiet," like Sarah, predisposed to silence through other choices, as Catarina does, or situationally silent, like Kurt and Jenna, their silences (and the discussions in which they exist) can easily become, as Kingston's narrator says, a misery.

While the students in this study did not make explicit connections between their perceptions of themselves, their silences, and their writing, Losey's research with Mexican American students offers a useful paradigm. She reads students' missing, late, short, or inadequate work and the failure to revise as a kind of silence. To what extent are these "failures" and silences a product of students' self-perceptions? If one believes "I'm not a writer," or "I'm not a good college writer," then can one realistically be expected to perform publically as one? How does the shift to college (or a new classroom) with new rules about writing affect students' confidence and ability to write well? Perhaps it is not surprising to find many students who, as the students in my study (and like those I see in other first-year classes), find themselves doubting their abilities as writers, even after successes as writers in high school. Some see themselves as less confident, less comfortable with the tasks they are given; many earn significantly lower grades in writing than they did in high school. (And, indeed, when they show me their thesis papers from high school, many do seem "less skilled" in their college writing than they were previously.) Unsurprising, students' responses often are negative: alarm, anxiety, resistance, even anger (particularly for those who saw themselves as "good writers" before entering college). The challenge for us as teachers, then, is to help students see this "de-skilling" as a response—and a common one—to a new writing environment that carries with it many new requirements that often go unspoken. We might do this through discussions of our own struggles with writing in new contexts, a collaborative inquiry into the differences between high school and college writing (perhaps with the assistance of former students), and ongoing discussions about rhetorical strategies used in different writing contexts. For me, the particular teaching strategies used are less important than the overall goal: to help students become conscious of the dislocation they may be feeling in a new context, and to assist them in identifying the new demands placed on them and their writing. This, I hope, will transcend the lessons of a College Writing classroom, to become one applied to any writing and learning situation.

Seeing Yourself: Confidence and Criticism

For many of us, it may be no great surprise that students' sense of themselves, their confidence (or lack of it), underlies their decisions to speak or to be silent. However, these complex internal negotiations point us toward central questions within composition pedagogy. Taking on many variations, students' reflections about speaking, definitions of the self, and knowledge (often figured in terms of the "right answer") evoke the work of Belenky and her colleagues in defining "received knowers . . . [who] have little confidence in their own ability to speak. Believing that truth comes from others, they still their own voices to hear the voices of others. . . . Things are right or wrong, true or false."[8]

Edward summarizes a prevalent sentiment this way: "Your response, I'd say, is pretty much tied to your confidence in yourself. If you're pretty confident in yourself, then I think you're going to respond. You're confident this is the right answer." Thus the vision of class discussion is a dualistic one—there are clearly right and wrong answers. And "being wrong" carries consequences. Hinting at these consequences, Edward theorizes, "Answering is a big risk . . . you're taking a leap of faith here, saying what you think you should say." Such a construction poses speaking as, essentially, an oral exam; silence allows you to avoid that testing. And speaking in a History class (Edward's major) carries extra weight. While he feels confident most of the time, if a teacher says

"no, that's not it, that's not what I was looking for, um, what else?"
You know, you feel like, "Oh, oh, oh, I should have known that."
And you just feel kind of dumb and it's, it's, it's just like being shot
down, I think. I don't know. It's just [that] you think you know
it. [When] you don't, you think, "Oh, OK, maybe I shouldn't try
anymore." . . . It's like, "I like this, I should have known it." You feel
dumb because you want to show you like this, it's like, "Yeah, I like
this!" And then you get it wrong, and it's like, "damn."

Sanjay worries about wrong answers too: "I think it's just the fear of
sounding silly, just sounding stupid, just being like shot down immediately. You
sit there and you formulate your own opinion and then you voice it. And it
would be devastating if someone said, 'uh, you're wrong.'" While most composition teachers probably seldom structure their classes around such a model, this
"middle-class" message (in Anyon's terms) about the construction of knowledge
has—for most students—permeated and shaped their school experience. That
is, while we may see our classes outside of this model, for students the distinction about what "counts" as knowledge may not be so clear. Rather, they equate
speaking in class with the demonstration of authorized knowledge (or, as many
fear, the lack of knowledge).

While their previous school experience seems to have been characterized
by those facets of education that Shor sees as profoundly silencing (traditional
classroom design, the lecturing voice of the teacher that disseminates knowledge, and undemocratic speaking opportunities), these students emphatically
do not perceive themselves as "Siberian exiles."[9] That is, they are conscious of
such experiences that Shor describes and of the moments when these shaped
their classroom decisions and behaviors. But these students seem remarkably
optimistic and resilient: to varying degrees, the students in this study see themselves *choosing to speak* in classrooms and wanting to participate in those ways
sanctioned by their teachers; they are not looking to escape or resist. This may
certainly be a product of their solidly middle-class backgrounds, previous successes in school, or their own unconscious identifications with the educational
system that lead them to believe that it is possible to get this—speaking in
class—"right" too.

While writing was generally perceived as a somewhat less public act than
speaking (and, therefore, not necessarily subject to the same reflexive public
critique—although peer feedback complicated this equation), students generally understood it to function similarly—as a process of "showing what you
know and what you don't," with right and wrong answers.

Compounding Lucy's self-consciousness and lack of confidence is the
cultural dislocation she experiences. Born and educated through her junior year
of high school in Israel, she is highly aware of the gap between her educational

background and that of the "typical" student in her classes now. She fears that her academic preparation—particularly in writing instruction—is inadequate for what she faces now: "MY life is totally different. . . . How am I going to fit in?" For Lucy, then, self-confidence (and her willingness to speak and to share her writing) is linked to her perception of how she compares to other students. Believing she is not "on the same level" as her peers makes speaking and sharing her writing a difficult prospect indeed.

One student makes this generalization about what she has observed about vocal and quiet students:

> I almost feel like they [quiet students] are just less confident because we always have students in classes who always talk and always say something. I don't always feel like it's a particularly smart thing or a very great answer. They just have more confidence to speak or to ask a question. . . . I just think the ones that speak are more confident and aren't necessarily, they don't necessarily know more. And I do sometimes sit there and am like, "Wow, that's great that they said that." And sometimes I'm just like, "Yeah I guess. That's a point too." But maybe, if I had that thought, I'd maybe think to myself, "Well, it's not important enough."

In this way, she makes a critical distinction: it is not that vocal students have "better" answers than she does, they just voice them more freely than she does.[10] Silence cannot—and should not—simply be equated with "not knowing," as *Women's Ways of Knowing* argues. Edward uses almost identical language to describe a particular discussion in our class. Thinking that his written responses "weren't exactly great by any stretch of the imagination," and that he would "probably look stupid if I [read] any of them out loud," he was surprised that others' responses were similar, sometimes identical, to his own.

An analogy might be made to those students who consistently volunteered to share their writing with the class, either orally or for the purposes of a class exercise. My teaching journal and the written reflections of several students reflect a curiosity about this: the habitual volunteers were not necessarily the strongest writers with the most profound insights or the most poetic voices. The willingness to "participate"—either in a discussion or by sharing writing—seemed, at best, tangentially related to any objective measurements of quality and more closely linked to a nebulous sense of self-confidence.

Measuring herself against a perceived standard, Lucy notes, "I always kind of felt like the things I wanted to say weren't important enough or not enlightening enough or just not relevant . . . a lot of times I found that I had things that I thought were important that I wanted to say, but I just wasn't confident enough to bring up." In this way, she is in a double bind. When she thinks her comments are important, her lack of confidence leaves her silent. But she sees that she has progressed, becoming more self-assured through her academic achievements during the first semester and by projecting an attitude of "I'm asking a question and I don't care what you think." In one sense, this probably is significant progress for Lucy; she feels new permission to speak in situations that used to leave her silenced and intimidated. However, I am hesitant to endorse the "progress" away from silence that necessitates ignoring the audience and the community.

While no students in the study explicitly made this connection, I observed a similar dynamic at play in their writing, particularly in research-based projects. For students struggling to move beyond summaries and reports of others' thinking, Lucy's dilemma ("What I have to say just isn't that important") aptly summarizes their predicament. One result were the papers dominated by citations and the ideas of her sources, the writer believing that her ideas just were not "enlightening or relevant"; another result—those papers, a polar opposite to that first category, that suggest "I don't care what you think" by eschewing research in favor of an ill-advised, underresearched, independent treatise. In both cases, we see the student-writer struggling unsuccessfully to find a place in an academic conversation that does not always easily admit new participants.

Finally, the pressure that students report feeling when deciding to speak seems silencing itself. As one student notes, "When I do want to make a comment, I feel like it has to be very well said and specific in order to actually be a real comment," and Allison only speaks when she has something "original" to say. For Edward to share an observation, it must be substantial and well developed, capable of "making an impact"; the positive feedback he receives has little effect on how he sees himself. Writers struggling with this pressure often find themselves "silent" at all stages of writing: unable to find a "special" or "real" topic or an original approach, struggling to develop an argument into something "substantial" or "capable" or "making an impact," incapable of finding words to adequately convey ideas. Such students, I contend, do not need more praise or critique but more practice and, I would argue, *ungraded practice* to see how their thinking and writing can grow through sustained experimentation with language. Small group work, student-led discussions, journals, freewrites, and drafts will all help students who experience these kinds of writer's and speaker's blocks.

But No Student Is an Island . . .

While many of the reflections discussed in the previous section pointed *inward* (Do I think this is a good answer? How do I feel about saying this? Do I think this is right?), many also subtly pointed *outward*, suggesting students' concerns for how speaking and writing might create, affect, and even damage their position within the classroom community. *Identity* and *community* are linked as central concerns in speaking and in writing as powerful currents of self-evaluation and self-criticism (about one's intelligence, personality, and even personal history) shaping students' decisions about what can be discussed orally and in writing. For example, Lucy worries that other students will "judge what I'm saying and think it's stupid, and then I'd feel really stupid." Thus one fundamental component of self-confidence is the question of intelligence—does my speaking make me look dumb? More precisely, does the *response* I receive make me feel silly, unintelligent, foolish? Or one might put this in terms reminiscent of the questions asked in *Women's Ways of Knowing*. How does what I say reveal what I know to those around me? What version of myself is revealed? Speaking and writing allow for public evaluation, and as Edward argues, "I don't want people to assess my intelligence." (Interestingly, he uses the same language—"making a fool of myself"—to describe answering in class, writing, and his theater performance. He clarifies the distinction: "You just do what you think is right in performing and . . . if it's not right, then you know that's not going to work, so you just try something else. It's just a trial-and-error kind of thing." So, for Edward, Theater classes and exercises allow for experimentation and growth; more traditional academic classes operate on a wholly different principle, in which speaking and writing can evoke uncomfortable, even debilitating, public assessment.)

While one might argue that such anxieties about intelligence are self-imposed limitations, I would suggest that these are nurtured by a school climate that is premised on evaluation (sometimes done publicly) and the dualistic construction of knowledge as "right" or "wrong." Edward and Lucy do recognize that they are more critical of themselves than many others, but all of the focal students and many others were concerned about how people might perceive them based on their words. Indeed, through many of the written reflections and interview transcripts, this concern for the evaluation and criticism that speaking and writing elicit is difficult to untangle, as self-perceptions often are interwoven with and inflected by the perceived judgments of other students. Lucy explores this dynamic in teasing out the ways that her identity is socially constructed:

> Sometimes if I catch myself thinking that [what I have to say isn't good enough] I say to myself, you know "Why? That's nonsense. They don't care. Why should I care, just say what you have to say." You know . . . *the way we perceive ourselves is really based on how other people perceive us, or how we think that they perceive us. Because it's really hard to say, "OK, I am whatever," without having in our mind what other people think of us, or what we think other people think of us* . . . what I *think* other people are hearing, or what I think other people are thinking. I think it's [me] kind of judging what I'm saying and feeling like it's not good enough or smart enough. (emphasis added)

In this way, Lucy's identity is inextricably linked to public perceptions. For her, self-image depends upon her sense of how others see her.

For Sanjay, the interaction between identity and community occurs in a different way. Particularly when sharing writing aloud, he believes there is a danger of "being too weird," a problem exacerbated by the lack of personal connection he feels in classes. He narrates:

> Every time you say something, it contributes to what someone else thinks of you. You say something, and someone else hears that and makes a judgment of you based on that. Now if you're going to be incredibly strange in what you write, you're going to have to accept the consequences of that probably being the only thing they've ever heard you say. They don't have any other context for why you're saying it . . . they'd have to make a judgment call based only on what they do know, which is that I just stood up and read the weirdest thing they've ever heard in their entire life. Now what they chose to think of me at that point is their own business, but I would like them to think positively of me. . . . It's hard to get that ratio of not too personal and not too deep.

Thus speaking and writing invite the evaluation not only of one's intelligence but of one's *identity*. Unlike Lucy, whose identity, in a sense, does not exist without that public construction, Sanjay maintains two identities, a private one that cannot safely be shared with his classmates and a public, "edited" one that is far less dangerous. This understanding necessitates a particular vigilance. *Am I revealing too much by what I say? Which parts of me are not safe for public consumption?* For Sanjay, self-evaluation is a critical step of self-preservation to establish and maintain functional relationships. In fact, to be able to read any of his writing out loud, Sanjay must make a conscious decision before beginning in order to produce something that is "safe" to share. For students such as Lucy and Sanjay, then, speaking and writing in class are premised on "Speakers' conscious and unconscious assessments of the risks and costs of disclosing their understandings of themselves and of others."[11]

Speaking in class requires the active negotiation of what one feels "safe" revealing. Sanjay ponders, "How do I describe it? . . . I have a tendency when I first meet someone not to spill my guts to them. . . . I don't necessarily want to be opening myself wide open to the entire class." Or, even more poignantly, Catarina "dislike[s] telling everyone around me everything about me," because "if I speak up too much, I might slip so[me] vital piece of secret information. I just can't stand to do that. So I only talk when I am absolutely positive that I can do no harm with what I am saying. I do not talk when I am nervous, I talk when I am sure of what is going to come out." And this cycle seems self-perpetuating:

"When I get nervous, I have no idea what I'm saying and I stumble and I go crazy." I am particularly struck by Catarina's formulation here: she herself is dangerous and must be contained, so her speaking (and ultimately her writing, if is to be shared) must be circumscribed as well.

While this can happen through class discussions, it is also intimately tied to sharing writing. As Edward suggests, it becomes necessary to "break down those fears of, you know, um, exposing yourself to other people. . . . And that's a big fear—showing someone your writing. But if you can break down those fears, then you can get more comfortable with that person because you've shown that person a little bit of who you are." Catarina echoes this sentiment as she reflects on the process of writing and sharing her narrative that makes quiet reference to tensions within her family and alludes to her mother's illness. Noting that in general she has a hard time sharing her writing, she recalls:

> It felt weird saying that kind of stuff to other people. We have a very small town at home and everyone either knew it or they didn't and you just didn't say anything about it. . . . I guess I generally just try to keep some things from other people knowing about them. So even when I wrote that essay about Thanksgiving, it was kind of vague in the fact that I didn't tell too much and a lot of people were going, "Well, what is with your mom?" *And I guess some people, myself included, tend to be really vague in their writing and not want to share it because they're afraid that it might reveal something that they don't really want other people to know.* (emphasis added)

Thus silence is not simply a function of oral discussion but permeates writing as well when a climate of "sharing" is enforced. While feedback seems to me a critical component in writing, perhaps more attention needs to be paid to the conditions under which this takes place. When "the talking circle represents an expression of disciplinary power—the regulation of the self through the internalization of the regulation of others,"[12] we must not naively assume that students feel equally free to "share" their writing and to give and receive feedback.

One objection I anticipate here is that students such as Catarina should not be writing personal narratives, that a first-year composition class is no place for the kinds of issues she wrestled in this paper and in the kinds of feedback she received. While I disagree with this on several levels, here I will just say this: other students faced the same kinds of discomfort in *all kinds of assignments*, from the more "personal" ones to the more traditionally academic ones— including ethnographic research, traditional arguments, and research-based papers. In each case, students were faced with the dilemma of choosing a topic, a point of view, and "evidence" they believed would be potentially persuasive in their classroom community. To present these (and their own identity revealed by them) might destabilize the fragile equilibrium of identity they had constructed for themselves. The task they faced was one all writers face: how to write about what matters to them carefully and thoughtfully, in a way that reflects their own views while taking into account the needs, values, and prejudices of their audience as well.

For Catarina, the subjects her classmates chose to write about were a barometer of people's comfort. She says, "It sounds kind of strange, but the topics people chose for their essays, that they felt all right with discussing with the class, some of them were really, really personal and they just, they weren't nervous to say this in front of the rest of the people and have it open for discussion." This suggests that *more* student control of topics is necessary, so those students who are willing to reveal themselves through highly charged topics can do so, and those who prefer less loaded subjects are not coerced into revealing what they wish to keep silent.

Such concerns about identity and community perception may seem relatively minor, even trivial, for the writing teacher and student to seriously contend with. Now substitute "voice" in writing for classroom identity, and this dilemma takes on a new urgency. In what ways do these concerns about identity and community evaluation shape students' willingness and ability to take on challenging, loaded subjects and develop distinctive voices in their writing? How much of this resistance is inflected by the shadowy presence of formal and informal peer evaluation? I do not want to argue against peer feedback or collaborative work by any means. Instead, I make more measured claims. We should not romanticize these pedagogical tools as the cure for what ails our students and their writing as one more "repressive fiction" about classroom dialogue.[13] Nor should we dismiss the anxieties that students experience in our writing classrooms that lead them to choose "safe" topics, comfortable voices, or even silence. As teachers, we would do well to acknowledge the ways that the voices and presence of others shape students' sense of identity and help them find productive ways to negotiate these challenges.

Hearing Others:
Student Response

Edward's reflections on how the performance of his identity through speaking puts him "at risk" point to another critical issue: a concern for other students' reactions as fundamentally shaping the decision to speak or to be silent. For Lucy, such responses do not necessarily have to be spoken. Even students "looking at me like 'What are you talking about?' . . . makes a big difference." Julia, one of the most vocal students in this class (in her estimation and mine), weighs other students' reactions the first time she speaks; if it is not "too traumatizing," then she is more able to ask questions in the future. Sarah recalls that being asked to read a sentence aloud from her research paper caused her profound anxiety about what other students might think of her topic.[14] (Sarah's anxieties were not ungrounded: several students *did* comment on her choice to me.) But both Lucy and Sarah find that in order to speak, they ultimately must *not care* what others in the class think of them. They share a conclusion of Elbow's—that when an audience is confusing or inhibiting, that when the anxieties about the reception of one's words become paralyzing, one can "close your eyes as you speak" in order to gain the confidence and permission to speak.[15]

However, formulations such as Lucy's and Sarah's are deeply troubling to me, particularly as they come from students who are deeply invested in their educations. In order to fulfill the *behaviors* associated with collaborative learning and critical pedagogy (participating in dialogue, critically examining one's experience), these students have profoundly unsettled their philosophical underpinnings: disconnecting themselves from the Contact Zone, dismantling a discourse community, and rendering our questions about consensus and dissensus moot. When Lucy and Sarah speak, if their classmates must also "disconnect," have they, have *we*, really made progress?

An analysis of the data reveals a daunting range of concerns about the potential for community evaluation of one's spoken or written words. Even the lack of a response is problematic. For example, Catarina tells this story about a highly vocal, outgoing friend who was met with paralyzing silence.

> The other people in the class kind of looked at her funny and were trying to decide whether or not they agreed with what she said. . . . She didn't raise her hand after that. She kind of kept her mouth shut, because she didn't like the idea that every single person in the class was kind of afraid to say anything after what she said. . . . So even the most outgoing person I know was kind of afraid to say anything.

Within our own class, Sanjay reports a similar occurrence regarding our daily routine of freewriting. Students brought in prompts each day, and we spent a few minutes in private writing. Based on the suggestion of a previous class that wanted freewriting to feel more integrated with the rest of the class, I regularly asked if anyone would like to read or share their thoughts. In this particular class, no one read aloud until Sanjay did on October 10 and 12. In my journal, I noted that he read, in his words, "'Because no one ever does.'" I speculated, "He's becoming more performative, find[ing] the class a willing and receptive audience." And this felt like a significant turning point to me. Gradually more students began to read their freewriting; in my construction, Sanjay was the catalyst. But during Sanjay's interview, he recalls he was "a little embarrassed to read" and had done so only as an experiment within the research context I had established. Laughing, he comments that his "expectation was that other people would immediately chime in and that didn't exactly happen . . . eventually I stopped . . . [afterward] I was kind of like, 'Wow, don't I feel like an ass.'" How wildly I misread Sanjay in my "*incomplete* and *interested* account"[16]; where I had seen confidence and satisfaction, he saw tension-filled silence that kept him from further "participation."

Students were also concerned about the possibilities of *misinterpretation* of their words. This was a particular concern for Catarina, since she believes all writing to be "really personal." She describes at length her fears at receiving feedback on her first essay; she remembers being worried that other students might "take it the wrong way . . . pick at it and think that there's a strange meaning behind the topic." While I certainly value sharing one's writing and receiving feedback as a key component in the writing process, Catarina's story asks me to reconsider what is gained by requiring students to read such weighty drafts to their peers. Would her final draft have been as strong had she not been required to share it? I don't know. Perhaps an argument can be made that students such as Catarina are strengthened by such discussions, both in their writing and in confronting subjects they consider taboo. However, I am uncomfortable with the possibility to which Catarina alludes: further alienation from the class community through the speaking and "sharing" I demand.

The concern for "fitting in" with the class community, and what can provoke the wrong sort of attention, runs through many students' reflections. Speaking, in fact, may create distance between a student and her classmates. Catarina never speaks first so she can "verif[y] what I was going to say was along the lines of what everyone else was discussing, so I wasn't completely off topic," an exaggerated (and seemingly unproductive) enactment of what Bruffee describes as collaborative learning, ". . . a group of people who accept, and whose work is guided by, the same code of values and assumptions."[17] Further, she fears that she will "sound strange" and people will think she is "weird." Sanjay must balance being "not too personal and not too deep," an intense intellectual engagement and a critical stance. For Catarina and her peers, what is at stake is the *appearance* of shared assumptions and values, making dialogue an empty, even dangerous, exercise in conformity. And as Edward assesses, it is not simply an answer that is judged. "People are worried about that they're going to think my answer is stupid so therefore I'm stupid and you know, maybe they think I'm just dumb and why am I here." Thus a student speaking in class allows for an evaluation not simply of what was said and who the student is but *whether (or how) the student belongs in this community,* just as Chiseri-Strater witnesses a student who can "earn her community membership"[18] by speaking, and as Villanueva can distinguish a student who "isn't much of a participator" through his silences.[19] The right to belong to the community is at stake in the decision to speak or to be silent.

Hearing Others:
Conflict, Criticism, and Confrontation

Many of our disciplinary descriptions of classroom communities are fairly optimistic ones: Bruffee envisions communities of knowledgeable peers, working and conversing to reach consensus.[20] Elbow and Belanoff's textbook is premised on the notion of "putting out words for readers," because "language is social and socializing"; by writing often and receiving feedback, one can learn to write better.[21] Patricia Bizzell figures community in terms of "initiation," in which "students [are] eager to enter the discourse community to which the teacher belongs."[22] Mary Louise Pratt, perhaps most optimistically, gives us the vocabulary of "safe houses for healing and mutual recognition."[23] While the design of my research did not give me the space to examine these visions of the classroom with the student participants, I suspect, given the previous discussions, that these definitions would not reflect their sense of classroom communities, which they see as often driven by unproductive and uncomfortable experiences of conflict, criticism, and confrontation.

Nearly all of the students expressed their concern for being publicly criticized, frequently choosing silence instead. Catarina does not want to have others "pick at" her responses, forcing her to defend herself; Sarah reflects that the students in our class "weren't really understanding of other people's opinions."[24] Kurt is concerned that people might think he is a "bad person" based on what he says in class. Edward, Sanjay, Christina, and Sarah frame their concern for criticism in terms of being teased, mocked, and laughed at. Sanjay offers this bleak comparison:

> I'm always amazed to see kindergarten children. The kindergarten children have no qualms about offering their opinions . . . maybe because they haven't had the experience of being laughed at yet. You'll never achieve the level of interactivity in a junior-year English class that you will in kindergarten storytime. . . . That level of participation is gone . . . it's kind of like, it's kind of similar to the loss of innocence.

For me, such issues are frustrating. I want my students to be better people, to treat each other and what they have to say with civility and dignity. I want my students to be stronger, not silenced, by a fear of confrontation or the inappropriate responses of others. Thankfully, many of the students say that this type of reaction is atypical in their college experience. But this does not mean that *criticism* disappears. In fact, I have come to see that this is an even more central preoccupation in a writing class in which student writing becomes the basis of discussion. Within this sample of students, peer feedback always carried with it the weight of criticism, regardless of what *I* said about the process. Just as students have experienced, in Sanjay's terms, a nostalgic "loss of innocence" about the safety of classroom interactions, we must also approach classroom activities without naïveté. Realistically, students may not be able to disentangle their critical censors and their egos from even the most purely descriptive feedback. Despite my using an Elbow-and-Belanoff-inspired approach of non-directive, response-driven questions, Lucy sees this as "correcting other people's papers," a process that leaves you "in a vulnerable position." Edward offers this further insight: "I think that it is intimidating to have to get up in front of several people and have to bare your soul (for writing is the window into one's soul). It's just too random: there's no real way of knowing what the result will be." The specter of evaluation is so powerful for Catarina that if she were asked to turn in an unfinished draft for feedback in a full-class workshop, she would not, opting for an F instead, perhaps explaining the surprising "silences" (to use Losey's term) of students who were consistently unprepared when they knew the class would be having a peer feedback session.

Faced with students such as Edward or Catarina, it is tempting to deplore or ignore their responses as unsophisticated or defensive, or to adopt a kind of boot-camp approach ("Peer feedback on the double!"). But in doing so, we miss several valuable opportunities. First, we fail to give students guidance on how to more effectively negotiate that vulnerability. And we overlook the chance to talk with students about the ways their writing *matters*—to the writers who might benefit from critical feedback and the readers who must carefully respond, as this writing shapes our view of ourselves and others. Rather than trying to "get over" such moments, it can be profoundly productive to dwell in these intersections between the writers' intentions and the meanings derived, to explore the tensions and discomforts for what they can suggest about the roles of writers and readers.

Considering this concern for the public criticism of one's speech, I was surprised that most students were willing to voice disagreement, even in those situations where their points of views were clearly marginalized. Perhaps their relative youth is what distinguishes them from the teachers Delpit writes about: these students represent themselves as eager to voice opposition, even when they know their ideas may not be popular. Sarah is "definitely open to conflict and disagreements," speaking up when her dissenting opinion "needed to be out there." Catarina considers joining the debate team as she enjoys "playing the devil's advocate." And Lucy relates this story of choosing to speak up in disagreement during a

> "Social Thought and Political Economy" class . . . that was a really hard class to be in. Because we were, I think about thirty, thirty students. And they were all very talkative. It was a discussion; it

wasn't a lecture. We kind of had to lead the class, so you had to talk. And people were coming up with all these ideas and theories. . . . I felt so stupid. And I felt like, "I can't believe I'm in this class. What am I doing here? I can never talk like this." . . . We had one class where we had a panel about Israel and Palestine. And I wasn't prepared for it because it wasn't on the syllabus or whatever. And I was really surprised.

So this moment includes a class that already felt intimidating because it required "discussion," which Lucy found uncomfortable; peers perceived by Lucy to be more competent; a "surprise" topic (allowing no preparation) on an issue charged with emotion for her; and a one-sided presentation that was mislabeled as a "panel discussion." Such a scenario might indeed prove disempowering, even silencing, for a student comfortable with speaking in class. Given my reading of Delpit's "The Silenced Dialogue," it does not seem unreasonable to expect Lucy to remain silent, perhaps growing increasingly frustrated, angry, or alienated. Lucy's response follows:

I had a lot to say because I know a lot about it. I was born there and I know a lot of the history. . . . It's my country, so I had so much to say and I was just sitting there. And I kind of felt like I was going to blow up, because I just had so much to say and I didn't know how to. And I felt so, I just, I don't know what the word is, I just felt like, these people were so much more confident than I was, or at least presented themselves as like a lot more sophisticated or maybe it was just my feeling, and *I just kind of had to talk*. (emphasis added)

So the decision does not even seem to be in Lucy's conscious control; she is compelled to speak up because this is so profoundly important to her. Lucy recalls that her classmates were surprised when she spoke up in response to the all-Palestinian panel. Eventually another student joined Lucy, and

it kind of became the two of us in front of these three people that were extremely angry and really had a lot to say and were really not open to listening. And that kind of also made me feel like, "I don't want to talk," because when someone is not open to hearing what you have to say, that's very discouraging. . . .

They never let us finish a sentence. They kind of jumped in all the time and just their tone of voice was very, I felt they weren't very respectful . . . of our feelings or thoughts. They wanted to get their point across, and maybe that's why it was a one-sided panel. . . . And that was, just, very unfair. . . .

He started talking after I started talking. And we kind of like, when I didn't know what to say he kind, we kind of helped each other out. . . . We both were getting really nervous because, because we weren't there to fight and we weren't there to argue. But I felt like we were both kind of put in that position of arguing over something we didn't really want to argue over, just because they were so angry and so attacking. . . .

I wanted to cry afterwards, because, because it was so personal and because it had a lot to do with my life and my family that does live in Israel and my friends and I did cry actually on the way back. I just, I just, I felt like I, I had shared so much with that class and it wasn't a good sharing environment . . . it really upset me. I felt really tired and kind of drained. It wasn't a good feeling. (emphasis added)

I repeat this story at length for several reasons. First, it seems inappropriate to take Lucy's charged words out of context and to inhabit her story to forward my own agenda. Also, I want to emphasize that Lucy's speaking out was impressive because of the interwoven layers of complexity she faced. A class community that already made her feel intimidated, the unexpected nature of a heated discussion on a personal and highly charged topic, and a resistant, even disrespectful, audience—these factors would be silencing for many of us. Yet Lucy spoke up, despite the costs to her.

Perhaps part of Lucy's willingness to speak up relates to the solidarity she felt with the other dissenting student. But from the beginning, she felt a sense of personal responsibility, even when she knew others might not be listening.

While I do not want to colonize Lucy's story for my own purposes, I do think her story points to an important issue: students who are *quiet* may not feel themselves *silenced*. (Indeed, as discussed in the last chapter, Lucy also related to me a story of interrupting a film in another class to express her discomfort both with the images presented and the discomfiting lack of reaction she perceived in her classmates.) Certainly it may be possible to argue that students do not construct themselves this way because this is not yet part of their vocabularies, or because they have not yet learned to see their worlds in terms of these power dynamics. On the other hand, I do think it is important to acknowledge that in their reflections, these students almost universally represent not speaking as a conscious choice, made after deliberation, rather than a lack of opportunity, or the sense, in Delpit's terms, that "no one is listening." Most compelling to me is that students grant the most power to teachers' dismissive or debilitating feedback. Choices such as this one of Lucy's profoundly challenge us to rethink the notion that our quiet students must be the victims of silencing.

Students also pay careful attention to how their oral and written words may affect others. For example, Michael points out that "it is difficult to speak when you are afraid you may hurt someone's feeling or even offend them." Sanjay's approach to this kind of conflict is a pragmatic one. How can one disagree with minimal repercussions? When is silence a wiser, more practical approach? He sees that expressing disagreement and inviting conflict have the potential to alter not just people's perceptions of him but also possible relationships within the classroom. While he is willing to express dissent, he is also aware that "if your opinions differ too greatly from other people's, it kind of sets up a roadblock to any type of connection." This became an issue for him in relation to sharing and receiving feedback on his two projects exploring religion and intolerance, including an observation of a community to which he did not belong. Writing these essays, he often found himself blocked, unable to develop an argument or complete drafts to his own standards.

> It just became difficult to say what I wanted to say. . . . I had to write and then have it edited by people who most certainly have different views than I did. . . . That definitely affected what I thought I could say . . . the way I would say it. There were so many times I wanted to say, "I disagree with this entirely." And I just had to stop myself, "No, I definitely don't want to say it that way." Because I have to at least have some semblance of tolerance, don't I, if I'm going [to] complain that no one else does.

Thus Sanjay's concern is not about *expressing* disagreement but in finding an appropriate and effective way to do so in his writing, particularly for readers who do not share his views. Often he found this an impossible task, leaving him silent both in discussions and in writing his essays. This proved especially troubling in a small group discussion that took place early in the semester. Sanjay's partner made a comment about the connections between crime and poverty, a comment he considered "ridiculous." He found it difficult to respond appropriately, to express his radical disagreement without "shooting her down." At stake was his sense of decorum ("it would have been terrible" to respond as passionately as he wished) and his own future in the class: "It was fear of jeopardizing a working relationship. Like if she had to edit one of my documents later, I wouldn't . . . want her to be biased [in] her editing, 'Oh this paragraph sucks, this paragraph sucks.'"

This is a critical insight. Not only is discussion in a writing class more loaded because the interaction often centers on a student-generated text, but classroom interactions and tensions may get (en)acted through those texts. The conflict and confrontation that can (and does) exist in any classroom is given a new arena when student texts are involved; student-writers are infinitely more vulnerable to their peers who now have access to more ammunition. As Sanjay points out, this can have profound consequences for the writer, his ego, and his development as a writer. Thus the fear of alienating others (and ultimately himself) through what he says is a powerful factor. As he says in his first written reflection:

> For the first week of English, I was simply nervous. People I'd never been around, never met, everything was so unfamiliar, I didn't want to alienate everyone by saying something stupid. . . . In a new environment, how do you know what to say and what not to say? Maybe your views won't be accepted by the class. That kind of rejection is hard to take, so better to play it safe and slowly "feel out" the "terrain."

In other words, Sanjay must balance his considerations of ethos and audience to foster a productive working relationship. Considering all of these concerns about conflict, the moments students relate about having no fear of criticism are revealing. For Lucy, the publication of a piece of writing that included a description of a particularly emotional confrontation with her stepmother was

> probably the one thing I didn't mind sharing at all. Because that story was um, just a really important story to me, and I kind of felt like, "OK no one can really judge this because this really happened and it's my story" . . . and I wrote it the way I felt it, and it was fine because it's something that was really important to me. So I kind of felt like whatever anyone else had to say didn't really matter because I felt good about it. And the other stories that I didn't necessarily feel as good about would have been harder to share.

In another instance, Sarah explores writing a speech for a local community meeting regarding a public safety concern when she felt

> like I was doing something. I was addressing an issue. And I felt like an authority and not just one of 500 students in a classroom. [Talking in class feels like you don't really have authority] because some students will say something and the teacher will be like, "No, no that's just all wrong." And what I had to say that day no one could really, they could disagree with it, but it was fact, so they couldn't really say that I was wrong.

What links these two stories for me is the locus of *authority*. Because Lucy's story is true, because Sarah is addressing an issue about which she has firsthand knowledge, they assume a new position of authority that they perceive is not available to them in the classroom. Any challenges they receive will be thoughtfully considered, but they feel they have the right to speak.

This highlights the importance of students writing about topics that matter to them, ones over which they feel some authority. Yes, it is important to challenge students to move beyond received knowledge and their comfort zones. But when we choose topics for students, when we decide what students *should* care about, we rob them of the sense of authority, determination, and curiosity that real writers have. Thus it is unsurprising that we receive lifeless essays that parrot our perspectives or weakly summarize a text. In Lucy's and Sarah's examples, I believe we see students using writing and dialogue in the most productive ways, as they take enormous chances with language and self-presentation because the topics matter, and they feel they have a right (even a responsibility) to speak.

Hearing Others:
The Importance of Intimacy

If the definitions of "community" proposed by Bruffee, Bizzell, and Pratt do not match my students' experiences (particularly in these definitions' failure to adequately account for the conflict, criticism, and confrontation that exist within the classroom on a daily basis), then in what productive ways can this community be constituted? First and foremost, many students stress the importance of "knowing" other students; such intimacy decreases the likelihood that they will choose to be silent in classes. I suspect this may be particularly important in a large university setting such as the University of Massachusetts, where relative anonymity is the norm, at least in introductory-level classes. The effect of this anonymity is so profound for Tom that he "just [does]n't have a lot to say to people" he does not know, as if the production of language depends on intimacy. For Lucy, when her classmates "know her," she has tacit permission to "really share" what she thinks, because "they understand the way I present things more." For Sanjay, intimacy allows for a fuller expression of his identity. He comments, "With my friends and my family I can be as weird as I want. . . . I guess how quiet I'll be is an inverse function of how familiar I am with the person."

The parallels to Lucy's and Sanjay's writing are apparent. For Lucy, this manifested in the development of a stable writing group over the second half of the semester with Tom and Allison, both inside and outside class. The influence of this group was tangible in Lucy's writing, as she began to take greater risks both in her topic and stylistic choices. In Sanjay's case, as he noted himself, he often felt conflicted about what was "appropriate" or "acceptable" to share with his peers, often resulting in short, underdeveloped exploratory and mid-process drafts. Before I interviewed him, I confess, I read this as a lack of effort and attention, particularly when his final drafts for me (and for grades) were typically far more sophisticated and nuanced, asking more difficult questions of himself and his readers.

But the value of a heightened sense of intimacy is not limited to an individual struggling with decisions about what she can say or write. Critical of the discussion sections associated with large lecture classes and their apparent anonymity, Edward notices this:

> You have twenty to twenty-five people in these classes, and you have a TA leading most of the discussion. Not everyone really knows each other. It's just a place you and twenty-four other people go that they are in the same lecture, God knows where they sit, you don't know these people . . . if you're in a class where you're comfortable with the people and you know the people I think you're more apt to be able to contribute, draw better conclusions.

In this way, then, *discussions themselves improve*; stronger, more rigorous academic work can be done when students feels a sense of comfort with their community. This trend was apparent to Sanjay in the progression of the discussions within our writing class. He says,

> [Although] I don't remember the discussions specifically, the only thing I remember is how they were held. Like at the beginning, I think we actually raised our hands. And towards the end that didn't seem necessary anymore. It seemed more like a conversation than it was like a discussion, if you catch the difference. . . . If someone offered a topic, no one was afraid to make a connection somewhere else, whereas in the beginning, people would try to stick on [a] subject and [you] would be a little afraid to deviate, because you didn't know if you were supposed to or not. Is that okay or not? It's just one of those things where the way you act becomes different over time, because you don't have to be so . . . *uptight* is too strong a word, but maybe conscious about what you're doing in everything. Like will the people here like what you're doing? Will the teacher like it? Is this acceptable behavior or not?

Thus the rules governing interactions evolve through a mutually constituted (if unspoken) sense of what "acceptable behavior" was, as greater intimacy decreased the need for silence. Sanjay continues, "As we get more familiar with one another, just by that fact alone, more topics open up for discussion"[25] and reflects that several discussions at the end of the semester could not have taken place without the development of intimacy and trust.

But what exactly do terms such as *familiarity* and *comfort* mean in this context for my students? I think it is easy to dismiss these terms as so broad as to be meaningless, or as concerns too unsophisticated to indulge our students in. After all, shouldn't they be "over it" by now? One key component is simply a sense of not being anonymous; silence, in the case of Edward's discussion section, is a protective measure in a rhetorically uncomfortable situation. Learning classmates' names asks students to acknowledge each other as individual, identifiable people rather than "just people in your discussion section. . . . I have never gotten to know . . . you have no idea where they're coming from, where they're going." Relying on his experience of Theater classes, during which emphasis is placed on "familiarity exercises," Edward concludes, "Once you can get used to these people that you're in class with, once you can start building relationships and breaking down walls, barriers . . . that's when you can really start to let go and start to take risks a lot easier." Speaking is one of those risks.

Sanjay finds that he is less inhibited about speaking in a class of friends because of their shared history and the safety and tolerance provided. He theorizes:

> If I make an exceptionally aggressive comment . . . my friends would understand why more readily than someone who just met me would understand. And if I make an exceptionally aggressive comment, how would I put it? The closest thing I can think of to say is that they'd be more inclined to forgive me for it. But that's not what I really mean. Yeah, OK, with my friends more radical comments would be treated with a greater tolerance, because they already know me and agree with me on other things.

Finally, the process of peer feedback becomes more productive with this greater intimacy. One student notes that peer feedback in college proves more challenging than in high school, because

> in your senior English class you've known these people forever, for the most part. And you're bound to have at least one person that you're decent friends with. I had a few friends in my senior English class. So you don't mind showing, like, "Hey check this out. What do you think?" And you can accept that kind of criticism from them. . . . And then you come here and you don't really know anyone, so you're just kind of getting familiar with them, and you've only known them as long as you've had the class, at least last semester. You just kind of have to go out on a limb.

Again, it seems important to note the construction of peer feedback that drives these responses—feedback is seen as *criticism*. Taking this perspective seriously, I think it is possible to see any response as the acceptance or rejection of an author's meaning. (While Elbow and Belanoff may argue that these are purely "descriptive," even "sayback" and "pointing" imply a kind of judgment, although the explicitly evaluative piece shifts back to the author: are readers "getting" what I am saying? By pointing to pieces of a text that are "striking," a reader implicitly suggests what is *not* noteworthy.) But even if I could convince students that feedback is not about evaluation, a level of trust and respect, intimacy, and comfort seems critical for the feedback process. Why should writers care about what readers they do not know or trust have to say about their drafts? Writers who have no faith in their readers may easily dismiss challenging feedback as the unreliable ramblings or hostile reactions of an untrustworthy reader. Likewise, readers may feel seriously inhibited in what they can say without a sense of how the author will react.

To my surprise, what most of my students want is not friendships with their classmates to make speaking easier. That is, their sense of community is not focused on creating personal, long-lasting relationships, nor do most students suggest that these will make for a better class. For example, Lucy (who did develop close friendships with two of her classmates) remarks:

> There were people I thought were really nice and I would just talk briefly with, but nothing ever happened beyond that. And that was fine with me, because you don't become best friends with everyone in your class. *And actually by finding two people that I feel really good with, I was happy to have [that] . . . I feel like I like having this real thing over kind of a fake-shallow-situation where everyone is really friendly because they're in the same class and smiling and whatever.* (emphasis added)

Thus it seems that what students are seeking is not necessarily friendship but what friendship provides—a context of safety and comfort when they speak. This desire surfaces in the repeated use of terms such as *clicking* and the *vibe* of the class, concepts that often were difficult for my students to conclusively define but easy to recognize when they encountered them. Some examples follow:

> It's just, it's just that the French might say, a "certain-I-don't-know-what." The class has to click. That's the biggest thing, I guess. There's no measurable factor . . . I think it's just, everybody has to be willing, in kind of the same mind-set to be, to get to know one another and accept one another.
> . . . the people in the class, even though I didn't *know* them, you could still kind of get a feeling what the *vibe* is.
> I guess it's just like when you meet new people . . . you click with them or you don't . . . from the way people are open to you or not, and if they want to hear what you have to say or don't or want to share stories. Because some people I feel like are just there, and

they don't really care. . . . *And so that kind of feeling makes you feel like, "I don't want to talk to these people if they have no interest in talking to me."* . . . I can tell when people speak in the class, if the rest of the students are looking at the person and . . . trying to get something from what they're saying or just doodling and not caring. (emphasis added)

Perhaps what links these attempts to define the "mentality" of the class is a sense of other students' willingness to listen, even to voices that disagree with theirs, to care, to engage. In retrospect, my need to pin down these terms seems matched by my students' sense that they are somehow undefinable and unmeasurable. Here Harris's metaphor of the classroom as a "city" seems particularly apt:

One does not need consensus to have community. . . . What I value instead is a kind of openness, a lack of plan, a chance both to be among others and to choose my own way. It is a kind of life I associate with the city, with the sort of community in which people are brought together more by accident or need than by shared values. A city brings together people who do not so much choose to live together as they are simply thrown together, and who must then make the best they can of their common lot. The core values of this loose form of community, it seems to me, are a tolerance of diversity and a respect for privacy.[26]

As one student suggests, ultimately "it is up to the class as a whole to take that final step," to determine the kind of citizenship one wishes to have in this community. Ultimately, these students define the classroom community in much the same terms as Harris does—as a willingness to work together on the common tasks of writing and a writing class—with consideration for each other's work and egos; as Allison succinctly argues, it is important to have "a tone of mutual respect between the students and teacher and the students with each other."

Hearing Others:
Group Size

Perhaps unsurprisingly, for nearly all of the students in this study, the *size of the group* had a significant effect on students' perceptions of discussions. Tom finds large groups "impersonal," echoing frequently cited concerns of self-consciousness and intimidation. And while Lucy is more likely to speak in smaller groups, she believes that in a larger class it may be easier to speak, because no one is likely to be paying attention to the speaker: "Who cares . . . you don't really mean anything in this class."

In composition, we may feel essentially free of this concern, since our classes are relatively small. While the size of writing classes has been growing steadily and may feel unmanageable to many teachers, these classes are blessedly not taught in large, anonymous formats like most other introductory-level and required courses. At the University of Massachusetts, composition classes of twenty-four students are likely to be the smallest (and sometimes the only small) class students have their first year. However, we should consider the choices that we make regarding student interaction, because even the relatively small size of our classes seems too large for many students. As Lucy comments, "Any more than twenty students . . . it's not a discussion." The extent of this issue is far-reaching. She concludes, "I think class size has a lot to do with whether it turns out to be a good class."

With the exception of two students, all of the students expressed a distinct preference for smaller groups. Edward (one of the exceptions) contends that larger groups provide a "forum" for a greater variety of responses. Interestingly, despite his appreciation for large-group discussions, Edward notes that he is not likely to talk unless he has something "pressing" to say.

Regarding the qualitative difference, Sanjay makes this analogy:

> Small groups as opposed to large groups? When is the last time you actually saw a protesting crowd actually talking to one other? It's just one guy up saying one thing, and everyone else is either agreeing or disagreeing. And that's what large groups and small groups are like. With a large group, you generally have a few select people who are really vocal, and they end up having a dialogue with each other. They have a small group with themselves within the large group.

In this analysis, large group discussions do not allow dialogue; they foster (and even create) factions and oversimplified arguments. Such a situation, according to Sanjay, offers little opportunity for vocal participation by those not part of that "small group." He realizes:

> It's hard to become a vocal member the farther along the discussion goes, because they [the vocal members] have the context behind them. You don't. They've been talking since the beginning. So for you to suddenly chime in would seem out of place, because you haven't contributed before. No one knows where you're coming from. You need to take an extra five minutes to qualify all of your statements. But with a small group it's much easier to participate in the conversation. It's much easier to have a dialogue that involves everybody.

So how do these students describe small-group discussions? Several point out that it is "impossible to hide," "forcing" them to speak. Sarah finds that she takes on a directive role in small groups, becoming "the leader . . . I just get the work done and give certain people work to do and make them talk." She concludes, "I participate more in small groups and give more effort than normal students." While I am intrigued by the possibility that different class structures offer students the opportunity to take on new roles, I am struck by Sarah's comparison of herself to so-called "normal" students. I am troubled that she sees herself in her relative quietness as deviant or abnormal. How powerful the message that speaking, and speaking alone, is equated with classroom participation.

Smaller groups also provide an important step of socialization into academic conversations. Catarina praises the higher interactivity of small groups, while Edward observes that small groups provide the opportunity for conversations that are deeper and more focused: "Where you're working with two or three other people . . . it becomes kind of a synthesis and a combination of what everybody thinks." This seems like an important step in the process of developing critical thinking and listening skills. Indeed, for Tracy, small groups are more productive, because other students "are actually listening." Likewise, Sanjay argues, "In a small group you can talk to one another and have better-quality conversation . . . *you just have a normal conversation*" (emphasis added). Beyond their artificial nature, Sanjay also suggests that large group discussions prove to be logistically difficult, as the time required for everyone to state their positions is prohibitive:

> In a real conversation, like, for example, a two-person conversation, I'm talking to someone else, well we're the only source of input and we're talking a lot. We're discussing our ideas a lot. Our personal ideas. In a large group, for everyone to state their opinion on just one topic takes a long time. And not everyone gets a chance to do it before someone continues the discussion a little further, at which point you can't really go back and say, "Well I think this," because the time is past, you've lost your chance. And so that just makes it difficult because once you go further along into the conversation and you say one thing, you didn't answer all the other questions, so no one has any idea what you're talking about now. "Why do you say that?" "Well let me go answer the fifteen questions that I didn't get a chance to talk on."

Sarah, too, finds that smaller groups provide more opportunities for genuine interaction and diminish the potential for conflict. In our class, "Working in small groups was the most helpful and the most useful . . . it just seemed like you could talk about so much more and discuss it in more detail in the small groups because you had less people wanting to say stuff."

Throughout these reflections, Sanjay and other students highlight their sense that small-group interactions can be "real discussions" and "real conversations." Perhaps what is most important in these reflections is the recognition of the artificial, contrived nature of what we do in our classes. Because we say a class is a "community," and because we say speaking in class is a "conversation," does not make it so. We would do well to explore this tension with our students explicitly—to deconstruct our expectations and their preconceptions. While I am skeptical that discussions with a group of twenty will become "real" or "genuine," our own and our students' efforts to understand their dynamics and their perceptions will improve these conversations.

Concluding Thoughts

What are the implications of these rich and varied stories about the relationships between silence, identity, and community my students have told? First, I think we must acknowledge the complex negotiations that these students experience—silence is not simply passivity or disengagement. Rather, these students are analyzing and weighing a range of factors—their own sense of identity; the possibility for criticism, misunderstanding, and the misconstruction of one's identity; the potential effects of speaking; the subsequent results of speaking on one's place in the classroom community; the connection (or lack of one) to the audience. Returning once again to the narrator of *The Woman Warrior*, I am struck by how succinctly and eloquently she encapsulates many of the themes and concerns that my students suggest influence their decisions to speak or to be silent in class. She connects her own silence to identity, knowing that it "had to do with being a Chinese girl." Although they do not link silence to a racial category or a visible difference, many students see speaking or silence as "natural," innate tendencies over which they have little control, or to some other identity category. And like the narrator, the shift to a new environment with unfamiliar rules has prompted students to reconsider their own silences. Some see in themselves a lack of self-confidence, as their voices are a mere "whisper with a little squeak coming out of my throat." And far too many have internalized the message that it is indeed a problem to be silent.

To frame these tensions in another, perhaps more optimistic, way, I argue that these silent students have considered in concrete terms many of the difficult lessons we try to teach in composition classes about ethos and identity, audience and authority. What might this reconsideration offer us? For teachers, I think it can make the silences of our students a bit less troubling. Rather than seeing them as resistant or unwilling, perhaps it is more useful to see these students as grappling with questions about how to best present themselves and their ideas in the spoken texts they produce. How do these students want to be perceived? With what authority do they speak, particularly when they know they will be evaluated for what they say? And to whom are they speaking? What are the conventions and expectations of this audience? What limitations (consciously or unconsciously) are imposed? How does the context shape what can be said?

How can student-speakers present their thinking in ways that engage rather than alienate their listeners?

I believe the issues these students consider in their decision to speak or to be silent in class might also provide a fruitful ground for a discussion of writing. For example, I have found the concept of "audience" difficult to teach in any systematic way. While some students seem to grasp this slippery concept after a variety of exercises, others find it frustrating. ("Why isn't the audience 'anyone'? Why does it matter who my reader is?") Asking students to apply the concerns they wrestle with in the decision to speak or to be silent may illuminate such writing questions in more immediate, practical terms. Sanjay certainly made this connection—finding it difficult to write about religious tolerance for peer readers who might not share his views.

Finally, if our goal as teachers is to have students speak frequently, then we need to seriously consider which issues of identity and community we can exert our teacherly control over. What can we do to promote a level of intimacy and respect? What do we ask students to reveal? While I am not arguing that we should avoid difficult topics, I have come to see that not every student will feel equally comfortable speaking (or may not even be able to speak). As the teacher, I need to respect those differences and, yes, a student's right to silence.

If different groups sizes and configurations provide students with new roles or offer different outcomes (what Edward sees as the distinctions between quality and quantity or synthesis and debate), then we should configure the opportunities for discussion with these in mind. Smaller groups may often be the best pedagogical option, as all five of the focal students reported their own willingness to speak more freely and frequently in them, with their experiences in these situations sounding more like opportunities for constructing meaning than for performing knowledge. As Edward suggests, small groups may have a cumulative effect on students, eventually affecting their oral participation in larger group discussions. He considers, "In this class, we do enough small group work that when it comes time to share with the class as a whole, there is no real intimidation from anyone, because we're all familiar with each other in one sense or another."

Chapter 7

Learning to See in a Whole New Light
Reimagining the Silences in Our Classrooms

Silence . . . is powerful. It is the dimension in which ordinary and extraordinary events take their proper places . . . silence is the sanctuary of sound. Words are wholly alive in the hold of silence; they are sacred.

—N. Scott Momaday, *The Man Made of Words: Essays, Stories, Passages*

It isn't a crime to be quiet.

—Edward, student

Silence. Belanoff contends, "We're a culture fearful of silence,"[1] a claim that resonates with me as I type this chapter, a CD playing in the background, my e-mail open, cordless and cell phones nearby. Despite these fears in contemporary American culture, I find that silence is surprisingly *present*. A few examples, among many others, follow:

- Silence is a legal right: the right to remain silent, guaranteed in Miranda warnings before a police interrogation, and the constitutional right to plead the Fifth Amendment are safeguards against incriminating oneself.
- The "strong, silent type" needs no explanation. As an image of masculinity, it prescribes a code in which one may feel much but can say little. In this image, a man's silence is a bit mysterious, attractive, even sexually charged.
- As a child, I came to associate silence with a particular religious gravity; profound prayer—and perhaps the answer to that prayer—comes

in silence. The nuns of my elementary school indelibly linked respect, reflection, and discipline for me and instilled the sense that silence was a necessary element of spirituality.

- In an episode of *Buffy the Vampire Slayer*, the shock following the death of the main character's mother is registered through several haunting minutes of utter silence. No speaking, no sound track, just wordless grief.
- There are those fleeting silences in a conversation, the unpleasant pauses when the lack of words unveils and instigates a more profound discomfort.
- Silence became, in the early weeks of fall 2001, eerily, impossibly more present. Moments of silence at memorial services, in Congress, at sporting events, and on the floor of the New York Stock Exchange punctuated an otherwise chaotic, media-saturated culture of instant information.

In each of these instances—the legally protected refusal to speak, an air of mystery, the silence of worship or silence in shock, a hiccup in a conversation, the temporary ceasing of activity in mourning—we *know* what silence means. It is not necessary to explain in these moments; to articulate what is unspoken inevitably diminishes the power of these silences. Indeed, some of these examples are so powerful precisely because of the implicit meanings we all share. How many times have we witnessed a parent's silent, paralyzing stare directed at a small, misbehaving child? Had an entire conversation with a lover communicated only through stolen glances? Felt another's heart break under the weight of grief? *We know what silence means.*

In the first chapter of *Reclaiming the Tacit Dimension: Symbolic Form in the Rhetoric of Silence*, Kalamaras eloquently summarizes the dilemma of silence:

> The concept of silence as a mode of knowing conflicts with the current Western perception of silence as a condition of annihilation ... silence is most often represented as a condition that the speaking subject must overcome, an abyss or lack that inhibits one's power to make meaning ... [the] feminist position of language against silence is understandable, and, I might argue, even necessary—at least with regard to certain *aspects* of silence—given the current and historical marginalization of women's voices, as well as those voices of ethnicity suppressed at the cultural and economic borders of an Anglo-, patricentric sensibility. If marginalized populations do not speak, contest, and argue, their voices are destined to go unheard.[2]

Such an understanding of silence underlies many of our pedagogical approaches to classroom silence. Perhaps simplistically put, we as teachers feel we need to move students "out of silence": beyond their resistances, beyond the marginalization that leaves them silenced. As a teacher, as a human being, as a gendered subject, as someone committed to social justice, this is a concern I share.

Where this position becomes troubling to me is in considering how differently students experience their own silences from the stories we tell ourselves about our classrooms. First, as their reflections implicitly argue, the sorts of active resistances we construct seem present far less often than *our* narratives suggest. Also, it seems critical to understand that students do not necessarily see their silences as inherently problematic. In other words, they do not generally see their silences in terms of unsuccessful attempts or thwarted desires to speak. Rather, this conflict is often framed in terms of failing to meet *teachers'* expectations. And this, I suspect, accounts for much of the tensions explored in chapters 5 and 6.

Am I proposing that we abandon our attempts to foster dialogue and ignore our own interpretations? Certainly, emphatically, not. But I am suggesting that we need to develop a clearer understanding of the contexts in which our students are working, learning, and speaking. That is, I believe that in our theorizing we also need to consider our students' negotiations of the multiple relationships in a classroom—between teacher and student; the categories of "teachers" and "students"; a student's educational context and an individual classroom; "knowledge" and authority; the constructions of "self" and community; speaking and silence—that are made more difficult, ironically, because many of the terms of these relationships remain tacit.

I want to argue, then, that we can maintain concern for the possible silencing that students may experience (what Erica Scheurer calls "monologic silences")[3] and work to create those conditions that might move students "out of silence," but our efforts need to take into account how students view speaking and silence. I think these more fully articulated understandings can lead us to strategies and practices that might help our students "find their voices" in our classes. Perhaps this will seem like an easy way out to my readers, but I will not presume to say what those practices should look like for every teacher. I can certainly draw conclusions about the particular practices that were successful in the class I studied (individual conferences; a freewriting routine that gave students control over what they shared; exercises that promoted familiarity with the community) and what deserves more of my attention (clearer explanations of why I value student interaction; a greater emphasis on small groups as "real" discussions; working to actively lessen the sense of evaluation around speaking). But it seems a profound misreading of my students to reduce the complexity of their stories to a list of "dos and don'ts" for all teachers. These stories identify, instead, the relationships that shape students' decisions to speak or to be silent and point to questions we as teachers might ask ourselves about how we foster (or hinder) those relationships. So I would argue that the practices a teacher develops need to be responsive to her students and internally consistent with the rest of her pedagogy and the persona she creates.

For example, if I encourage my students to think of their classmates as a "writing community" on which they rely for fair readings of their work because they have achieved some level of comfort and intimacy and because they respect each other as readers, writers, and thinkers, then where am *I* situated? During the first few years I taught, I found myself uncomfortably outside: my students worked well in small groups, but as a full class, we sometimes seemed uncomfortable, strained. I could ask the very same kinds of questions of the whole class that I would ask them to consider in small groups. Silence. The bad kind. The looking-at-desks-avoiding-my-eyes-checking-watches kind of silence. Was it me? Was my graduate student presence inhibiting, intimidating, silencing? (How could that be?) When I grew more comfortable with myself as a teacher (not coincidentally when the difference between my students' ages and my own had grown to a more comfortable margin), my relationship with my students grew easier. When I asked students to introduce each other to the class, I participated. When students wrote in class, I did too. When I invited students to read aloud from unfinished pieces, I did as well, sharing my embarrassingly sentimental attempts at poetry or very incomplete drafts. If students were putting pieces together for a class magazine, then it seemed only fair and responsible that I take that same risk and share my writing as well. I do not mean to suggest that I collapsed the distance between teacher and student, that I gave up my authority, or that I "empowered" my students. (All of those seem like potentially dangerous formulations and problematic propositions, particularly for teachers who are not seen as inherently, institutionally authoritative.) But what I do think happened is that I became more "me"—teller of dumb jokes, watcher of bad television shows, mystery reader, person who cries over "Olympic moments"—by allowing myself to become more a part of that classroom community I was trying so hard to create with and among my students. In being more myself, I grew to be a better teacher, one students found they could trust with their writing and their voices.

But there is a second argument I want to make, one that in some ways contradicts (or at the very least complicates) this argument about creating circumstances that encourage students to speak. It is this: while maintaining these concerns and working to effect positive change, we also need to be open to the possibility that the *decision to be silent is a legitimate, reasoned one.* As Glenn argues, "Silence is more than the negative of not being permitted to speak, of being afraid to speak; it can be a deliberative, positive choice."[4]

I believe we should spend at least as much energy in developing the silences in our classrooms as we do in fostering dialogue. While part of this claim is rooted in my conscious effort to respect the individual who may not fit our model of the vocal "good student," I think there is a practical dimension as well. "Ultimately the current productive emphasis on rich and varied talk in the classroom merges with the productive uses of silence ... [to create] a continuum of instructional practices,"[5] to foster what Belanoff calls "an interlaced pattern of reflection and action [that] constructs literacy and learning."[6] Along with Anne Ruggles Gere, I argue against the common positioning of speech and silence as opposites, with silence as something to be broken or overcome. Rather, "We can conceive of it [silence] as part of speech located on a continuum and put one in dialogue with the other."[7] Likewise, I believe we need to begin conceptualizing and more skillfully deploying those different kinds of silences, to take advantage of the possibilities implicit in silence. Like Glenn, I believe, "we must locate, discover, stumble over, and then open up silences."[8] As teachers of language, we *know* the power of written and oral voices. But we also need to help ourselves and our students find in silence the tools and possibilities for contemplation and negotiation, meditation and mediation, and formulation and creation.

In an attempt to reread silence not merely (or not only) as lack, Magda Gere Lewis weaves together feminist theory, literary criticism, and composition pedagogy in *Without a Word: Teaching beyond Women's Silences*. She points out:

> If we are to propose pedagogical strategies that really might make a difference for women, we need to find a way of understanding the discursive meaning of women's silence and not dismiss it as an example of women's lack and absence out of which we need to be recovered. . . .
>
> Might we not equally see women's silence as practice directed toward social transformation?[9]

The challenge Lewis offers here is one of critical reexamination and relistening, one that asks us to consider alternative ways of interpreting students, their silences, and our own classrooms and practices. While Lewis offers little in terms of specific methodology or what such "social transformation" might look like, her point is a useful one. Instead of simply seeing silence as a lack (an assumption that ultimately underlies many of the texts I discussed in chapter 2), Lewis asks for a fundamental redefinition of the terms we use to describe our students' audible voices. Rather than pathologizing silence as lack or absence and further marginalizing those students we choose to label as "silent," we need to investigate the critical and transformative potential of silence.

Considering Contexts

Linguistic research invites such a reinterpretation by offering an alternative framework for understanding silence. Linguists such as Muriel Saville-Troike, Deborah Tannen, and Adam Jaworski argue that silence is an ambiguous symbol dependent on context for an appropriate reading. While the Oxford English Dictionary's definitions of silence (and most of its associations) are rooted in the notion of absence, "Both speech sounds and speech silences are symbolic in nature, and the meaning of silence is thus also derived by convention within particular speech communities . . . silence (like all nonverbal communication) is more context-embedded than speech, that is more dependent on context for its interpretation."[10] Silence offers no explicit statement, there is no overt denotation, and by its very nature, "pure" silence does not invite redefining or the active negotiation of meaning. While I do not mean to suggest that it is impossible to *assign* meaning to silence or to imply infinite interpretive indeterminacy, it is critical to remember that *any* reading of silence is contingent upon understanding the multiple factors that create its context (or overlapping contexts).

One important consideration is that of cultural definitions of silence. In this section, I focus on stories Lucy tells about her decision to speak or to be silent. One might argue that she does not represent the "typical" student.[11] This is true: her background is strikingly different from many of her classmates in her College Writing class who were born and raised in suburban and rural Massachusetts. But her narrative offers a consideration of a wide range of issues reflecting themes from the stories of other students and posing critical questions to consider for all of our students.

Lucy sees quietness as an essential part of her identity in the same way several other students such as Catarina, Sandra, Sarah, and Renee do. She speculates:

> I don't know if it's been since I was little, but I've always been more of a listener than a talker when there are a lot of people. . . . that's how I get to know people, by what they have to say. . . . [But] I've never felt like you have to hear my voice in order to know who I am. I feel like I almost want people to know me more as a listener than as someone who wants to control the conversation all the time. Because I don't [want to control the conversation]. I really want to hear what they have to say.

In this framework, then, Lucy's silence is *not* problematic; it is the way she chooses to interact with other people. It is only in classrooms in the United States that her identity as a "listener" has become troubling.

This identity has its roots in both her family and cultural contexts. She notes that while she was growing up, it was not common in her family to discuss particularly emotional or introspective issues. Within a larger frame, Lucy sees a profound sociocultural influence on her silences. Born and raised in Israel, her move to the United States at age sixteen revealed to her the role of silence in her home culture. She theorizes, "It's really a culture that is so focused around death, because of the army and because there's constant dying. So everything is quick, and there's no long-term plans . . . you never really know." Lucy sees that one of the cultural responses to this instability is the frequent use of the Hebrew phrase meaning "It'll be fine": "They [Israelis] say that about everything from the . . . simplest things like dinner plans [up] to death. 'It'll be fine.' It's a kind of a culture that just says, 'Don't dwell. Move on. It's fine.'" For Lucy, this is a remarkable contrast to American culture, in which "there's much more long-term plans and digging into things and finding 'what is it that made this happen?'" She sees the worldviews shaping respective interaction styles; the "just move on" attitude shapes the content and depth of conversations in Israel as well. In this context, the directive of college classrooms toward close reading, analysis, and "dwelling" is complicated indeed.

The clash of home and school cultures emerges in other students' stories as well. For example, Catarina sees in her family a strong directive toward silence. Her mother's illness encouraged her and her brother

> to be quiet in the house. And when we were around family members, we had to be quiet, sit down, and wait for someone else to tell us to talk, and then we talked. And if everybody else was talking, we could go around and play, yell, and scream. But [at] family get-togethers, it was just kind of known that we sit down and wait until somebody else comes and tells us we could go play.

These family messages were compounded for Catarina by both a school system and a religious tradition that had an expectation of silence and limited space for speaking and participation. She relates:

> I was brought up very, very, very rigidly religious in a Baptist church [where] you sing when everyone else is singing. When anyone else is talking, you listen. And when you're expected to talk, you talk, and [then] you sit down and wait for somebody else to go. . . . I guess it was just kind of understood when I was little that there were times you talked and times you were quiet, and I just had to kind of learn when those times were.

Thus it seems that all of Catarina's "training" previous to college leads her to view silence as natural, in her words "a pattern. I just learned to be kind of quiet." In Catarina's world, these very strict rules about speaking combine with the lessons of school (to give the answer that mimics the teacher's lecture during the five-minute concluding "discussion"), making the relatively freewheeling discussions of college classrooms quite alien indeed. Catarina's success was dependent, in large part, on her ability to discern the tacit rules that governed these conversations.

In the cultural adaptation of college classes, students such as Lucy and Catarina are asked to make a profound (and, I would wager, sometimes confusing) shift from their home cultures where silence is the expectation, the rule. I want to point out here that Lucy and Catarina are both eager to understand the tacit rules for interaction here: they are working to engage with these new cultural norms that may contradict their expectations about speaking and silence. They *want* to do what teachers expect. My concern is that this shift asks students to abandon the messages of home without adequate preparation for what constitutes the "times you talk" or respect for those alternate models of being and interacting.

Further, Helen Fox's *Listening to the World* offers an important perspective: how might a student's home culture and its construction of silence shape her understanding of speech and silence within classrooms? Fox explores the patterns that characterize the written discourse of world-majority students (immigrants, children of immigrants, and traditionally underrepresented U.S. groups—those typically labeled "minorities"). These patterns include indirectness and "respectful omissions"; the emphasis on consensus and harmony in cultures that do not foreground individuality (at least as it is understood in the American construction); and the deferral to "original" wisdom, coupled with a sense of one's position within a hierarchy.[12] Such patterns are generally considered flaws or failures in American academic discourse. More work needs to be done in composition studies (perhaps in conjunction with communication or anthropology studies) to understand how such cultural patterns of respect shape the voices and silences of students in our classrooms, as well as how we can teach the patterns of academic discourse *as* valid discursive choices.

Dismantling the Active-Passive Dichotomy

Palmer believes, "We need to abandon the notion that 'nothing is happening' when it is silent, to see how much new clarity a silence often brings."[13] Confirming this, the students in my study resist the interpretation that silence signals disengagement or passivity. Many admit that this is certainly *possible*, reflecting on classmates whose silence may be a "staring at the walls thing" or "tuning out." While Sanjay sees listening as "inherently passive," he contends that silence does not mean there is no "mental activity . . . there *is* something getting done there." And at least one-third of the class spoke in their written reflections of their desire to *listen* and *absorb*, often accomplished only by being silent. Catarina defines her own silences "as reflectiveness . . . trying to pay attention and soak in the material. I don't think everyone does the whole staring at walls thing. . . . They're being quiet to just listen and pay attention." Such constructions evoke Olsen's praise of natural silences that are a "necessary time for renewal, lying fallow, gestation, in the natural cycle of creation."[14] While I think Olsen's formulation is helpful in reconsidering our definitions of silence, I am troubled that it too seems to rely on a notion of silence as *not producing* anything, a time where nothing is cultivated in preparation for later productivity. Quite differently, in my students' constructions, silence is itself the space, the energy, and the mindfulness of mental engagement.

For Lucy, silence signals that she is working to understand what others are saying. She says, "I just think it's really important for [teachers] to know . . . if you're quiet, it doesn't mean that you're not trying hard enough or that you're not a good student or that you're not paying attention. I almost feel like, because I'm quiet, *I am paying more attention* because I'm really trying to focus and really trying to understand." Silence, then, can be a process of active engagement with the ideas of others, "making meaning via language via others."[15]

I think it can be problematic to frame this (as many students did) in terms of "absorbing what has been said," because this casts thinking and "understanding" as passive processes. Rather, in these student reflections, I see a dynamic and engaged effort to take on the perspective of another through active, rhetorical listening: how and why might someone believe this? What leads her to this conclusion? Ratcliffe furthers this definition in describing the potential for rhetorical listening as "'a code of cross-cultural conduct' . . . listening signifies not only respect but also asks listeners to acknowledge, to cultivate, and to negotiate conventions of different discourse communities."[16]

My students' descriptions also evoke Elbow's "believing game," which necessitates "listening, affirming, entering in, trying to experience more fully, and restating—understanding from the inside."[17] Although different from typical academic discourse (what Elbow calls the "doubting game"), this should not be mistaken as being easier or less energetic than the more culturally acceptable "good student" behaviors. I also connect the type of active listening my students describe to isometric exercises in which muscles contract against some immovable object, but there is no motion in the affected joints and no reaction in the outside object. (One example of isometric exercise is tightening muscles by pushing against a wall.) So there is engagement, "flexing," without a visible display such as lifting a weight. Although it may appear as though little is happening, this type of training is "effective for developing total strength of a particular muscle or group of muscles. . . . This kind of training can provide a relatively quick and convenient method for overloading and strengthening muscles."[18] In this way, we might understand the energy of silence as "strengthening mental muscles" without an outward, measurable display.

Sandra advances the distinction about listening being "active," claiming, "I can bet that I pay much more attention to what is going on in class or around me than people who are speaking and adding to the conversation. . . . A talkative student does not always pay attention. Sometimes they are too involved with what they want to say to really comprehend what is happening in class." In this way, Sandra sees that to enter actively into the perspective of another, to "listen with the intent to receive,"[19] requires focused energy that necessitates concentration and, yes, silence. Sandra makes two critical distinctions between *mentally engaging* and *demonstrating* that engagement through speaking, between the narrowing in vision that may happen in speaking and the capacity to see multiple possibilities through silent reflection. Such constructions ask us to consider the sorts of mental interaction that discussion allows. When does a discussion leave space for a genuine engagement of ideas? How can we structure these interactions to allow us to entertain a range of possibilities without seeking closure into a unified, singular conclusion ("This is my position . . ." or "The truth is . . . ," etc.)? And when is the interaction we promote in class discussions a surface one—where words are exchanged, but little substantial effect is made?

Michael Heller's short "Proposal for Silence" offers one response to these questions. He envisions a "Concentration in Silence," an academic discipline of "inward-directed experiences" promoting reflective contemplation. He says, "We want our students to value and nurture their processes for finding wisdom, their spiritual lives, clarity, and creativity . . . contemplative education moves students *beyond the role of being passive listeners*."[20] Such a claim opposes the traditional construction that positions silence *as* passivity. While Heller's proposal may strike some as extreme, it invites us to consider what spaces for reflective contemplation are permitted within our classrooms. The pedagogy that Heller proposes suggests that we must have faith in students' motives and in their internal lives that cannot be measured, quantified. Unless we can abandon our need to quantify student behaviors, I am skeptical that Heller's radical proposal will have widespread appeal.

Reframing Silence as
Internal Conversation

For other students, choosing to be silent is not only a way to "stand under" the discourses and the perspectives of others, but it is also a means of figuring out one's own position. The Bakhtinian concept of "internalized voices" offers a useful framework in which to consider these students' reflections. Frank Farmer argues that Bakhtin's vision imagines

> a necessary striving with the voices we have internalized or assimilated from others—many of which we find compatible with our situated purposes, many of which we do not. The important point is that at any given moment, the voice we choose to call our own is made possible by all those other voices which vie for hegemony in our consciousness, which form the chorus of voices against which our own may be heard. It follows then, that what we call consciousness is dialogic through and through.[21]

But what do students see happening in this silence of listening? For Edward, it allows him time to maybe not develop a complete argument or a complete thought . . . but mull it about a bit. . . . I know that personally, when I'm quiet in this class, I'm taking in others' points of view on a certain discussion topic, thinking about it and trying to apply it to my own thoughts. . . . Or, sometimes if I'm having a hard time coming up with a thought or viewpoint on something, hearing others speak their mind motivates me to think and gives me something to work from.

In this way, silence is a space of possibility; choosing to be silent allows for the active construction of one's perspective through considering others' insights, using those as "something to work from," and "applying it to my own thoughts." So Edward's voice—his consciousness—whether externalized through speech or not, is "made possible" by witnessing the interaction of those competing discourses. His reflections bear out James Moffett's claim that "sustained attention to inner speech reveals ideas one did not know one thought, unsuspected connections that illuminate both oneself and the outside objects of one's thought."[22]

Belanoff describes silence as "intense, aroused attention, a set of mind that turns over and paws at, fingers experiences, emotions, events, and sensations within an enclosing silence."[23] In essence, silence invites critical thinking and engagement on multiple levels. Edward supports this claim, seeing his own silences in classes as "observing on so many levels. Observing your learning as well. Learning about the material. But you're also observing people. Their mannerisms. And you're getting a feel for them too. And that works into the whole 'clicking with the class.'" He and other students suggest such metacognition is not possible while speaking; contrary to our community wisdom, silence is the necessary medium through which one engages with and interacts critically with one's world.

For Edward, this observation is a particularly important activity in a writing class in which the discussion of anyone's paper may provide critical insight about his own writing. But more than that, remaining silent allows him the crucial opportunity to reflect on his learning, the classroom community, and the interrelationships developed there. Further, in light of the discussion in chapter 6, I believe it is possible to argue that the development of the classroom community as a space in which one might choose to speak is contingent for some students only upon this observation conducted through silence. Thus as O'Reilley asserts, "silent reflection and verbal witness"[24] are important, not simply as a personally directed endeavor, but because "a certain kind of contemplative life is synonymous with responsible behavior in a community."[25]

Several students express their preference for silence as "internal dialogue," a conversation one holds with oneself. Lucy says, "If it was up to me, I would just sit and listen all the time, answer questions in my head, to myself and my notebook." And Jenna notes that her "normal commenting . . . remains in my head."

But beyond that, silence can also be the space of working with one's multiple languages. Again, Lucy's reflections provide a vivid example, one that highlights a struggle experienced by students who feel they do not have adequate access to academic language. Believing that she lacks the English vocabulary and linguistic proficiency of other students, Lucy frequently feels intimidated, lacking "control over language." Framing this struggle as a process of "learning to be articulate,"[26] she describes the difference between speaking in the two languages like this:

> I grew up there [in Israel], so . . . I'm in control of the language and everything that comes along with that. . . . I don't have to stop and think of how to say what I'm thinking. When it's your first language, it's a lot easier to just articulate whatever is in your mind. It just comes out. Whereas now, I sometimes have to sit and process it. And I think, "OK, this is what I'm trying to say," and think if it makes any sense in English. Because sometimes I say things and I know that I am translating directly from Hebrew, [and] I know it's not the right way of saying it.

While her concerns are about literal translation, I suspect that such descriptions of the process of articulation may also resonate for those who do not see themselves as verbal thinkers. For example, a student who is primarily a visual thinker may encounter similar difficulties in shifting from visual imagery to a different symbolic system that lacks congruent expressions.

It is not simply a matter of familiarity with English that Lucy must negotiate. She says:

> A lot of times I think in Hebrew and there are words . . . that don't translate . . . especially feelings and words for emotions that you don't have in English. . . . It is, it's hard, because it just, it's so different, I mean the languages are so different . . . *words in different languages make you feel differently* because when there are words in English that I can't explain, I can't think of certain things that I think of in Hebrew. Because I can't translate it, so I just don't think of it. (emphasis added)

In some ways, Lucy faces an unwieldy task in translating the untranslatable— as she sees some concepts available to her only in her first language. It seems to me a tremendous loss when I consider where this often leaves Lucy—because of the difficulties of translation and the time this would entail, her capacity to think is limited to the language shared in oral discussion. Silence, then, is the only medium through which the range of Lucy's thinking can flourish, in which she is able to draw on her multiple discourses and their attendant ways of thinking.

There is often a second step to this translation process. If Lucy is able to move from Hebrew to English, then she must also move from English to Academic English by paying attention to "even just the words [other students] use. I try to connect my words to theirs and see if there's any common theme going there, and if not, I try to articulate it in a different way." Sometimes this struggling with internalized voices means working to locate a precise word; at other times, it might entail seeing how "her English" fits within an academic conversation. Such a challenge, I suspect, faces many students who perceive a distance between their home language and that of the classroom. Likewise, students not raised in middle-class or academically oriented homes may simply feel a nearly unbridgeable gap between their own language and that of the academy, of which they perceive their classmates to be fluent users. This linguistic struggle and negotiation make silence a precious commodity, important not just for discussion purposes but also for a student's development of academic discourse.[27]

Ultimately this leads me to reconsider not just the importance of student silence but also teacher-directed silence. Although infrequent (and infrequently mentioned in their interviews or written reflections), these silences have a profound impact for some students. They are

> positive when people are reflecting on what's going on . . . I think it's definitely a good thing when people are thinking about what's happening or what someone has just said. [And] just kind of thinking about, for me, thinking about what I'm going to say.

Catarina narrates the practice of one teacher who

> is always trying to get the class to speak and always trying to motivate the class to keep on topic and just discuss a film that we just watched or something that we just listened to. A lot of the times, though, right after he'll have read a passage or we'll have watched a really moving movie, everyone just kinds of sits and thinks about it for a little while. And the teacher never gets on our case to start talking right then. Because I think it's just kind of understood that we're thinking and gathering thoughts.

In this instance, then, there is a tacit agreement between the teacher and students about the importance of silence within a conversation. For Catarina this is clearly active space, one in which the work of the class *is* being done, albeit in a different form than is typically expected in the academy. In this way, she, her teacher, and her classmates are engaging in what Kalamaras sees as "natural silences [that] are not opposed to language but help to shape it in dynamic and generative ways."[28] Or, as Gere frames the relationship in "Revealing Silence," "Silence [can] engender speech."[29]

Another student narrates at length a similar moment she observed in another class. Students had been discussing an issue, but eventually the teacher

> just shut off the lights and we . . . were quiet for ten minutes. Kind of meditating, but not really, just looking into what we were thinking and then sharing it. . . . I think [the meditation time changes how people respond], because it makes me feel more grounded and kind of more confident because I feel like I can gather my thoughts, calm down, breathe, relax, and think what I have to say, and put it in order. And if I want to say, I say it, and if I don't, I don't. It just kind of, it's like gathering yourself . . . sometimes when I'm in a class where I get nervous, it's hard to gather myself. I feel like my mind is somewhere else, my body is nervous, and it's just impossible to talk.

For this student who registers nervousness and this reconnection as physical sensations, to gather herself when her mind is "somewhere else," such silence is essential.[30]

These practices of silence run counter to our mission of production—of texts, of interpretations, of words. O'Reilley connects the "noisiness" of education to the mandate for *quantity*: the impulse toward mastery of an enormous body of texts can often overload students, leaving them little space and time for reflection.

Perhaps one lesson to take from these student reflections is this: "requiring" less might paradoxically produce more.

Challenging Our Definitions of Speaking, Silence, and Learning

Another way to frame a redefinition of classroom silence is through assessing students' learning effected through speaking and silence. In their reflections, many students, including those who self-identify as quiet students, wrote of their own need to speak in order to learn, although not necessarily in the terms we teachers use. Michael notes that while he seldom speaks during his classes, "Students often take the discussion beyond the classroom. I have many times walked out of a class and talked to a classmate about a topic without ever speaking in class." Another student notes, "When I talk about something that's the easiest way for me to prepare myself for an exam. Because it makes things clearer for me to hear them out loud, instead of just reading or scanning [the material] in your mind . . . you kind of explain it to yourself in your own mind." But because she prefers not to speak in class, she has developed a study group in which each person explains concepts from their classes. In these situations focused on academic material, she finds she does not experience the same silences and struggles for language: "I talk about it in my language and the way that I understand it, so it's probably less polished than the way it's presented in class . . . it's very different from what happens in class. It's almost like I look back at what the professor said and what I understood and my notes, and [then] I put it all together in my own words and explain it." Such comments suggest to me how limited my own sense of learning is—unconsciously, I have believed that academic conversations and "real" learning only happen in the presence of a teacher who is guiding, shaping, and evaluating that conversation.

The comments of several students problematize for me our disciplinary assumptions about the value of speaking in class. As discussed in previous chapters, these students generally see discussion as a way of demonstrating to the teacher the knowledge that one has already mastered—that one can get the "right answer." And for some, their motivation to speak comes from a need to stay focused on the course material. For instance, Christina finds that she "gets sidetracked" easily when she is only listening and thus prefers more "hands-on" activities. And Julia notes, "Talking during class keeps me from getting bored, and it also keeps me interested in what we're doing. If I don't talk during class, then I get really bored and don't really listen a lot." When speaking's primary value is its capacity to maintain the attention of the speaker, I think we may be shortchanging our students and ourselves in not teaching them how to be better listeners—how to be more fully and actively present through other ways of being in the classroom.

Along with several other students, Julia theorizes that this learning-through-speaking does not work for everyone equally well. As Sarah notes, "I think some people need to speak in order to understand things. They get a connection when they're discussing something. But I don't really know because I don't need to do that." Such comments provide an important caution about conflating our goal (the construction of knowledge) with an outward manifestation. As these students point out, learning can take place in many modes; no one style of learning fits all students. A more useful construction might be Kalamaras's: "As an authentic mode of knowing, silence is not opposed to language, which I define as the human capacity for vocal and written utterance. Rather, silence and language act in a reciprocal fashion in the construction of knowledge."[31] Understood in this way, both silence and language are necessary in our classrooms to reach the range of learners.

Pushing the connection between silence and the construction knowledge in a different direction, Sarah contends that the speech of quiet students feels inherently weightier: "When they finally do speak up, it's obviously something important to say . . . the statement they are saying will be much more profound than something another student says [who] is always participating or just saying something to say something." I don't want to endorse a simplistic dichotomy of quality of speech versus quantity of speech. But I do agree that for a quiet student to move beyond her typical silence, listeners may assume this statement is somehow more significant, a distinction that changes how that utterance is heard. Elbow echoes Sarah's construction. In "Silence: A Collage," in which he connects the generative power of freewriting and silence, Elbow claims an interest in "the silent ones. *When* they say something, their words often seem remarkably powerful: more umph, more conviction, more presence—their words more 'gathered up.'"[32]

Catarina offers one final way to reconsider the silences in our class. Reflecting on the common silences that followed after someone read a piece of writing, she says, "Simply because we don't want to share the writing should be a sign that we are actually taking heart in them and not using them trivially. In that way, I can't believe that the silence in that instance is all bad. I think it is wonderful." In this way, silence became a crucial way for Catarina to measure students' seriousness about their writing and their exploration of important and challenging topics. Such an interpretation runs exactly counter to my own: early in the semester I had worried that these silences indicated disengagement with, even disdain for, the practice. Catarina hypothesizes that more people might

> like to say something, but they are in awe of something thought-provoking that has already occurred. Personally I feel like I don't want to disturb the aura that comes into the room when someone says something truly unique or special. I like that feeling that people get when they are truly understanding a person's point of view.

Silence, then, becomes a sign of respect for what has been said and for the power of another person's words. For students to take each other's writing and speaking that seriously seems like a powerful learning experience indeed.

The work of Anne French Dalke supports Catarina's rereading of silence. In her work on women writers of the early twentieth century, Dalke claims that silence, rather than connoting absence and lack, indicates a "fullness," a space of possibility and openness that *cannot* be fulfilled by speech. Rather, "Silence [is] a gift . . . when we do not speak, we may listen, hear, understand, even communicate in other ways. Silence may function as an altogether alternative means of communication, not dependent on speech for fulfillment."[33] Or, as Gere argues, "Seeing silence in continuity with speech invests it with qualities of affirmation and fullness."[34] While such interpretations of silence directly challenge our values of how classrooms are supposed to work, they simultaneously offer us ways to reimagine the dynamics of such classes that often *do not* work as we hope. In such visions and voices, there is indeed a hope for new kinds of conversations that respect the voices and silences of all students.

Embracing Silence?
Some Implications for Teaching

The rest is silence.

—William Shakespeare, *Hamlet*

I return to the quote from Edward's interview with which I began this chapter: "It isn't a crime to be quiet." I think this simple assertion is one of the most important insights I gained from this research, one of the things I most want other teachers and theorists to understand. *It isn't a crime to be quiet.* The stories we tell about the silences in our classrooms—ones that focus on silence as absence or lack—are not the only ones that can be told.

Committed to dialogue as a means of knowing, I think it is possible and responsible for teachers to work to create those conditions and opportunities in which students can and will choose to speak. The data that form the basis of this project lead me to conclude that our sustained attention to the relationships within the classroom can positively influence students' decisions to speak and may simultaneously provide us with concrete ways to talk about rhetorical issues in writing. But our stories should be augmented and complicated by those that our students tell about their active choices to speak or to be silent.

What concerns me more than the occasional student whose silence does mark passivity or resistance are the students such as Catarina, Edward, Lucy, Sarah, Sanjay, and many of their classmates. While they are using the space of silence as a space of engagement to actively enter into the ideas of others, to consider and construct their responses, to translate their thoughts into the language of the classroom, they have learned that to be silent is a risky prospect; most likely it is not adequate, at least in their teachers' estimations. I worry that we may "lose" students like these through what may feel like an overwhelming pressure to demonstrate their thinking and to perform in a particular model, one that simply does not work for all students. And, as those who have sat through a "quiet" class can attest, their silences can become increasingly, devastatingly problematic for us and for them. I worry that we may, at times, lose sight of our goal—students' engagement and learning—for *one* of the ways to reach that goal—dialogue.

So along with Belanoff, I find that what I ultimately am "campaigning for is space and time in our classrooms and in our scholarly lives for looking inward in silence."[35] Such a commitment respects the individual student's "right to silence" and also actively incorporates practices of silence in our classroom, acknowledging that "silence . . . already exists in each of our classrooms; it can become rich and productive."[36]

In the dialogue between students' versions and the authorized ones in our discipline I have presented in this chapter, it seems clear that silence *can* generate speech. But silence also invites thinking, deliberative engagement, reflection, and the negotiation of internalized voices. Powerful silences. However one frames this active, internal process, I believe this is a critical skill to foster in all of our students, not just those we view as "silent." Thus we need to develop and implement strategies and pedagogies that foster such generative silences. Perhaps the first challenge in this process is a change of vision for both teachers and students, because

> in most places where people meet, silence is a threatening experience. It makes us self-conscious and awkward; it feels like some kind of failure. So the teacher who uses silence must understand that a silent space seems inhospitable at first to people who measure progress by noise. Silence must be introduced cautiously; we must allow ourselves to be slowly re-formed in its discipline before it can become an effective teaching tool. But once the use of silence is established with a group, once we learn that we make progress in being quiet . . . then silence becomes a potent space for learning.[37]

How very different this classroom might feel (and work) from those that measure "progress" in the quantity of dialogue and seek to avoid the "problem" of silence.

So what would these practices designed to foster reflection and generative silences look like? How might we foster and incorporate such dialogic silences?

Freewriting is one of the more obvious possibilities, in which the absence of structure, audience expectations, or rhetorical limitations invites reflective, meditative explorations. From personal experience, the stories of my students, and our professional literature, I believe this practice can be a liberating experience. On the other hand, I suspect that many students are unwilling or incapable of allowing themselves the freedom to write incoherently, to commit to paper the vagaries of their minds. So freewriting can only form one part of a range of teaching practices that will invite introspection and reflection.

I would also like to explore essay assignments and classroom activities that ask students to engage with the ideas of others. Collages, essays in which students are encouraged to engage with the ideas of the text *and* work out their own thinking, and inkshedding that invites students to respond to both texts and other students all seem to be promising possibilities to explore in their emphasis on dialogic thinking. However, it seems important to also recognize that the potential of these kinds of assignments may be limited. The encouragement toward meditation and reflection, toward engaging and making the sorts of connective leaps these students experience in silence, may not "fit" with traditional models of what a good essay—what "good academic thinking"—looks like. Reflection and meditation are often seen as brief developmental stages that help students get to a strong, clear thesis and the demonstration of knowledge, not as ends in themselves.

I do not want to belabor the process-product argument, but I do want to acknowledge how complicated it may be to conceive a pedagogy that invites silence. In a slant way, this pedagogy challenges some of our deepest-held notions about good writing and good thinking.

I believe, as well, that I need to place a greater emphasis on activities that foreground active listening as an integral part of dialogue and learning. Ratcliffe's work challenges us to create a space for listening as a productive, but generally overlooked, rhetorical strategy. But even very small gestures, such as asking students to directly respond to a previous speaker or to frame their comments in connection to another contribution, can effect positive change in developing the active practice of silence.

In addition, teacher-directed silences provide an important resource for developing dialogic silences as well. For example, I am eager to experiment with building into my class more frequent and extended deliberate silences. Several students in my study suggested how powerful those moments can be when teachers ask students to *simply think*. I suspect such mindful silences will result in deeper engagement, more intense thinking, and ultimately better discussions.

I will work as well to be more conscious of not filling all of those uncomfortable pauses in class with my own or my students' voices. Recently I heard a colleague assert that only thirty to sixty seconds of silence could be tolerated in a classroom. I agree to some extent: when my model of the good classroom is one of constant conversation, I get nervous. Each second can feel like a new failure. Such silences will not be easy; I do not mean to suggest that they are. But silences, even (or especially?) the uncomfortable ones, invite participants to *do* something. Keeping in mind that

> reflection often grows out of discomfort even though it may afford
> delight and thrive in mystery and paradox. Educational settings
> have to create some level of dis-ease, some disruptions of student
> and teacher expectations: ways to disrupt our students' routines and
> cause them discomfort, which is undoubtedly going to cause us
> discomfort too.[38]

Rather than seeing silence as requiring the antidote of speech, I might more fruitfully see it as a productive disruption of expectations. And as my students' stories suggest, it is possible to understand those silences not as signifying tension but as a space where *work is being done*.

This short list of possible practices to incorporate silence more deliberately and more mindfully is by no means exhaustive. Just as our discipline has worked to foster dialogue, I believe we need to pay attention to creating productive silences. We should also detangle assessment and evaluation from speaking because it simply does not serve our larger goals, particularly when we devote so little time to *teaching* speaking in our classes. Catarina felt an "aura of dread" permeating our class when students learned they had to "talk a lot." If "encouraging" dialogue should promote genuine learning and engagement, and we do so through measures that are, for so many students, inordinately anxiety producing and disruptive, then we have found a profoundly counterproductive "solution" to this perceived problem. Allison protested the connection she sees enacted in her classes and suggested that teachers develop alternate forms of evaluation. Her suggestion seems worth exploring. If evaluation of classroom performance is a priority, then our definition of "participation" must include all of those behaviors that comprise good class citizenship: respectful, active listening; feedback to peers; participation in writing activities; and self-assessment. Still other students questioned the "science" of evaluation. Do quality and quantity matter? Does one "really good" contribution matter more or less than several "less good" observations? What standards does a teacher use? How can a teacher assess the "participation" in small-group discussions?

Belanoff contends that "Silence, meditation, reflection, and contemplation are being pushed aside by the growing octopus tendrils of standards and assessment" and remarks, ironically, "Students ought to reflect on their own time, not on ours. Anyway, how on earth can we grade/assess/evaluate silence or create standards for it?"[39] Together, Allison, Catarina, and Belanoff point to a serious difficulty I face in proposing a pedagogy that invites silence. As a teacher, how can I monitor what is happening? Whether anything is happening? How can I see, measure, and encourage progress? And how can I justify this practice to my students and colleagues?

Perhaps I need to have more faith—in my students, in myself, and in silence.

Finally, I am led to consider the importance of talking with my students about speaking and being silent in classes. The profound mismatch between students' visions and my own has led me to realize how little I (and probably many other teachers) have made explicit about teachers' expectations, goals, and values. When I introduced this project to my class, one student I had reflexively labeled "painfully quiet" asked *why teachers had never asked them about their silences before*. In some ways, this tension reminds me of Tompkins's comparison between learning to teach and sex: one is supposed to be good at it, but one is certainly not encouraged to talk about it.

So at the risk of sounding corny, I think I need to implement an ongoing dialogue about dialogue with my students. Speaking and silence and the pressure to "participate" in the classroom loom larger than the proverbial elephant in the corner. I ask students to speak, and they may comply, resist, or fail to meet my expectations; they may disappoint, delight, or astonish me. I put requirements on my syllabi. I may consider this "participation" in their grades, but if there is no real conversation about classroom conversation, about the values my students and I have, the goals we have for such conversations, and the criteria against which students are going to be assessed, then how can I ethically evaluate students' oral participation?

I can see several important areas for further research as well, including a companion study to this current one, in which I would investigate the perspectives of highly vocal "good" students or a project that explores constructions of silence across several classes, disciplines, or institutions. It is not enough to do research about silence in my classroom; I need to investigate it *with* my classes.

At times during this research, I frankly wondered if my students and I were looking at and thinking about the same class. Without a clearer sense of my goals, my students will inevitably misread me, and I will, in all probability, misread them too. And I will, in a sense, continue fumbling in the dark alone, trying to "fix" a dynamic I do not fully understand. In light of the conversations I have had with colleagues over the years of this research, I know I am not the only one struggling with this isolated, isolating endeavor.

While I am not envisioning the sort of in-depth conversation that went into this research, one of the ways to begin to bridge this gap is through more explicit discussion and co-investigation with my students about speaking and silence in classrooms. What do I want to happen through discussion? What makes a "good discussion"? How is this different in an academic setting from other sorts of conversations? What do students see happening in class discussions—those they see as successful, uncomfortable, interesting? What expectations do students have about how classes should "work"? Why do I think it is so important for students to speak anyway? What encourages their speech? Why does silence trouble me? What value do they see in speaking or being silent?

Some of this conversation certainly might take place in oral dialogue. The overwhelming number of students who volunteered to participate in the second part of my research suggests that students are willing, even eager, to talk about their speaking and silence in classes. Beyond that, I think it is important to ask students to become more aware of their own behaviors and attitudes, just as I do in becoming self-reflective about my values and my pedagogy. As some of the students in my study reported, writing informal reflections invited them to become self-aware and helped them identify patterns in their behavior of which they had not been aware. In doing so, they were able to confront difficult dynamics, to understand their learning styles more clearly, and, sometimes, to feel encouraged to speak more frequently. In short, to speak or to be silent became a more conscious, powerful choice.

I think it is important, then, to acknowledge that there is more than one way to be a contributing member of a class, more than one way of learning and engaging. In her research paper investigating the causes of shyness and quietness, Sarah offers this metaphor: "Some were too shy to sing. That's why poetry was born." I believe it is my responsibility not to abandon dialogue but to acknowledge *both* the singing and the poetry my students create.

Not long before I began this chapter, I saw this advertisement in a magazine: four children with shaved heads, clad in the traditional orange robes of Buddhist novice monks sit in prayerful postures, their hands in their laps. The three boys in the background have closed eyes and contemplative expressions; even their posture exudes silent serenity. The smallest child in the center looks at the camera, the giant bubble of his chewing gum only partially obscuring his joyful grin. The caption is: "I see laughter in a moment of silence." This notion of silence, whose meaning is so apparent, provides a symbolic shift, a vehicle through which a person "can see the world differently."

The advertisement for Transitions Lenses extols a product that allows people "to see life in a whole new light." While I am more than a little squeamish over both the use of religious metaphors in commercial enterprises and finding my critical insights in a magazine, I find myself identifying a bit with that impish little gum chewer. Given our culture's "privileging of sight,"[40] I want to borrow this metaphor briefly to help us learn to hear silence in a new register, a new tone.

What can happen when we think about silence through these new contexts my students propose? What is gained by changing our dominant metaphors? What if the filters we use to hear silence are shades of openness, not signs of failure? Can we teachers do the same—see silence in a whole new light? Can we look beyond our shared meaning of the "problem of silence" to see—and hear— its possibilities as well?

Glenn concludes *Unspoken: A Rhetoric of Silence* with this:

> Silence . . . is an invitation into the future, a space that draws us forth. There is not one but rather many silences, and like the spoken or written, these silences are an integral part of the strategies that underlie and permeate rhetoric. Thus, silence is at once inside the spoken and on its near and far sides as well. In a hallway, a committee meeting, a courtroom, at a news conference, on a mesa, a reservation, or in a classroom, silence is a linguistic art, one that needs only to be named in order to be understood.[41]

Catarina contemplates, "I can't believe silence . . . is all bad. I think it is wonderful." It is my hope that we as teachers can learn to see and hear silence the way Catarina does—full of wonder, beyond our doubts, encompassing awe and inquisitiveness, surprise and speculation.

Appendix
Teaching Practices

One might assume that the focus and goal of this book—to problematize the notions of student silence within pedagogies of dialogue—would mean that I do not value student discussion. But in fact I place a great deal of emphasis on student interaction as a primary teaching and learning strategy. A substantial portion of time in the classes I teach is spent in student interaction, in a variety of forms. My grounding in feminist theory, critical teaching, expressivist theories, and collaborative learning leads me to value the interaction of student voices as a means of constructing knowledge; sharing, testing, and complicating assumptions; and improving writing.

However, within my teaching I attempt to be conscious of several things and take these into account as I plan class activities and evaluate students' participation in them. Many of these practices will be explored directly and indirectly here through my students' reflections on their experiences in classrooms.

1. *Each student has a unique sense of what is safe and comfortable in the classroom.*

As a teacher, I try to respect these boundaries, even if they make difficult what *I* want to do. Therefore, it is rare that I will require a particular student to speak. If I do, it is part of an exercise in which I ask everyone in the class to contribute something. In these instances, I will typically give students a moment to write in journals or to talk to a partner to prepare to speak aloud. Such "round-robin" discussions are prompted by an open-ended question. For example, after reading two short pieces about Northampton, Massachusetts, I asked my students to offer their insights about what they liked, disliked, agreed with, disagreed with, questioned, or responded to in either piece. In doing so, I hoped to have offered a range of possible types of response from observation to analysis. This kind of discussion tends to move very slowly; there is repetition, and sometimes little follow-up. However, I believe that this practice emphasizes that everyone's voice is equally valuable, and that many types of contributions are important in developing our thinking.

Some may argue that it is not necessary or productive to focus on students' comfort in this way, that it is by being made *uncomfortable* that we grow and learn. My concern, supported by the research in this book, is that the discomfort students experience in being required to speak often proves to be counterproductive, silencing.

2. *Dialogue can happen in many ways.*

In conjunction with my first premise—that students have particular boundaries that should be respected—and in light of my research, I strive to balance the types of discussion forums and formats I create. Most of the students I have interviewed about classroom silence have expressed their preference for smaller, more intimate discussion groups. However, some have found this format less productive. Some students prefer specific, narrowly defined tasks, while others thrive on an open task that gives them a maximum degree of self-direction.

To accommodate these diverse learning styles, I strive to vary the classroom format as much as possible (and as is reasonable). Therefore, in a typical semester, I ask students to work in groups ranging from pairs to the full class, with projects stretching from responding to a specific set of questions to more amorphous tasks with various ways they might be completed, in formats where I (or another student) moderate/direct to more free-form discussions. My expectation is that this will provide students with circumstances that are amenable to their own boundaries; my hope is that this may challenge students to try out new roles in a range of circumstances.

3. *Although it is often seen in opposition to "discussion," writing in the classroom can indeed be a dialogue.*

This point, more often (and more easily) assumed in a computer classroom, leads me to several "dialogue activities" that take place in silence as students use writing as a means of discussion. In one activity, each student briefly summarizes in writing his research interests, central focus, and what draws him to this topic. The abstract is then passed to other students who respond with their own questions and suggestions for resources. As the exercise progresses, students begin connecting their responses to previous ones, highlighting particular previous responses, and so on. At the end, each student receives feedback that is essentially a dialogue in print on his research topic. I find frequently that students who are less likely to orally contribute suggestions are willing to share their thoughts in writing.

Another activity I like to use to suggest that writing does indeed "count" as dialogue is inkshedding. I find this works best when students bring in a short piece of writing, perhaps a reading response or an analytical piece on some common assignment such as a publication response. In class, students pass their writing to another student who will read and respond to it by commenting in the margins, highlighting resonant passages, and so on. As with the previous exercise, often a dialogue takes place as students comment on the initial writing as well as the responses forming a thoughtful, written conversation.

4. *It is important to give space to various class formats—individual work, small groups, and large-group work.*

In a typical class, I try to blend these three groupings so as not to suggest that one is more or less important than another. Each format has a specific task and purpose; one is not preparation for another. In doing so, I suggest that thinking and learning happen in all sorts of settings, even those without the presence (and direction) of a teacher.

5. *When students work in small groups, it is important to have these groups "report in" to the larger group about what they explored.*

From a practical standpoint, this means that many perspectives will be heard and the class will develop a broader, shared understanding or knowledge base. It is also critical because it is an additional way of hearing student voices. That is, students elected spokespersons will share not just their own perspectives but also those of various group members. In doing so, a forum is provided whereby quieter students' voices are heard in a large group, even if *they* themselves do not choose to share. I believe that for students who are less confident, such validation becomes critical.

6. *Sometimes teachers can be most effective as agents of learning by saying little; their silence may invite more active engagement by students.*

This has seemed a particularly effective strategy in student conferences. Rather than use these as a space where I offer my oral evaluation of a student's essay (that could easily be translated into written feedback), I try to background my authoritative teacher-voice to leave space for the student's. This practice models a type of learning where a student is not most concerned with absorbing the right answer, at least according to the teacher.

7. *Listening is participating too; it should be acknowledged as being as important as speaking.*

To give credit for listening is difficult; some students' body language and expressions indicate attention to a speaker, while others' simply do not. However, in my syllabus, I emphasize listening as a contribution to classroom interaction. For all students, I attempt to "teach listening" through various strategies. A particular one is the practice of linking one's comments to a previous one. This is particularly effective when small groups are reporting their findings to the large group. This encourages attention to the words of others, as students seek opportunities to fit their responses into a larger framework. I am also particularly struck by the practice of asking students, during a full-class interaction, to frame their contributions as a direct response to a previous speaker. In doing so, I believe students begin to *listen to each other* rather than performing for the teacher. This encourages students to engage in a more genuine dialogue, where ideas are developed, explored, and challenged through the words of other students.

8. *Silence in the classroom can be seen as productive.*

I work, each class day, to build in moments of silence. While noise and energy signify that work is being done and that learning is happening, so too can concentrated silence. To this end, I build in freewriting time each day. For some students, this quiet can be disorienting; *this* cannot be learning. After asking one class about their reactions to freewriting, many students suggested that I extend the time devoted to this exercise because it gave them space to think and write and explore: to learn about what was in their own heads. I adopted another of their suggestions as well: to provide time for students to share their freewriting if they chose—to acknowledge and honor what can be done in those brief moments of silence. In this way, what appears a "private" activity, one that does not foster dialogic interaction, is "sociable."[1]

Because this practice has proven so useful, I strive to integrate silence in other ways. For instance, I often pose a question and ask students to wait silently for a period of time before speaking. I also experiment in other ways. What happens when group dialogue is stopped and transferred to writing, either private or shared? What is the effect of the *teacher's* silence in a dialogue? And, indeed, I think it is important not to follow every silence with speaking. Speaking is not the opposite or antidote to silence; rather, it is another valid form of thinking.

Notes

Chapter 1

1. Linda Brodkey, "Writing Critical Ethnographic Narratives," in *Writing Permitted in Designated Areas Only* (Minneapolis: University of Minnesota Press, 1996), 113.

2. In brief, Finkel's position is that such a model of the Great-Teacher-as-Teller focuses on teaching as the goal as the genuine objective of education: "*Good teaching is the creating of those circumstances that lead to significant learning in others*" (Donald L. Finkel, *Teaching with Your Mouth Shut* [Portsmouth, NH: Boynton/Cook, 2000], 8, emphasis added.)

3. John Dewey, *Experience and Education* (New York: Collier Books, 1938), 19.

4. Paulo Freire, *Pedagogy of the Oppressed,* trans. Myra Bergman Ramos (New York: Continuum, 1994), 70–74.

5. Kenneth Bruffee, "Collaborative Learning and the 'Conversation of Mankind,'" *College English* 46, no. 7 (1984): 642.

6. Hebzibah Roskelly, "The Risky Business of Group Work," in *The Writing Teacher's Sourcebook*, ed. Gary Tate, Edward P. J. Corbett, and Nancy Myers (New York: Oxford University Press, 1994), 141.

7. Along with Roskelly, I "believe in group work" and the learning that takes place. Dialogue and constructed learning are a central theoretical underpinning in my teaching. I try to incorporate varied formats that ask students to draw on different types of speaking and responding. (For example, I try to validate the importance of hearing *each* student's voice through practices such as asking every student to offer any sort of comment or response to a text. In addition to larger discussions, my class also spends a great deal of time working in small groups of various sizes with different principles of organization: completely

random, student selected, teacher selected, etc.) I also suggest alternate models of conversation—through inkshedding and dialogues that take place in written, rather than spoken, form.

In addition to oral discussion, I try to emphasize other skills and behaviors that I believe are crucial to dialogue and constructed learning. What space is there for reflective thinking within the classroom? In his proposal for an academic "Concentration in Silence," Michael Heller claims, "Contemplative education moves students beyond the role of being passive listeners" (Michael Heller, "A Proposal for Silence," *Friends Association for Higher Education* [1996–1997], 7). With this in mind, I try to build into my class space for *thinking*, what Kenneth Bruffee calls "internal dialogue." For example, I typically offer time to consider a topic before beginning oral discussion or another interaction, or I ask for reflective writing at the end of class to consider its content or interaction. Also, I try to emphasize the importance of listening. Through strategies such as asking students to link their oral contributions or their unvocalized thoughts to a previous one, I believe I can help them see their own ideas within a context, inflected by the voices and discourses that surround them.

The appendix at the end of this book offers a fuller description of some of my teaching practices, and chapter 4 gives a brief overview of the writing class in which this study took place.

8. Janet Collins, *The Quiet Child* (London: Cassell, 1996), 3.

9. Collins, *The Quiet Child*, 148.

10. Michelle Fine and Lois Weis, eds., *Beyond Silenced Voices: Class, Race, and Gender in United States Schools* (Albany: State University of New York Press, 1993), 1.

11. Robin Patric Clair, *Organizing Silence: A World of Possibilities* (Albany: State University of New York Press, 1998), 47.

12. The work of Kay M. Losey (*Listen to the Silences: Mexican American Interaction in the Composition Classroom and Community* [Norwood, NJ: Ablex, 1997]) is an exception that emphasizes my point: Losey's project is to explore the silences of Mexican-American students in a California community college. Notable to me is the minimal place the voices of the students occupy in this text, despite her professed interest in silent students' voices.

13. Linda Brodkey, "Introduction: Poststructural Theories, Methods, and Practices," in *Writing Permitted in Designated Areas Only* (Minneapolis: University of Minnesota Press, 1996), 8, emphasis in origianal.

14. Mimi Orner, "Interrupting the Calls for Student Voice in 'Liberatory Education': A Feminist Poststructuralist Perspective," in *Feminisms and Critical Pedagogy*, ed. Carmen Luke and Jennifer Gore (New York: Routledge, 1992), 83.

15. Stephen M. Fishman and Lucille Parkinson McCarthy, "Boundary Conversations: Conflicting Ways of Knowing in Philosophy and Interdisciplinary Research," *Research in the Teaching of English* 25, no. 4 (1991): 419–68; Nancie Atwell, "Everyone Sits at a Big Desk: Discovering Topics for Writing," *English Journal* 74, no. 5 (1985): 35–39; Marcia Curtis and Elizabeth Klem, "The Virtual Context: Ethnography in the Computer-Equipped Writing Classroom," in *Re-Imagining Computers and Composition: Teaching and Research in the Virtual Age*, ed. Gail E. Hawisher and Paul LeBlanc (Portsmouth, NH: Boynton/Cook, 1992), 155–72; Lester Faigley, "Subverting the Electronic Notebook: Teaching Writing Using Networked Computers," in *The Writing Teacher as Researcher: Essays in the Theory and Practice of Class-Based Research*, ed. Donald A. Daiker and Max Morenberg (Portsmouth, NH: Boynton/Cook, 1990), 290–311.

16. Joy Ritchie, "Confronting the 'Essential' Problem: Reconnecting Feminist Theory and Pedagogy," in *Feminisms and Composition: A Critical Sourcebook*, ed. Gesa E. Kirsch, Faye Spenser Maor, Lance Massey, Lee Nickoson-Massey, and Mary Sheridan-Rabideau (Boston, MA: Bedford/St. Martin's Press, 2003), 79.

17. E. David Wong, "Challenges Confronting the Researcher/Teacher: Conflicts of Purpose and Conduct," *Educational Researcher* 4, no. 24 (1995): 23.

18. Owen van den Berg, "The Ethics of Accountability on Action Research," in *Ethical Issues in Practitioner Research*, ed. Jane Zeni (New York: Teachers College Press, 2001), 85.

19. Suzanne M. Wilson, "Not Tension but Intention: A Response to Wong's Analysis of the Researcher/Teacher," *Educational Researcher* 24, no. 8 (1995): 20.

20. Jane Zeni, "Introduction," in *Ethical Issues in Practitioner Research*, ed. Jane Zeni (New York: Teachers College Press, 2001), xv.

21. Marian M. Mohr, "Drafting Ethical Guidelines for Teacher Research in School," in *Ethical Issues in Practitioner Research*, ed. Jane Zeni (New York Teachers College Press, 2001), 3.

22. Floyd Hammack, "Ethical Issues in Teacher Research," *Teachers College Record* 99, no. 2 (Winter 1997): 249.

23. This class, taught in a dorm in the Orchard Hill section of the University of Massachusetts at Amherst campus, met on Tuesdays and Thursdays from 11:15 to 12:30. It represented a cross-section of majors and was composed entirely of first-semester students.

24. Hammack, "Ethical Issues in Teacher Research," 254.

25. The decision to designate this core group of interviewees as the "focal" students was a deliberate one, as I hope to shift our attention away from vocal students to explore the experiences of this other population in our classes.

26. Stephen R. G. Jones, "Was There a Hawthorne Effect?," *The American Journal of Sociology* 98, no. 3 (November 1992): 451.

27. These experiments of workplace behavior took place at the Hawthorne Plant of the Western Electric Company in the 1920s and 1930s; they were designed to test whether workers' behavior and performance change following increased attention or changes in working conditions. "The Hawthorne effect has come to occupy a central role in the methodology of experiments and continues to have a widespread influence in social science . . . and especially in the research of the psychology of education" (Jones, "Was There a Hawthorne Effect?," 451).

28. Gordon Diaper, "The Hawthorne Effect: A Fresh Examination," *Educational Studies* 16, no. 3 (1990): 264.

29. Keith Basso, "'To Give Up on Words': Silence in Western Apache Culture," *Southwestern Journal of Anthropology* 26, no. 3 (Autumn 1970); Cheryl Glenn, *Unspoken: A Rhetoric of Silence* (Carbondale: Southern Illinois University Press, 2004); Carol Gilligan, *In a Different Voice: Psychological Theory and Women's Development* (Cambridge, MA: Harvard University Press, 1982); Mary Field Belenky, Blythe McVicker Clinchy, Nancy Rule Goldberger, and Jill Mattuck Tarule, *Women's Ways of Knowing: The Development of Self, Voice, and Mind* (New York: Basic Books, 1986).

30. Berg, "The Ethics of Accountability on Action Research," 86.

31. Madeline R. Grumet, "The Politics of Personal Knowledge," in *Stories Lives Tell: Narrative and Dialogue in Education*, ed. Carol Witherell and Nel Noddings (New York: Teachers College Press, 1991), 69.

32. Some students took this invitation to tell stories quite literally and narrated identifiable, individual moments. Others read this request more broadly and wrote in less specific terms about common occurrences or typical behaviors and reactions. I see these as stories about students' educational experiences, although perhaps different in content and intent than those about particular events.

33. Kathleen Casey, "The New Narrative Research in Education," *Review of Research in Education* 21, no. 1 (1995): 220.

34. Paul Anderson, "Simple Gifts: Ethical Issues in the Conduct of Person-Based Composition Research," *College Composition and Communication* 49, no. 1 (1998): 75.

35. Because this process of commenting explicitly on another student's behavior seems particularly complicated, I was conscious to keep these reflections private and to use pseudonyms to protect both the writer and the subject

of the reflections. In several instances I chose not to include material that reflected negatively and unproductively on another student's behavior, since both the writer and subject were easily identifiable.

36. Gesa E. Kirsch, *Ethical Dilemmas in Feminist Research: The Politics of Location, Interpretation, and Publication* (Albany: State University of New York Press, 1999), 14; Fishman and McCarthy, "Boundary Conversations," 424.

37. Anne J. Herrington, "Reflections on Empirical Research: Examining Some Ties between Theory and Action," in *Theory and Practice in the Teaching of Writing: Rethinking the Discipline*, ed. Lee Odell (Carbondale: Southern Illinois University Press, 1993), 40.

38. Fishman and McCarthy, "Boundary Conversations," 423.

39. I. E. Seidman, *Interviewing as Qualitative Research: A Guide for Researchers in Education and the Social Sciences* (New York: Teachers College Press, 1991), 3; Michael Quinn Patton, *Qualitative Evaluation and Research Methods* (Newbury Park, CA: Sage, 1990), 278; Fishman and McCarthy, "Boundary Conversations," 423; Herbert J. Rubin and Irene S. Rubin, *Qualitative Interviewing: The Art of Hearing Data* (Thousand Oaks, CA: Sage, 1995), 1; Kirsch, *Ethical Dilemmas in Feminist Research*, 4.

40. Seidman, *Interviewing as Qualitative Research*, 7.

41. Patton, *Qualitative Evaluation and Research Methods*, 282.

42. Ruth Ray, "Composition from the Teacher-Researcher Point of View," in *Methods and Methodology in Composition Research*, ed. Gesa Kirsch and Patricia A. Sullivan (Carbondale: Southern Illinois University Press, 1992), 175–76.

43. More extensive introductions will be provided in chapter 4.

44. That is, I eliminated two students from the interview pool based on their atypical or outlying responses that seemed to connect only tangentially to the central questions of the study. Such responses would certainly help me map out the outer margins of this population, but I suspected that interviews with these students might not provide an adequate quantity of focused data to produce a nuanced picture of that student's perceptions of speaking and silence within a composition classroom. With my relatively small data sample, it seemed more important and more useful to explore the trends rather than the isolated cases within the class.

45. Patton, *Qualitative Evaluation and Research Methods*, 390.

46. Ibid.

47. For instance, students' references to calling on students, lecturing, first-day-of-class activities, seating arrangements, peer feedback, in-class writing,

small group work, and so on seemed to me logically in a related grouping of "teaching practices."

48. Patton, *Qualitative Evaluation and Research Methods*, 384.

49. Robert E. Stake, "Case Studies," in *Handbook of Qualitative Research*, ed. Norman K. Denzin and Yvonna S. Lincoln (Thousand Oaks, CA: Sage, 1994), 237.

50. Many students spoke of unfamiliar subject matter as potentially leading them to (temporary) silences, but few moved beyond these initial statements, suggesting that this was not a particularly useful avenue for my exploration. Likewise, the theme of "difference" showed up only briefly in response to direct questions from me.

51. Brodkey, "Writing Critical Ethnographic Narratives," 113.

52. Kirsch, *Ethical Dilemmas in Feminist Research*, 14.

Chapter 2

1. Hedris of Cornwall, *Silence: A Thirteenth-Century French Romance*, ed. and trans. Sarah Roche-Madhi (East Lansing, MI: Colleagues Press, 1992), l. 3012, 3116.

2. When Silence is outwardly male, a masculine pronoun is used.

3. Hedris of Cornwall, *Silence: A Thirteenth-Century French Romance*, l. 2068.

4. Linda Brodkey, "Telling Experiences," in *Writing Permitted in Designated Areas Only* (Minneapolis: University of Minnesota Press, 1996), 150.

5. Eleanor Kutz and Hepzibah Roskelly, *An Unquiet Pedagogy: Transforming Practice in the English Classroom* (Portsmouth, NH: Boynton/Cook, 1991), 45.

6. Cheryl Mattingly, "Narrative Reflections on Practical Actions: Two Learning Experiments in Reflective Storytelling," in *The Reflective Turn: Case Studies in and on Educational Practice*, ed. Donald A. Schön (New York: Teachers College Press, 1991), 237.

7. Joseph Trimmer, "Telling Stories about Stories," in *Narration as Knowledge: Tales of the Teaching Life*, ed. Joseph Trimmer (Portsmouth, NH: Boynton/Cook, 1997), 57.

8. Patricia Shelley Fox, "Finding the Selves We Set Aside," in *Narration as Knowledge: Tales of the Teaching Life*, ed. Joseph Trimmer (Portsmouth, NH: Boynton/Cook, 1997), 42.

9. Kim Stafford, "Pilgrimage at the Penitentiary," in *Narration as Knowledge: Tales of the Teaching Life*, ed. Joseph Trimmer (Portsmouth, NH: Boynton/Cook, 1997), 29.

10. Lynn Bloom, "Teaching College English as a Woman, *College English* 54, no. 7 (1992): 825.

11. Kutz and Roskelly, *An Unquiet Pedagogy*, 3.

12. Ibid., 4–5.

13. Elizabeth Chiseri-Strater, *Academic Literacies: The Public and Private Discourse of University Students* (Portsmouth, NH: Boynton/Cook, 1991), 39.

14. Victor Villanueva Jr., "Shoot-Out at the I'm OK, You're OK Corral," in *Narration as Knowledge: Tales of the Teaching Life*, ed. Joseph Trimmer (Portsmouth, NH: Boynton/Cook, 1997), 44.

15. Sharon J. Hamilton, "Nancy's Promise," in *Narration as Knowledge: Tales of the Teaching Life*, ed. Joseph Trimmer, (Portsmouth, NH: Boynton/Cook, 1997), 101.

16. Joy Passante, "Up River, Down River, and Across the Aegean," in *Narration as Knowledge: Tales of the Teaching Life*, ed. Joseph Trimmer (Portsmouth, NH: Boynton/Cook, 1997), 19.

17. Lad Tobin, "Reading Students, Reading Ourselves: Resisting the Teacher's Role in the Writing Class," *College English* 53, no. 3 (1991): 343.

18. Kutz and Roskelly, *An Unquiet Pedagogy*, 4–5.

19. Elizabeth Rankin, *Seeing Yourself as a Teacher: Conversations with Five New Teachers in a University Writing Program* (Urbana, IL: NCTE Press, 1994), 1.

20. Nancy Sommers, "Editor's Choice: The Language of Coats," *College English* 60, no. 4 (1998): 424.

21. Fox, "Finding the Selves," 35.

22. Brodkey, "Introduction," 20.

23. Charles Moran, "'From a High-Tech to a Low-Tech Writing Class, and Back: A Study in Transition' Or, 'You Can't Go Home Again,'" Presentation, Conference on College Composition and Communication, March 1996, 3, emphasis in original.

24. Herman Melville, "Bartleby, the Scrivener: A Story of Wall Street," in *Great Short Works of Herman Melville*, ed. Warner Berthoff (New York: Harper and Row, 1969), 57.

25. Bonnie TuSmith, "The Englishes of Ethnic Folk: From Home Talkin' to Testifyin' Art," *College English* 58, no. 1 (1996): 49.

26. TuSmith, "The Englishes of Ethnic Folk," 50.

27. Ira Shor, *Empowering Education: Critical Teaching for Social Change* (Chicago: University of Chicago Press, 1992), 2.

28. Shor, *Empowering Education*, 2.

29. Ira Shor, *When Students Have Power: Negotiating Authority in a Critical Pedagogy* (Chicago: University of Chicago Press, 1996), 12.

30. Brodkey, "Introduction," 8, emphasis in original.

31. Mattingly, "Narrative Reflections on Practical Actions," 236.

32. U.S. Constitution.

33. *Rock the Vote Blog*, "Afghans Killed for Registering to Vote," http://www.blog.rockthevote.com/2004_06_27_archive.html (accessed August 10, 2004).

34. bell hooks, *Talking Back: Thinking Feminist, Thinking Black* (Boston, MA: South End Press, 1989), 12.

35. Fox, "Finding the Selves," 34.

36. Moran, "'From a High-Tech to a Low-Tech Writing Class,'" 2, emphasis in the original.

37. Passante, "Up River, Down River, and Across the Aegean," 37.

38. Sondra Perl, "Facing the Other: The Emergence of Ethics and Selfhood in a Cross-Cultural Writing Classroom," in *Narration as Knowledge: Tales of the Teaching Life*, ed. Joseph Trimmer (Portsmouth, NH: Boynton/Cook, 1997), 182.

39. Trimmer, "Telling Stories about Stories," 59.

40. Hunter McEwan, "Narrative Understanding in the Study of Teaching," in *Narrative in the Study of Teaching, Learning, and Research*, ed. Hunter McEwan and Kieran Egan, (New York: Teachers College Press, 1995), 166.

41. Carol Witherell and Nel Noddings, "Prologue: An Invitation to Our Readers," in *Stories Lives Tell: Narrative and Dialogue in Education*, ed. Carol Witherell and Nel Noddings (New York: Teachers College Press, 1991), 4.

42. Brodkey, "Introduction," 8.

43. Villanueva, "Shoot-Out at the I'm OK," 48.

44. Ibid., 49, emphasis in original.

45. Trimmer, "Telling Stories about Stories," 59.

46. Jane Tompkins, *A Life in School: What the Teacher Learned* (Reading, MA: Addison-Wesley, 1996), 114.

47. Hamilton, "Nancy's Promise," 2.

48. Rankin, *Seeing Yourself as a Teacher*, 29.

49. Alan Brinkley, Betty Dessants, Michael Flamm, Cynthia Fleming, Charles Forcey, and Eric Rothschild, "Classroom Discussions," *The Chicago Handbook for Teachers: A Practical Guide to the College Classroom* (Chicago: University of Chicago Press, 1999), viii.

50. Brinkley et al., "Classroom Discussions," 33.

51. Freire, *Pedagogy of the Oppressed*, 77.

52. Mikhail Bakhtin, "Marxism and the Philosophy of Language," in *The Rhetorical Tradition: Readings from Classical Times to the Present*, ed. Patricia Bizzell and Bruce Herzberg (Boston, MA: Bedford Books,1990), 938.

53. Katerina Clark and Michael Holquist, *Mikhail Bakhtin* (Cambridge, MA: Harvard University Press, 1984), 348.

54. Kenneth Burke, *Grammar of Motives* (New York: Prentice Hall, 1945).

55. Shor, *Empowering Eduation*, 87.

56. bell hooks, *Teaching to Transgress: Education as the Practice of Freedom* (New York: Routledge, 1994), 8.

57. Mary Rose O'Reilley, *The Peaceable Classroom* (Portsmouth, NH: Boynton/Cook, 1993), 32–33.

58. David Bartholomae and Anthony Petrosky, "Preface" in *Ways of Reading: An Anthology for Writers*, 3rd ed. (Boston, MA: Bedford Books, 1993), ix.

59. Becky Ropers-Huilman, "Still Waters Run Deep: Meaning of Silence in Feminist Classrooms," *Feminist Teacher* 10, no. 1 (1996): 3, emphasis added.

60. Although the equation of silence with absence is certainly a dominant paradigm in feminist theory, it is important to acknowledge that not all theorists see silence as inherently problematic. For example, in *Unspoken: A Rhetoric of Silence*, Glenn argues persuasively that silence is "the most undervalued and *under*-understood traditional feminine site and concomitant rhetoric art" (2, emphasis in original); silence can be a powerful, persuasive form of communication. I explore such readings in the final chapter.

61. Muriel Saville-Troike, "The Place of Silence in an Integrated Theory of Communication," in *Perspectives on Silence*, ed. Deborah Tannen and Muriel Saville-Troike, (Norwood, NJ: Ablex, 1985), 9–10.

62. Sociolinguist Adam Jaworski offers a similar interpretation: "A kind of macro silence is the desired state for most political dictatorships . . . silence is an indicator of misfortune and crime and allows tyrants to do anything they desire as long as their activities are not exposed to the public, commented on,

or protested against. The silence of oppression is a desirable state for all power groups that are afraid that the mere expression and exchange of opinions or the free flow of information will threaten the existing status quo. This is why there are often legal measures introduced for not allowing political opponents to speak out" (*The Power of Silence: Social and Pragmatic Perspectives* [Newbury Park, CA: Sage Publishers, 1993], 115–16).

63. Magda Gere Lewis, *Without a Word: Teaching beyond Women's Silence* (New York: Routledge, 1993), 41.

64. Tillie Olsen, *Silences* (New York: Delacourt Press, 1978), 6.

65. Clair, *Organizing Silence: A World of Possibilities*, 47.

66. Myra Sadker and David Sadker, *Failing at Fairness: How Our Schools Cheat Girls* (New York: Touchstone Books, 1995), 170.

67. Jill McLean Taylor, Carol Gilligan, and Amy M. Sullivan, *Between Voice and Silence: Women and Girls, Race and Relationships* (Cambridge, MA: Harvard University Press, 1995), 3.

68. Ibid., 40.

69. Ibid., 44–45.

70. Belenky et al., *Women's Ways of Knowing: The Development of Self, Voice, and Mind*, 24–25.

71. These are Anyon's terms, created via an examination of the students' parents' incomes, occupations, and other related data.

72. Jean Anyon, "From Social Class and the Hidden Curriculum of Work," in *Rereading America: Cultural Contexts for Critical Thinking and Writing*, ed. Gary Columbo, Robert Cullen, and Bonnie Lisle (Boston, MA: Bedford Books, 1995), 57.

73. hooks, *Teaching to Transgress*, 149.

74. Shor, *Empowering Education*, 94.

75. Henry Giroux, *Theory and Resistance in Education: A Pedagogy for the Opposition* (New York: Bergin and Garvey, 1983), 66.

76. Shor, *When Students Have Power*, 12–13.

77. Sadker and Sadker, *Failing at Fairness*, 172.

78. Chiseri-Strater, *Academic Literacies*, 64.

79. Ibid., 16.

80. hooks, *Teaching to Transgress*, 39–40.

81. Ibid., 41.

82. Bruffee, "Collaborative Learning," 89.

83. Taylor et al., *Between Voice and Silence.*

84. Losey, *Listen to the Silences: Mexican American Interaction in the Composition Classroom and Community,* 150.

85. Clair, *Organizing Silence,* 53.

86. Losey, *Listen to the Silences,* 152.

87. Frank D. Walters, "Writing Teachers Writing and the Politics of Dissent," *College English* 57, no.7 (1995): 833.

88. Elizabeth Ellsworth, "Why Doesn't This Feel Empowering?: Working through the Repressive Myths of Critical Pedagogy," in *Feminisms and Critical Pedagogy,* ed. Carmen Luke and Jennifer Gore, (New York: Routledge, 1992), 106–107.

89. James Berlin, "Composition and Cultural Studies," in *Composition and Resistance,* ed. C. Mark Hurlbert and Michael Blitz (Portsmouth, NH: Boynton/Cook, 1991), 53–54.

90. Ellsworth, "Why Doesn't This Feel Empowering?" 107.

91. James Berlin, "Poststructuralism, Cultural Studies, and the Composition Classroom: Postmodern Theory in Practice," in *Professing the New Rhetorics: A Sourcebook,* ed. Theresa Enos and Stuart C. Brown (Englewood Cliffs, NJ: Blair Press, 1994), 478.

92. Orner, "Interrupting the Calls for Student Voice," 77.

93. Barney G. Glaser and Anselm L. Strauss, *The Discovery of Grounded Theory: Strategies for Qualitative Research* (New York: Aldine de Gruyter, 1967).

Chapter 3

1. Peter Elbow's description of freewriting resonates here:

> Unfocused exploring is probably my main use of freewriting: I have a thought, perhaps out of the blue and perhaps in the midst of writing something (even while writing something else), and I give myself permission to pursue it on paper in an uncontrolled way wherever it wants to go, even if it digresses (as it usually does). This kind of freewriting is precious to me because my mind seems to work best—at the level of ideas as well as syntax—when I allow it to be uncontrolled and disorganized. *I cannot find as many perceptions if I try to stay on one track or be organized. And the not-stopping seems to build mental momentum,* helps me get wound up or get rolling so that more ideas come.

See Elbow, "Toward a Phenomenology of Freewriting," in *Everyone Can Write: Essays toward a Hopeful Theory of Writing and Teaching Writing* (New York: Oxford University Press, 2000), 118, emphasis added.

Although I resist the idea that my thought processes are unorganized or uncontrolled, Elbow's assertion, that active control in writing and thinking processes limits possibilities and the space to pursue these possibilities, can indeed build a "mental momentum" that might not be possible otherwise seems an accurate description of my own thinking. For me, this suggests a crucial distinction between my thinking and *demonstrating* that thinking.

2. Irene Papoulis, "Appearance as Shield: Reflections about Middle-Class Lives on the Boundary," in *Writing Ourselves into the Story: Unheard Voices from Composition Studies*, ed. Sheryl Fontaine and Susan Hunter (Carbondale: Southern Illinois University Press, 1993), 274–75.

3. Ibid., 281.

4. Susan Kirtley, "The Woman behind the Curtain: Reflections of a Female Teaching Assistant," unpublished paper.

5. Parker Palmer, *To Know As We Are Known: A Spirituality of Education* (San Francisco: Harper and Row, 1983), 80.

6. Krista Ratcliffe, "Rhetorical Listening: A Trope for Interpretive Invention and a 'Code of Cross-Cultural Conduct,'" *College Composition and Communication* 51, no. 2 (1990): 205–206, emphasis in original.

7. Palmer, *To Know as We Are Known*, 81.

8. David Bartholomae, "Writing with Teachers: A Conversation with Peter Elbow," *College Composition and Communication* 46, no. 1 (1995): 62–71; Patricia Bizzell, *Academic Discourse and Critical Consciousness* (Pittsburgh, PA: University of Pittsburgh Press, 1992).

Chapter 4

1. University of Massachusetts, Amherst, Office of Institutional Research, *UMass at a Glance 2000–2001*, http://www.umass.edu/oapa (accessed May 19, 2005).

2. University of Massachusetts, Amherst, Student Activities Center, *Registered Student Organizations*, http://www.umass.edu/campact/category/html (accessed May 19, 2005).

Chapter 5

1. Tobin, "Reading Students, Reading Ourselves," 343.

2. TuSmith, "The Englishes of Ethnic Folk," 39.

3. Kutz and Roskelly, *An Unquiet Pedagogy*, 4.

4. Rankin, *Seeing Yourself as a Teacher*, 29.

5. Joseph Harris, *A Teaching Subject: Composition since 1966* (Upper Saddle River, NJ: Prentice Hall, 1997), 106, 109.

6. Michel Foucault, "The Means of Correct Training," in *The Foucault Reader*, ed. Paul Rabinow (New York: Pantheon Books, 1984), 197.

7. Ibid., 199.

8. Trimmer, "Telling Stories about Stories," 57.

9. Erica Scott, "Composing as a Person: Gender, Identity, and Student Writing," *WILLA* 10 (2001), http://www.scholar.lib.vt.edu/ejournals/WILLA/fall01/scott.html, 8 (accessed May 15, 2005).

10. It seems important to note, however, that for this student resistance to "work" to any substantial degree, it needs to be a collective effort. And while I do not mean to diminish the impact of such resistance, a teacher's power always trumps students' power, if only through the power to grade.

11. hooks, *Teaching to Transgress*, 205.

12. Ibid., 204.

13. O'Reilley, *The Peaceable Classroom*, 97.

14. Susan Kirtley, "What's Love Got to Do with It?: Eros in the Writing Classroom," in *A Way to Move: Rhetorics of Emotion and Composition Studies*, ed. Dale Jacobs and Laura Micciche (Portsmouth, NH: Boynton/Cook, 2003), 66.

15. hooks, *Teaching to Transgress* 13, 21.

16. Sometimes plans that go awry can have unexpected benefits: I had planned to "sit out" this exercise to allow students to interact without my interference beyond establishing the initial parameters for the exercise. But when I saw a student who remained unpaired and who did not join another group, I asked that student to work with me. Later in the chapter, I discuss her responses to this activity and others; she calls into question the interpretation that this was an unqualified success, despite what Catarina says.

17. O'Reilley, *The Peaceable Classroom*, 90.

18. hooks, *Teaching to Transgress*, 203.

19. Ibid., 194.

20. This feels like an unwieldy situation to me: part of me *wants* to agree with Edward and argue that students should feel free to explore and express their identities within the confines of the classroom. But where is the line? And how do I, as a teacher, negotiate it? Part of the process of schooling is a process of socialization, learning how to fit in with the rules and norms of school.

Perhaps part of my occasional resistance to Edward's behavior and humor is this: I often ended up feeling that he should "know better." As he acknowledges, he was "flying in my face," aware of the boundaries of acceptable behavior but pushing at them anyway. I want to be able to view these expressions of identity with equanimity, to see these, in Robert Brooke's terms, as a productive underlife. And yet it did not always *feel* that way, as I often feared an utter loss of control if I did not stop Edward and a shutting down (by Edward and others) if I did.

21. Taylor et al., *Between Voice and Silence*, 40.

22. Bartholomae, "Response," 85.

23. Ellsworth, "Why Doesn't This Feel Empowering?," 101.

24. Peter Elbow, *University of Massachusetts Writing Program Newsletter*, Amherst, MA. October 1999, n.p.

25. O'Reilley, *The Peaceable Classroom*, 106.

26. Orner, "Interrupting the Calls for Student Voice," 87.

27. Peter Elbow, "Inviting the Mother Tongue: Beyond 'Mistakes,' 'Bad English,' and 'Wrong Language,'" in *Everyone Can Write: Essays Toward a Hopeful Theory of Writing and Teaching Writing* (New York: Oxford University Press, 2000), 326–29.

28. Ibid., 324.

29. Brodkey, "Writing Critical Ethnographic Narratives," 113.

30. Peer feedback and small groups will be discussed further in the next chapter, when I examine community relationships in greater depth.

31. O'Reilley, *The Peaceable Classroom*, 107.

32. Lester Faigley, "Competing Theories of Process: A Critique and a Proposal," *College English* 48, no. 6 (1986).

33. Roskelly, "The Risky Business of Group Work," 141.

34. Catherine E. Lamb, "Beyond Argument in Feminist Composition," *College Composition and Communication* 42, no. 1 (1991): 13, 18–19, emphasis in original.

35. Mike Rose, *Lives on the Boundary: A Moving Account of the Struggles and Achievements of America's Educationally Underprepared* (New York: Penguin Books, 1990), 47–48.

Chapter 6

1. Shor, *When Students Have Power*, 10.

2. Rankin, *Seeing Yourself as a Teacher*, 29.

3. Villanueva, "Shoot-Out at the I'm OK," 43, emphasis in original.

4. It is tempting to locate students' perceptions of "identity" along the expressivist-social construction faultline (or the extreme representations of it) that defines much of composition.

Do students' perceptions correspond to the early work of so-called expressivists, in which a great deal of attention is paid to the connection between writing, the development (or expression) of identity, and personal experience? For example, Donald Murray's seminal work, *A Writer Teaches Writing* (Dallas, TX: Houghton Mifflin, 1985), offers students a journal exercise for recording experience and personal development. And Peter Elbow's work also seems appropriate to consider. In his discussion of five meanings of voice, he connects resonant voice to identity: "Aristotle clearly implies what common sense tells us: we are not persuaded by [an] implied author as such—that is, by the creation of a dramatic voice that has a skillfully trustworthy *sound*; we are actually only persuaded if we believe that dramatic voice *is* the voice of the actual speaker or author" (Elbow, "What Is Voice in Writing?," in *Everyone Can Write* [Oxford: Oxford University Press, 2000], 214.)

Do students understand identity in postmodern terms, "the self, not as signifier of one 'I', but the coming together of many 'I's'"? (See bell hooks, *Yearning: Race, Gender, and Cultural Politics* [Boston, MA: South End Press, 1992.])? Do students understand that identity is socially constructed, as many compositionists, including John Trimbur, Lester Faigley, and Patricia Sullivan, have explored in their work on the composition classroom? Do they see the classroom, in Mary Louise Pratt's terms, as a Contact Zone in which "cultures meet, clash, and grapple with each other, often in contexts of highly asymmetrical relationships of power"? (See Mary Louise Pratt, "Arts of the Contact Zone," *Profession* 91 [1993]: 34).

Here I want to be precise about the ways I am using the term *identity* in this text, given that my students' definitions are not entirely congruent with many of the prevailing definitions that circulate in our professional discourse. I follow the lead of the students I interviewed and use the term to mean "*who I perceive myself to be, at any given moment in time, as it is constituted in this social world.*" For many, this concept of identity seemed, paradoxically, to be both fixed and responsive, with self-definition coexisting with (and being shaped by) the constructions of others. In short, these students often seemed to balance competing theories of identity, blending Romantic individualism and postmodern sensibilities. While many were skeptical that one's identity is already written by culture, a socially constructed product, they held that "the individual is a constituent of culture." (See Lester Faigley, "Competing Theories of Process," 535.)

Interestingly, when I instigated conversations about the role that *difference* might play in identity, such as the role of gender or race in relation to speaking and silence, students were notably, resoundingly silent.

Most participants in the study articulated the notion that each person has some core identity, personality, "self"—a set of characteristics analogous to blood type or eye color. However, this identity can (and often does) change in response to one's environment and outside influences. For example, during their interviews, some students spoke of particular identities (in the postmodern sense) shaping their behaviors, attitudes, and perceptions of themselves. For example, Catarina traced the influence of her Baptist upbringing, while Lucy investigated how her Israeli worldview distinguished her from her "typical American classmates." Both, however, acknowledge that one year of college has begun to influence them; each sees herself as "different" from when she began college, shaped by these experiences as well as by how others define her. Thus many of the students implicitly drew on a notion of identity congruent with Robert Brooke's use of Erving Goffman's work—in particular, in the ways identity is a function of social interaction and social organizations, providing roles that imply certain kinds of identities.

The term *community*, likewise, has multiple definitions: students in a particular major; those from a geographic region; and those who shared a distinctive characteristic, religion, race, style of dress, preference in music, and so on, or participated in a shared activity (such as Marching Band) could be (and often were) explicitly considered a "community." However, the definition that my students (and therefore I) relied upon was essentially, "*those people I have something in common with because we are members of the same class and have a set of shared experiences.*" Being a member of this community does not depend on choice or more significant interpersonal connections, although for many these did develop.

I argue that if these representations of identity and community shape how students interact in our classrooms, then it is important for us to understand the terms they use and the questions they ask in constructing those narratives. For me to move ahead to critique—of their naive, Romantic notions, for example—is to blithely replace one narrative with another, one partial view of the interactions in a classroom with another, without finding a way to address students' concerns and my own.

5. Research on patterns of interaction (including that of Myra Sadker and David Sadker and Deborah Tannen) suggests that women students would experience this newfound silence more extensively. However, students in this class described the move to college in remarkably similar ways, often using identical terms to describe their experiences.

6. Shor, *When Students Have Power*, 42.

7. In the final chapter, I explore some American cultural perspectives on silence.

8. Belenky et al., *Women's Ways of Knowing*, 37.

9. Shor, *When Students Have Power*.

10. In fact, Julia, a highly vocal student, says, "Basically, I would say that *whenever I feel like saying something, I say it*" (emphasis added). This suggests an area for further exploration: Julia constructs her speaking in terms of feeling and reaction, while many of the quieter students speak of the thinking and analytical processes that shape their decision to speak or to be silent. Does this pattern hold true for other students? If so, what might this tell us about how we value those highly vocal students?

11. Ellsworth, "Why Doesn't This Feel Empowering?," 105.
Many scholars, including bell hooks, Kay Losey, and Myra Sadker and David Sadker, argue that women and students of color fear being judged intellectually inadequate by their peers and consequently do not speak in class, while their white male counterparts continue to be highly vocal. My research corroborates their findings, given the frequency of such anxieties reported by Lucy (born in Israel) and Sanjay (of Indian descent). What is less apparent, though, are the challenges to these gender- and race-based propositions, namely, that all of the students, including the white men, report similar concerns. (I have not included them here to avoid repetition.) The most significant differences I could discern upon closer reading were these: both Lucy and Sanjay had developed productive ways to deal with, even control, their concerns about their peers' evaluation of their speech and writing. Sanjay assesses the rhetorical situation, makes informed choices about "appropriate" topic choices, and focuses on the audience, ethos, and meaning in revision. Lucy's concerns for perceived deficits lead her to seek additional guidance from instructors and to create study groups with classmates—two strategies that increased both her knowledge base and her self-confidence and substantively improved her writing.

12. Orner, "Interrupting the Calls for Student Voice," 83.

13. Ellsworth, "Why Doesn't This Feel Empowering?," 107.

14. This comment was particularly striking to me. I often ask students to share a sentence from the final draft of a paper because I think of this as an eminently low-stakes way to speak in class and a "celebratory" conclusion to a project.

15. Peter Elbow, "Closing My Eyes When I Speak," in *Everyone Can Write: Essays Toward a Hopeful Theory of Writing and Teaching Writing* (New York: Oxford University Press, 2000), 97.

16. Brodkey, "Introduction," 8.

17. Bruffee, "Collaborative Learning," 642.

18. Chiseri-Strater, *Academic Literacies*, 39.

19. Villanueva, "Shoot-Out at the I'm OK," 44.

20. Bruffee, "Collaborative Learning," 642, 645.

21. Peter Elbow and Pat Belanoff, *A Community of Writers: A Workshop Course in Writing*, 3rd ed. (Boston, MA: McGraw-Hill, 2000), xxvii, xxiii.

22. Bizzell, *Academic Discourse*, 136.

23. Pratt, "Arts of the Contact Zone," 40.

24. I was interested to note that she cited the last day of class as an example of this intolerance. We had a discussion led by students about the final publication. I had seen this discussion as fairly engaged: students spoke passionately about what they liked about essays in the publication (generally about style or the revisions that led to these products), occasionally dipping into what I saw as a good-spirited exchange about the *ideas* of the essays. One essay in particular—dealing with teenagers' choice of clothing and construction of a particular image—garnered this sort of attention. In my teaching journal, I wrote this:

> Nicole spoke immediately, asking a question about how people responded to Kurt's essay and the issues the essay brought up. (Something like, "We feel like it's okay to criticize people who have money and spend it on clothes from the Gap, but are we willing to see people who go to the Salvation Army in the same way? And how come?") Interesting—lots of response, although not directly in response to her questions. More about the issue of clothes and image. Both pro and con. And at some point there was a bit of debate, people responding directly to each other. It's the conversation I find myself fantasizing about as "good teaching"—there's this intense interaction, not because I've forced it or directed it or done very much except provide the conditions for it to happen. (OK, occasionally I asked a question or tried to redirect to Nicole's original question.)
>
> Interesting. Meg said, "It's the last day of class! Let's not fight, OK?" And people quieted down a bit. This was a pretty telling moment. Confrontation as some way destructive of community?
>
> Nicole asked Kurt (eventually) if it was OK that we talked about his essay. He seemed somewhat surprised that she even asked.

As I recall, I had felt satisfied with this: the class ended on an engaged yet critical note, focused on student writing. In my excitement over that, I essentially ignored the issue that Meg pointed out and Sarah later reflected on.

25. He also points out that greater intimacy may ultimately close some topics, since participants know how others will respond to a particular topic. Citing an example relating to an ongoing discussion about a floormate's relationship, he muses:

> It got to the point, we had tried to tell her so many times and she just wasn't listening, to the point where she told us to stop telling her or else she'd move off the hall. And so no one discusses that anymore. And that wouldn't have happened if we didn't know her. If we had just met her, then

it wouldn't have been our business. And so, one, the topics never would have come up, and, two, we would have never [thought] to put it in [that] way. It's kind of a catch-22, don't you think?

26. Harris, *A Teaching Subject*, 106–107.

Chapter 7

1. Pat Belanoff, "Silence: Reflection, Literacy, Learning, and Teaching," *College Composition and Communication* 52, no. 3 (2001): 400.

2. George Kalamaras, *Reclaiming the Tacit Dimension: Symbolic Form in the Rhetoric of Silence* (Albany: State University of New York Press, 1994), 1, 4–5, emphasis in original.

3. Erica Scheurer, *"A Vice for Voices": Emily Dickinson's Dialogic Voice from the Borders*. PhD diss., University of Massachusetts at Amherst, 1993.

4. Cheryl Glenn, *Rhetoric Retold: Regendering the Tradition from Antiquity through the Renaissance* (Carbondale: Southern Illinois University Press, 1997), 176.

5. Charles Suhor, "The Pedagogy of Silence in Public Education: Expanding the Tradition," in *Presence of Mind: Writing and the Domain beyond the Cognitive*, ed. Alice Glarden Brand and Richard L. Graves (Portsmouth, NH: Boynton/ Cook, 1994), 36.

6. Belanoff, "Silence: Reflection, Literacy, Learning, and Teaching," 417.

7. Anne Ruggles Gere, "Revealing Silence: Rethinking Personal Writing," *College Composition and Communication* 53, no. 2 (2001): 206.

8. Glenn, *Unspoken*, 151.

9. Lewis, *Without a Word*, 40–41, 47.

10. Saville-Troike, "The Place of Silence," 10–11.

11. Of course, this raises a question about what makes a student "typical" and suggests that there is in fact some model student.

12. Helen Fox's work (*Listening to the World: Cultural Issues in Academic Writing* [Urbana, IL: NCTE Press, 1994]) reminds me of one student in my study who eventually confessed his confusion when I asked for feedback about the class. From his writing, I knew that he was critical, engaged, and insightful. Yet his responses to me were minimal. After several interactions (and my growing irritation), he pointed out to me that in his home culture, it simply "isn't done" to question a teacher in the ways I was inviting.

13. Palmer, *To Know As We Are Known*, 80.

14. Olsen, *Silences*, 6.

15. Ratcliffe, "Rhetorical Listening," 208.

16. Ibid., 210.

17. Peter Elbow, "The Believing Game: A Challenge after Twenty-Five Years," in *Everyone Can Write: Essays toward a Hopeful Theory of Writing and Teaching Writing* (New York: Oxford University Press, 2000), 77.

18. Micromedex, Inc., "Isometric Exercise," *Hendrick Health System*, http://www.ehendrick.org/healthy/00047540.html (accessed March 2, 2002).

19. Ratcliffe, "Rhetorical Listening," 209.

20. Heller, "A Proposal for Silence," 7, emphasis added.

21. Frank Farmer, *Saying and Silence: Listening to Composition with Bakhtin* (Logan: Utah State University Press, 2001), 60.

22. James Moffett, "Writing, Inner Speech, and Meditation," *College English* 44, no. 3 (1982): 235.

23. Belanoff, "Silence," 404.

24. O'Reilley, *The Peaceable Classroom*, 32.

25. Ibid., 77.

26. This construction is troubling to me, as Lucy's writing throughout the semester and her extensive reflections in her interviews reveal to me that she is both highly inquisitive and articulate. Self-reflective about her own behaviors and experiences, she has provided me with much rich and complex data.

27. A related example of this comes from Catarina's reflections on being in the chorus for several years. This has "just kind of ingrained in me that you rehearse everything." She finds this carries over to her classroom behaviors ("I'm just very used to thinking about what I'm going to say and when I have a presentation to do for a class, I rehearse it at least forty times just so that I'm very positive I know what I'm going to say and I just can't do things on the fly . . .") and other sorts of communication, such as leaving phone messages at work for her supervisors.

28. Kalamaras, *Reclaiming the Tacit Dimension*, 5.

29. Gere, "Revealing Silence," 218.

30. Lucile Burt narrates a similar experience in "Liberty Bell," *Teacher Magazine* 13, no. 3 (2001). Upon ringing a bell at the beginning of her class, followed by a period of silence, she could "make myself present for a new class . . . silence, blissful silence, in days otherwise cluttered with noise. When class began, it always did so from a calm place" (43).

31. Kalamaras, *Reclaiming the Tacit Dimension*, 8.

32. Peter Elbow, "Silence: A Collage," in *Everyone Can Write: Essays toward a Hopeful Theory of Writing and Teaching Writing* (New York: Oxford University Press, 2000), 174, emphasis in original.

33. Anne French Dalke, "'On Behalf of the Standard of Silence': The American Female Modernists," *Soundings: An Interdisciplinary Journal* 78, nos. 3–4 (1995): 465.

34. Gere, "Revealing Silence," 207.

35. Belanoff, "Silence," 420.

36. Ibid., 419.

37. Palmer, *To Know As We Are Known*, 241.

38. Belanoff, "Silence," 420.

39. Ibid., 418.

40. Ratcliffe, "Rhetorical Listening," 201.

41. Cheryl Glenn, *Unspoken*, 160.

Appendix

1. Elbow, "Toward a Phenomenology of Freewriting," 120.

Bibliography

Anderson, Paul. "Simple Gifts: Ethical Issues in the Conduct of Person-Based Composition Research." *College Composition and Communication* 49, no. 1 (1998): 63–89.

Anyon, Jean. "From Social Class and the Hidden Curriculum of Work." In *Rereading America: Cultural Contexts for Critical Thinking and Writing*, edited by Gary Columbo, Robert Cullen, and Bonnie Lisle, 45–60. Boston, MA: Bedford Books, 1995.

Atwell, Nancie. "Everyone Sits at a Big Desk: Discovering Topics for Writing." *English Journal* 74, no. 5 (1985): 35–39.

Bakhtin, Mikhail M. *The Dialogic Imagination: Four Essays*. Edited by Michael Holquist. Translated by Caryl Emerson and Michael Holquist. Austin: University of Texas Press, 1981.

———. "Marxism and the Philosophy of Language." In *The Rhetorical Tradition: Readings from Classical Times to the Present*, edited by Patricia Bizzell and Bruce Herzberg, 63–74. Boston, MA: Bedford Books, 1990.

Bartholomae, David. "Response." *College Composition and Communication* 46, no. 1 (1995): 84–87.

———. "Writing with Teachers: A Conversation with Peter Elbow." *College Composition and Communication* 46, no. 1 (1995): 62–71.

———, and Anthony Petrosky. "Preface." In *Ways of Reading: An Anthology for Writers*, edited by David Bartholomae and Anthony Petrosky, v–xiii. 3rd ed. Boston: Bedford Books, 1993.

Basso, Keith. "'To Give Up on Words': Silence in Western Apache Culture." *Southwestern Journal of Anthropology* 26, no. 3 (Autumn 1970): 213–30.

Belanoff, Pat. "Silence: Reflection, Literacy, Learning, and Teaching." *College Composition and Communication* 52, no. 3 (2001): 399–428.

Belenky, Mary Field, Blythe McVicker Clinchy, Nancy Rule Goldberger, and Jill Mattuck Tarule. *Women's Ways of Knowing: The Development of Self, Voice, and Mind*. New York: Basic Books, 1986.

Berg, Owen van den. "The Ethics of Accountability on Action Research." In *Ethical Issues in Practitioner Research*, edited by Jane Zeni, 83–91. New York: Teachers College Press, 2001.

Berlin, James. "Composition and Cultural Studies." In *Composition and Resistance*, edited by C. Mark Hurlbert and Michael Blitz, 47–55. Portsmouth, NH: Boynton/Cook, 1991.

———. "Poststructuralism, Cultural Studies, and the Composition Classroom: Postmodern Theory in Practice." In *Professing the New Rhetorics: A Sourcebook*, edited by Theresa Enos and Stuart C. Brown, 461–80. Englewood Cliffs, NJ: Blair Press, 1994.

———. "Rhetoric and Ideology in the Writing Class." *College English* 50, no. 5 (1998): 477–94.

Bizzell, Patricia. *Academic Discourse and Critical Consciousness*. Pittsburgh, PA: University of Pittsburgh Press, 1992.

Bloom, Lynn. "Teaching College English as a Woman." *College English* 54, no. 7 (1992): 818–25.

Böll, Heinrich. "Murke's Collected Silences." In *The Stories of Heinrich Böll*, translated by Leila Vennewitz, 495–513. New York: McGraw-Hill, 1986.

Booth, Wayne C. "The Ethics of Teaching Literature." *College English* 61, no. 1 (1998): 41–55.

Brady, Philip. "Teaching TuFu on the Night Shift." *College English* 57, no. 5 (1995): 564–69.

Brinkley, Alan, Betty Dessants, Michael Flamm, Cynthia Fleming, Charles Forcey, and Eric Rothschild. "Classroom Discussions." In *The Chicago Handbook for Teachers: A Practical Guide to the College Classroom*. Chicago: University of Chicago Press, 1999.

Brodkey, Linda. "Introduction: Poststructural Theories, Methods, and Practices." In *Writing Permitted in Designated Areas Only*, 1–24. Minneapolis: University of Minnesota Press, 1996.

———. "Telling Experiences." In *Writing Permitted in Designated Areas Only*, 150–52. Minneapolis: University of Minnesota Press, 1996.

———. "Writing Critical Ethnographic Narratives." In *Writing Permitted in Designated Areas Only*, 106–13. Minneapolis: University of Minnesota Press, 1996.

Brooke, Robert. "Underlife and Writing Instruction." *College Composition and Communication* 38, no. 1 (1987): 141–53.

Bruffee, Kenneth. "Collaborative Learning and the 'Conversation of Mankind.'" *College English* 46, no. 7 (1984): 635–52.

Burke, Kenneth. *Grammar of Motives*. New York: Prentice Hall, 1945.

Burt, Lucile. "Liberty Bell." *Teacher Magazine* 13, no. 3 (2001): 32–43.

Casey, Kathleen. "The New Narrative Research in Education." *Review of Research in Education* 21, no. 1 (1995): 211–53.

Chiseri-Strater, Elizabeth. *Academic Literacies: The Public and Private Discourse of University Students*. Portsmouth, NH: Boynton/Cook, 1991.

Clair, Robin Patric. *Organizing Silence: A World of Possibilities*. Albany: State University of New York Press, 1998.

Clandinin, D. Jean, and F. Michael Connelly. "Personal Experience Methods." In *Handbook of Qualitative Research*, edited by Norman K. Denzin and Yvonna S. Lincoln, 413–27. Thousand Oaks, CA: Sage, 1994.

Clark, Katerina, and Michael Holquist. *Mikhail Bakhtin*. Cambridge, MA: Harvard University Press, 1984.

Collins, Janet. *The Quiet Child*. London: Cassell, 1996.

Curtis, Marcia, and Elizabeth Klem. "The Virtual Context: Ethnography in the Computer-Equipped Writing Classroom." In *Re-Imagining Computers and Composition: Teaching and Research in the Virtual Age*, edited by Gail E. Hawisher and Paul LeBlanc, 155–72. Portsmouth, NH: Boynton/Cook, 1992.

Dalke, Anne French. "'On Behalf of the Standard of Silence': The American Female Modernists." *Soundings: An Interdisciplinary Journal* 78, nos. 3–4 (1995): 463–81.

Dangerous Minds. Directed by John N. Smith. Don Simpson/Jerry Bruckheimer Films, 1995.

Dead Poets Society. Directed by Peter Weir. Buena Vista Pictures, 1989.

Delpit, Lisa. "The Silenced Dialogue: Power and Pedagogy in Educating Other People's Children." *Harvard Educational Review* 58, no. 3 (1988): 180–298.

Dewey, John. *Experience and Education*. New York: Collier Books, 1938.

Diaper, Gordon. "The Hawthorne Effect: A Fresh Examination." *Educational Studies* 16, no. 3 (1990) 261–67.

Elbow, Peter. "Being a Writer vs. Being an Academic: A Conflict in Goals." *College Composition and Communication* 46, no. 1 (1995): 72–83.

———. "The Believing Game: A Challenge after Twenty-Five Years." In *Everyone Can Write: Essays toward a Hopeful Theory of Writing and Teaching Writing*, 76–80. New York: Oxford University Press, 2000.

———. "Closing My Eyes As I Speak." In *Everyone Can Write: Essays toward a Hopeful Theory of Writing and Teaching Writing*, 93–112. New York: Oxford University Press, 2000.

———. "Inviting the Mother Tongue: Beyond 'Mistakes,' 'Bad English,' and 'Wrong Language.'" In *Everyone Can Write: Essays toward a Hopeful Theory of Writing and Teaching Writing*, 323–50. New York: Oxford University Press, 2000.

———. "A Map of Writing in Terms of Audience and Response." In *Everyone Can Write: Essays toward a Hopeful Theory of Writing and Teaching Writing*, 28–47. New York: Oxford University Press, 2000.

———. "Silence: A Collage." In *Everyone Can Write: Essays toward a Hopeful Theory of Writing and Teaching Writing*, 173–83. New York: Oxford University Press, 2000.

———. "Toward a Phenomenology of Freewriting." In *Everyone Can Write: Essays toward a Hopeful Theory of Writing and Teaching Writing*, 113–36. New York: Oxford University Press, 2000.

———. *University of Massachusetts Writing Program Newsletter*. Amherst, MA. October 1999.

———. "What Is Voice in Writing?" In *Everyone Can Write: Essays toward A Hopeful Theory of Writing and Teaching Writing*, 184–221. Oxford: Oxford University Press, 2000,

———. *Writing without Teachers*. New York: Oxford University Press, 1973.

———, and Pat Belanoff. *A Community of Writers: A Workshop Course in Writing*. Boston, MA: McGraw-Hill, 2000.

———. *Sharing and Responding*. Boston, MA: McGraw-Hill, 2000.

Ellsworth, Elizabeth. "Why Doesn't This Feel Empowering?: Working through the Repressive Myths of Critical Pedagogy." In *Feminisms and Critical Pedagogy*, edited by Carmen Luke and Jennifer Gore, 90–119. New York: Routledge, 1992.

Faigley, Lester. "Competing Theories of Process: A Critique and a Proposal." *College English* 48, no. 6 (1986): 527–42.

———. "Subverting the Electronic Notebook: Teaching Writing Using Networked Computers." In *The Writing Teacher as Researcher: Essays in the*

Theory and Practice of Class-Based Research, edited by Donald A. Daiker and Max Morenberg, 290–311. Portsmouth, NH: Boynton/Cook, 1990.

Farmer, Frank. *Saying and Silence: Listening to Composition with Bakhtin.* Logan: Utah State University Press, 2001.

Ferris Bueller's Day Off. Directed by John Hughes. Paramount Pictures, 1986.

Fine, Michelle, and Lois Weis, eds. *Beyond Silenced Voices: Class, Race, and Gender in United States Schools.* Albany: State University of New York Press, 1993.

Finkel, Donald L. *Teaching with Your Mouth Shut.* Portsmouth, NH: Boynton/Cook, 2000.

Fishman, Stephen M., and Lucille Parkinson McCarthy. "Boundary Conversations: Conflicting Ways of Knowing in Philosophy and Interdisciplinary Research." *Research in the Teaching of English* 25, no. 4 (1991): 419–68.

———. "Is Expressivism Dead?: Reconsidering Its Romantic Roots and Its Relation to Social Constructionism," *College English* 54, no. 6 (1992): 647–61.

Foucault, Michel. "The Means of Correct Training." In *The Foucault Reader*, edited by Paul Rabinow, 188–205. New York: Pantheon Books, 1984.

Fox, Helen. *Listening to the World: Cultural Issues in Academic Writing.* Urbana, IL: NCTE Press, 1994.

Fox, Patricia Shelley. "Finding the Selves We Set Aside." In *Narration as Knowledge: Tales of the Teaching Life*, edited by Joseph Trimmer, 34–42. Portsmouth, NH: Boynton/Cook, 1997.

Freire, Paulo. *Pedagogy of the Oppressed.* Translated by Myra Bergman Ramos. New York: Continuum, 1994.

Gere, Anne Ruggles. "Revealing Silence: Rethinking Personal Writing." *College Composition and Communication* 53, no. 2 (2001): 203–23.

Gilbert, Sandra M., and Susan Gubar. *The Madwoman in the Attic: The Woman Writer and the Nineteenth Century Literary Imagination.* New Haven, CT: Yale University Press, 1979.

Gilligan, Carol. *In a Different Voice: Psychological Theory and Women's Development.* Cambridge, MA: Harvard University Press, 1982.

Giroux, Henry. *Theory and Resistance in Education: A Pedagogy for the Opposition*, 7–41. New York: Bergin and Garvey, 1983.

Glaser, Barney G., and Anselm L. Strauss. *The Discovery of Grounded Theory: Strategies for Qualitativ* New York: Aldine de Gruyter, 1967.

Glenn, Cheryl. *Rhetoric Retold: Regendering the Tradition from Antiquity through the Renaissance*. Carbondale: Southern Illinois University Press, 1997.

———. *Unspoken: A Rhetoric of Silence*. Carbondale: Southern Illinois University Press, 2004.

Gradin, Sherrie L. *Romancing Rhetorics: Social Expressivist Perspectives on the Teaching of Writing*. Portsmouth, NH: Boynton/Cook, 1995.

Grumet, Madeline R. "The Politics of Personal Knowledge." In *Stories Lives Tell: Narrative and Dialogue in Education*, edited by Carol Witherell and Nel Noddings, 67–77. New York: Teachers College Press, 1991.

Half-Nelson. Directed by Ryan Fleck. Hunting Line Films, 2006.

Hamilton, Sharon J. "Nancy's Promise." In *Naration as Knowledge: Tales of the Teaching Life*, edited by Joseph Trimmer, 98–106. Portsmouth, NH: Boynton/Cook, 1997.

Hammack, Floyd. "Ethical Issues in Teacher Research." *Teachers College Record* 99 no. 2 (Winter 1997): 247–65.

Harris, Joseph. *A Teaching Subject: Composition since 1966*. Upper Saddle River, NJ: Prentice Hall, 1997.

———, and Jay Rosen. "Teaching Writing as Cultural Criticism." In *Composition and Resistance*, edited by C. Mark Hurlbert and Michael Blitz, 58–67. Portsmouth, NH: Boynton/Cook, 1991.

Heath, Shirley Brice. *Ways with Words: Language, Life, and Work in Communities and Classrooms*. Cambridge: Cambridge University Press, 1983.

Heldris of Cornwall. *Silence: A Thirteenth-Century French Romance*, edited and translated by Sarah Roche-Madhi. East Lansing, MI: Colleagues Press, 1992.

Heller, Michael. "A Proposal for Silence." *Friends Association for Higher Education* (1996–1997): 2, 7.

Herrington, Anne J. "Reflections on Empirical Research: Examining Some Ties between Theory and Action." In *Theory and Practice in the Teaching of Writing: Rethinking the Discipline*, edited by Lee Odell, 40–70. Carbondale: Southern Illinois University Press, 1993.

hooks, bell. *Talking Back: Thinking Feminist, Thinking Black*. Boston, MA: South End Press, 1989.

———. *Teaching to Transgress: Education as the Practice of Freedom*. New York: Routledge, 1994.

———. *Yearning: Race, Gender, and Cultural Politics*. Boston, MA: South End Press, 1992.

Hurlbert, C. Mark, and Michael Blitz. "Resisting Composition." In *Composition and Resistance*, edited by C. Mark Hurlbert and Michael Blitz, 139–44. Portsmouth, NH: Boynton/Cook, 1991.

Jaworski, Adam. *The Power of Silence: Social and Pragmatic Perspectives*. Newbury Park, CA: Sage, 1993.

Johnson, Cheryl L. "Participatory Rhetoric: The Teacher as Racial/ Gendered Subject." *College English* 56, no. 4 (1994): 409–19.

Jones, Stephen R. G. "Was There a Hawthorne Effect?" *The American Journal of Sociology* 98, no. 3 (1992): 451–68.

Kalamaras, George. *Reclaiming the Tacit Dimension: Symbolic Form in the Rhetoric of Silence*. Albany: State University of New York Press, 1994.

Kingston, Maxine Hong. *The Woman Warrior: Memoirs of a Girlhood among Ghosts*. New York: Vintage Books, 1989.

Kirsch, Gesa E. *Ethical Dilemmas in Feminist Research: The Politics of Location, Interpretation, and Publication*. Albany: State University of New York Press, 1999.

Kirtley, Susan. "What's Love Got to Do with It?: Eros in the Writing Classroom." In *A Way to Move: Rhetorics of Emotion and Composition Studies*, edited by Dale Jacobs and Laura Micciche, 56–66. Portsmouth, NH: Boynton/Cook, 2003.

———. "The Woman behind the Curtain: Reflections of a Female Teaching Assistant." Unpublished paper.

Kutz, Eleanor, and Hepzibah Roskelly. *An Unquiet Pedagogy: Transforming Practice in the English Classroom*. Portsmouth, NH: Boynton/Cook, 1991.

Lamb, Catherine E. "Beyond Argument in Feminist Composition." *College Composition and Communication* 42, no. 1 (1991): 11–24.

Lewis, Magda Gere. *Without a Word: Teaching beyond Women's Silence*. New York: Routledge, 1993.

Lincoln, Yvonna S., and Egon G. Guba. *Naturalistic Inquiry*. Beverly Hills, CA: Sage, 1985.

Losey, Kay M. *Listen to the Silences: Mexican American Interaction in the Composition Classroom and Community*. Norwood, NJ: Ablex, 1997.

Lu, Min-Zahn, and Bruce Horner. "The Problematic of Experience: Redefining Critical Work in Ethnography and Pedagogy." *College English* 56, no. 4 (1998): 259–77.

Mattingly, Cheryl. "Narrative Reflections on Practical Actions: Two Learning Experiments in Reflective Storytelling." In *The Reflective Turn: Case*

Studies in and on Educational Practice, edited by Donald A. Schön, 235–57. New York: Teachers College Press, 1991.

McEwan, Hunter. "Narrative Understanding in the Study of Teaching." In *Narrative in the Study of Teaching, Learning, and Research*, edited by Hunter McEwan and Kieran Egan, 166–83. New York: Teachers College Press, 1995.

———, and Kieran Egan. "Introduction." In *Narrative in the Study of Teaching, Learning, and Research*, edited by Hunter McEwan and Kieran Egan, vii–xv. New York: Teachers College Press, 1995.

Melville, Herman. "Bartleby, the Scrivener: A Story of Wall Street." In *Great Short Works of Herman Melville*, edited by Warner Berthoff, 39–74. New York: Harper and Row, 1969.

Micromedex, Inc. "Isometric Exercise." *Hendrick Health System*. http://www.ehendrick.org/healthy/00047540.html (accessed March 2, 2002).

Moffett, James. "Writing, Inner Speech, and Meditation." *College English* 44, no. 3 (1982): 231–46.

Mohr, Marian M. "Drafting Ethical Guidelines for Teacher Research in School." In *Ethical Issues in Practitioner Research*, edited by Jane Zeni, 3–12. New York: Teachers College Press, 2001.

Momaday, N. Scott. *The Man Made of Words: Essays, Stories, Passages*. New York: St. Martin's Press, 1997.

Moran, Charles. "'From a High-Tech to a Low-Tech Writing Class, and Back: A Study in Transition,' or, 'You Can't Go Home Again.'" Presentation. Conference on College Composition and Communication, March 1996.

Murray, Donald. *A Writer Teaches Writing*. 2nd ed. Dallas, TX: Houghton Mifflin, 1985.

Olsen, Tillie. *Silences*. New York: Delacourt Press, 1978.

O'Reilley, Mary Rose. *The Peaceable Classroom*. Portsmouth, NH: Boynton/Cook, 1993.

Orner, Mimi. "Interrupting the Calls for Student Voice in 'Liberatory Education': A Feminist Poststructuralist Perspective." In *Feminisms and Critical Pedagogy*, edited by Carmen Luke and Jennifer Gore, 74–89. New York: Routledge, 1992.

Palmer, Parker. *To Know As We Are Known: A Spirituality of Education*. San Francisco: Harper and Row, 1983.

Papoulis, Irene. "Appearance as Shield: Reflections about Middle-Class Lives on the Boundary." In *Writing Ourselves into the Story: Unheard Voices from*

Composition Studies, edited by Sheryl Fontaine and Susan Hunter, 269–88. Carbondale: Southern Illinois University Press, 1993.

Pascal, Blais. *Pensées*, edited and translated by Roger Ariew. Indianapolis, IN: Hackett, 2004.

Passante, Joy. "Up River, Down River, and Across the Aegean." In *Narration as Knowledge: Tales of the Teaching Life*, edited by Joseph Trimmer, 12–24. Portsmouth, NH: Boynton/Cook, 1997.

Patton, Michael Quinn. *Qualitative Evaluation and Research Methods.* Newbury Park, CA: Sage, 1990.

Perl, Sondra. "Facing the Other: The Emergence of Ethics and Selfhood in a Cross-Cultural Writing Classroom." In *Narration as Knowledge: Tales of the Teaching Life*, edited by Joseph Trimmer, 173–90. Portsmouth, NH: Boynton/Cook, 1997.

Pratt, Mary Louise. "Arts of the Contact Zone." *Profession* 91 (1991): 33–40.

Rankin, Elizabeth. *Seeing Yourself as a Teacher: Conversations with Five New Teachers in a University Writing Program.* Urbana, IL: NCTE Press, 1994.

Ratcliffe, Krista. "Rhetorical Listening: A Trope for Interpretive Invention and a 'Code of Cross-Cultural Conduct.'" *College Composition and Communication* 51, no. 2 (1990): 195–224.

Ray, Ruth. "Composition from the Teacher-Researcher Point of View." In *Methods and Methodology in Composition Research*, edited by Gesa Kirsch and Patricia A. Sullivan, 172–89. Carbondale: Southern Illinois University Press, 1992.

Reason, Peter, and Peter Hawkins. "Storytelling as Inquiry." In *Human Inquiry in Action: Developments in New Paradigm Research*, edited by Peter Reason, 79–101. London: Sage, 1988.

Rich, Adrienne Cecile. "Cartographies of Silence." In *The Dream of a Common Language: Poems, 1974–1977*, 16–20. New York: W. W. Norton, 1993.

Ritchie, Joy. "Confronting the 'Essential' Problem: Reconnecting Feminist Theory and Pedagogy." In *Feminisms and Composition: A Critical Sourcebook*, edited by Gesa E. Kirsch, Faye Spenser Maor, Lance Massey, Lee Nickoson-Massey, and Mary Sheridan-Rabideau, 79–102. Boston, MA: Bedford/ St. Martin's Press, 2003.

Rock the Vote Blog. "Afghans Killed for Registering to Vote." http://www.blog.rock thevote.com/2004_06_27_archive.html (accessed August 10, 2004).

Ropers-Huilman, Becky. "Still Waters Run Deep: Meaning of Silence in Feminist Classrooms." *Feminist Teacher* 10, no. 1 (1996): 3–7.

Rose, Mike. *Lives on the Boundary: A Moving Account of the Struggles and Achievements of America's Educationally Underprepared.* New York: Penguin Books, 1990.

Roskelly, Hebzibah. "The Risky Business of Group Work." In *The Writing Teacher's Sourcebook,* edited by Gary Tate, Edward P. J. Corbett, Nancy Myers, 141–46. New York: Oxford University Press, 1994.

Royster, Jacqueline Jones. "The Other Side of Speaking: Claiming the Right to Response." Presentation. Conference on College Composition and Communication, April 2000.

Rubin, Herbert J., and Irene S. Rubin. *Qualitative Interviewing: The Art of Hearing Data.* Thousand Oaks, CA: Sage, 1995.

Sadker, Myra, and David Sadker. *Failing at Fairness: How Our Schools Cheat Girls.* New York: Touchstone Books, 1995.

Saville-Troike, Muriel. "The Place of Silence in an Integrated Theory of Communication." In *Perspectives on Silence,* edited by Deborah Tannen and Muriel Saville-Troike, 3–18. Norwood, NJ: Ablex, 1985.

Scheurer, Erica. *"A Vice for Voices": Emily Dickinson's Dialogic Voice from the Borders.* PhD diss. University of Massachusetts at Amherst, 1993.

Scott, Erica. "Composing as a Person: Gender, Identity, and Student Writing." *WILLA* 10 (2001): 17–22. http://www.scholar.lib.vt.edu/ejournals/WILLA/fall01/scott.html (accessed May 15, 2005).

Seidman, I. E. *Interviewing as Qualitative Research: A Guide for Researchers in Education and the Social Sciences.* New York: Teachers College Press, 1991.

Shakespeare, William. *Hamlet.* London: Penguin Books, 1980.

Shor, Ira. *Empowering Education: Critical Teaching for Social Change.* Chicago: University of Chicago Press, 1992.

———. *When Students Have Power: Negotiating Authority in a Critical Pedagogy.* Chicago: University of Chicago Press, 1996.

Simon, Paul, and Art Garfunkel. "Sounds of Silence." *Sounds of Silence.* Legacy Records, compact disc, 2001.

Sommers, Nancy. "Editor's Choice: The Language of Coats." *College English* 60, no. 4 (1998): 421–25.

Spellmeyer, Kurt. "Knowledge against 'Knowledge': Freshman English, Public Discourse, and the Social Imagination." In *Composition and Resistance,* edited by C. Mark Hurlbert and Michael Blitz, 70–80. Portsmouth, NH: Boynton/Cook, 1991.

Stafford, Kim. "Pilgrimage at the Penitentiary." In *Narration as Knowledge: Tales of the Teaching Life*, edited by Joseph Trimmer, 25–-33. Portsmouth, NH: Boynton/Cook, 1997.

Stake, Robert E. "Case Studies." In *Handbook of Qualitative Research*, edited by Norman K. Denzin and Yvonna S. Lincoln, 236–47. Thousand Oaks, CA: Sage, 1994.

Suhor, Charles. "The Pedagogy of Silence in Public Education: Expanding the Tradition." In *Presence of Mind: Writing and the Domain beyond the Cognitive*, edited by Alice Glarden Brand and Richard L. Graves, 31–37. Portsmouth, NH: Boynton/Cook, 1994.

Tannen, Deborah. "Silence: Anything But." In *Perspectives on Silence*, edited by Deborah Tannen and Muriel Saville-Troike, 93–111. Norwood, NJ: Ablex, 1985.

Taylor, Jill McLean, Carol Gilligan, and Amy M. Sullivan. *Between Voice and Silence: Women and Girls, Race and Relationships.* Cambridge, MA: Harvard University Press, 1995.

Tobin, Lad. "Reading Students, Reading Ourselves: Resisting the Teacher's Role in the Writing Class." *College English* 53, no. 3 (1991): 333–48.

Tompkins, Jane. *A Life in School: What the Teacher Learned.* Reading, MA: Addison-Wesley, 1996.

Trimbur, John. "Consensus and Difference in Collaborative Learning." *College English* 51 no. 6 (1989): 602–16.

Trimmer, Joseph. "Telling Stories about Stories." In *Narration as Knowledge: Tales of the Teaching Life*, edited by Joseph Trimmer, 51–60. Portsmouth, NH: Boynton/Cook, 1997.

TuSmith, Bonnie. "The Englishes of Ethnic Folk: From Home Talkin' to Testifyin' Art." *College English* 58, no. 1 (1996): 43–57.

United States Constitution, Fifth Amendment.

University of Massachusetts, Amherst. Office of Institutional Research. *UMass at a Glance 2000–2001.* http://www.umass.edu/oapa (accessed May 19, 2005).

University of Massachusetts, Amherst. Student Activities Center. *Registered Student Organizations.* http://www.umass.edu/campact/category/html (accessed May 19, 2005).

University of Massachusetts. Writing Program. Syllabus, Fall 2000.

Villanueva, Victor Jr. "Shoot-Out at the I'm OK, You're OK Corral." In *Narration as Knowledge: Tales of the Teaching Life*, edited by Joseph Trimmer, 43–50. Portsmouth, NH: Boynton/Cook, 1997.

Walters, Frank D. "Writing Teachers Writing and the Politics of Dissent." *College English* 57, no. 7 (1995): 822–39.

Weiner, Harvey. "Collaborative Learning in the Classroom: A Guide to Evaluation." In *The Writing Teacher's Sourcebook*, edited by Gary Tate, Edward P. J. Corbett, and Nancy Myers, 132–40. New York: Oxford University Press, 1994.

Wilson, Suzanne M. "Not Tension but Intention: A Response to Wong's Analysis of the Researcher/Teacher," *Educational Researcher* 24, no. 8 (1995): 19–22.

Witherell, Carol, and Nel Noddings. "Prologue: An Invitation to Our Readers." In *Stories Lives Tell: Narrative and Dialogue in Education*, edited by Carol Witherell and Nel Noddings, 1–12. New York: Teachers College Press, 1991.

Wong, E. David. "Challenges Confronting the Researcher/Teacher: Conflicts of Purpose and Conduct." *Educational Researcher* 4, no. 24 (1995): 22–28.

Zeni, Jane. "Introduction." In *Ethical Issues in Practitioner Research*, edited by Jane Zeni, xi–xxi. New York: Teachers College Press, 2001.

Zimbardo, Philip G. *Shyness: What It Is, What to Do about It.* New York: Addison-Wesley, 1977.

Index